THE 9 DISCIPLINES OF A FACILITATOR

Leading Groups by Transforming Yourself

Jon C. Jenkins

Maureen R. Jenkins

JOSSEY-BASS
A Wiley Imprint
www.josseybass.com

Published by Jossey-Bass
A Wiley Imprint
989 Market Street, San Francisco, CA 94103-1741   www.josseybass.com

Credit lines are on page 310.

Readers should be aware that Internet Web sites offered as citations and/or sources for further information may have changed or disappeared between the time this was written and when it is read.

Jossey-Bass books and products are available through most bookstores. To contact Jossey-Bass directly call our Customer Care Department within the U.S. at 800-956-7739, outside the U.S. at 317-572-3986, or fax 317-572-4002.

Jossey-Bass also publishes its books in a variety of electronic formats. Some content that appears in print may not be available in electronic books.

Library of Congress Cataloging-in-Publication Data
Jenkins, Jon C.
    The 9 disciplines of a facilitator: leading groups by transforming yourself / by Jon C. Jenkins,
Maureen R. Jenkins.
        p. cm.
    Includes bibliographical references and index.
    ISBN-13: 978-0-7879-8068-9 (cloth)
    ISBN-10: 0-7879-8068-4 (cloth)
    1. Leadership. 2. Self-management (Psychology) 3. Organizational effectiveness.
4. Organizational sociology. I. Jenkins, Maureen R., 1946- II. Title. III. Title: Nine disciplines
of a facilitator.
    HD57.7.J45   2006
    658.4'092—dc22

                                                                          2006014168

Printed in the United States of America
FIRST EDITION
HB Printing   10 9 8 7 6 5 4 3 2 1

The Jossey-Bass
Business & Management Series

Contents

Preface vii

The Authors ix

Introduction 1

Part One: The Context

1   Leadership: A Matter of Spirit 15

2   Trends in Employee Participation 45

3   The Skills of a Facilitative Leader 55

4   The Future of Facilitation 67

Part Two: The Disciplines

5   Detachment: Stepping Back 79

6   Engagement: Committing to the Group 102

7   Focus: Willing One Thing 127

8   Interior Council: Choosing Advisors Wisely 147

9   Intentionality: Aligning the Will to Succeed 170

10 Sense of Wonder: Maintaining the Capacity
    to Be Surprised 194

11 Awareness: Knowing What Is Really Going On 215

12 Action: Effective Doing 242

13 Presence: Inspiring and Evoking Spirit in Others 262

References 285

Index 295

PREFACE

The Ecumenical Institute (E.I.) of Chicago developed from a World Council of Churches initiative in the 1950s. In 1962, six families moved to Chicago from Austin, Texas, to form a community that staffed the E.I. The Institute had three focuses: practical research in society, culture, and theology; training in these same areas; and demonstration projects in communities and organizations that applied the insights gained through the training and research. In the mid-1970s the E.I. created the Institute of Cultural Affairs, by which the Institute is now known.

Maureen and Jon joined the community in May 1968 and left in 1988. Over that period we participated in all three areas of work—research, training, and demonstration projects. In the summer of 1968 the Institute built a model it named the "New Religious Mode." The New Religious Mode was an attempt to understand the vows and practices of traditional religious life as applied to contemporary life. It looked at the vows of poverty, chastity, and obedience; the practices of meditation, contemplation, and prayer; and what the Institute called the journeys: knowing, doing and being. Each of these were looked at from a phenomenological perspective. The staff of the Institute experimented with a number of practices during the model's development. This work has continued to inform our life and work in the years since. This model has provided inspiration for the nine disciplines described in *The 9 Disciplines of a Facilitator.*

In conferences of the International Association of Facilitators in Stockholm, Utrecht, Fort Worth, and Ottawa, and in our ongoing advanced facilitation courses, we have led workshops in which managers and facilitators told us about the personal disciplines they follow in order to become more proficient in their roles as leaders. We have been intrigued at the number of similarities in people's struggles across different circumstances, professions, and cultures. Although the contexts are different across different industries and cultures, recognizable themes recur. We have decided in this book to share our thinking. We have attempted to share as clearly as possible a number of disciplines we know, practice, and have practiced to build personal discipline as facilitative leaders.

A key issue is the word *discipline* itself. Why is this a book about discipline, rather than practices or attitude or something else? In this we give the floor to Peter Senge, from his book *The Fifth Discipline* (1990):

> By "discipline," I don't mean "enforced order," or "means of punishment" but a body of theory and technique that must be studied and mastered to be put into practice. A discipline is a developmental path for acquiring certain skills or competencies. As with any discipline, from playing the piano to electrical engineering, some people have an innate "gift," but anyone can develop proficiency through practice. (pp. 10–11)

We hope that this book results in more conversations about the internal disciplines and practices of facilitative leadership. Perhaps there are disciplines you have that you would like to share with others. This could become an online discussion process or a Web site. In any case, please feel free to contact us at jon@imaginal.nl or maureen@imaginal.nl if you have thoughts on this matter.

May 2006   Jon C. Jenkins
Groningen, The Netherlands   Maureen R. Jenkins

The Authors

Jon C. Jenkins is a project leader, trainer, and facilitator. He has more than thirty-five years experience in micro-level social change in developing and developed countries and in training in the fields of short- and mid-term planning, community development, team building, motivation, and methods of education. He led or helped lead participative consultations in nineteen projects in eleven countries. He was project director or assistant project director for one- to two-year on-site residences in three communities. He has taught more than one hundred two- to three-day modules on individual and social change, community development, and education methods. He has designed curriculum or programs for KPN (the Dutch telephone company), The Netherlands; The International Criminal Tribunal for the Former Yugoslavia, The Netherlands; Shell International Exploration & Production, The Netherlands; and the Institute of Cultural Affairs in India, the United States, and Europe. He has developed open programs for local communities, businesses, and service organizations. He has also written or edited a number of articles and books on business and social problems. He is the Coordinator of Publications and Communications on the board of directors of the International Association of Facilitators (IAF). He is the editor of the IAF Methods Database, an open source Web site dedicated to providing group facilitation methods to managers, team leaders, and facilitators. He is on the board of directors for the Union of International Associations.

Maureen R. Jenkins has designed and facilitated international change processes since 1968. Between 1968 and 1988, she held various positions with the Institute of Cultural Affairs, including as a member of the International Board of Managers and codirector of the Lima and Rome Areas. She participated in teams developing the Technology of Participation strategic planning process, the Social Process Triangles, and many training and facilitation programs. In 1988 she formed Imaginal Training, a soft skills training and group facilitation consultancy based in The Netherlands. She was part of the Action Learning Team at Shell International Exploration & Production (SIEP), where she facilitated workshops for self-managing teams and trained facilitators. She now facilitates for the Drilling the Limit and Servicing the Limit performance improvement initiatives of SIEP. She has designed and delivered the basic and advanced training courses for all facilitators for the Dutch Ministry of Public Works. Most recently, Maureen is one of five International Facilitators for Shell's Core Leadership Development Program, focused on emerging leaders across the world. She co-facilitates basic training for online facilitators. Maureen has written or edited a number of articles and books on group processes, and is past chair of the International Association of Facilitators.

Introduction

What takes place in the head and heart of an effective facilitative leader? How do these individuals find the inner resources they need to carry out their responsibilities? What is the source of their powerful effect on people and situations? Where do they find their strength? In this book, we explore these questions and enable readers to develop their own answers.

As we all know, the nature of organizations is changing. There is a call for new levels of personal commitment, creativity, and contribution from organization members. Employees expect meaningful work, significant participation, and quality of social interaction in the workplace. A new way of leading is emerging: facilitative leadership.

The Facilitative Leader

We use the term *facilitative leader* to include both facilitators who find themselves in leadership roles and leaders who are more facilitative than directive in their interaction with colleagues. Facilitative leadership is not *making* people do things, but rather *enabling* them to release their energies.

The most difficult thing any facilitative leader can do is to master himself or herself. Every leader experiences doubt, anxiety, cynicism, and his or her own dark side. Facilitative leaders need to restore their personal energy, maintain respect for both colleagues and themselves, find new sources of ideas and inspiration, and battle the human propensity toward self-limitation, caution, mediocrity, and dependency.

1

Facilitative leaders require from themselves personal dedication, imagination, and charisma. They also must call forth these qualities from their colleagues. In order for this to happen, today's facilitative leaders require new kinds of self-mastery. This book describes nine ways to build self-mastery regarding others, yourself, and the world.

Peter Koestenbaum, in an interview by Polly LaBarre of *Fast-Company*, states

> One of the gravest problems in life is self-limitation: We create defense mechanisms to protect us from the anxiety that comes with freedom. We refuse to fulfill our potential. We live only marginally. This was Freud's definition of psychoneurosis: We limit how we live so that we can limit the amount of anxiety that we experience. We end up tranquilizing many of life's functions. We shut down the centers of entrepreneurial and creative thinking; in effect, we halt progress and growth. But no significant decision—personal or organizational—has ever been undertaken without being attended by an existential crisis, or without a commitment to wade through anxiety, uncertainty, and guilt.

> That's what we mean by transformation. You can't just change how you think or the way that you act—you must change the way that you will. You must gain control over the patterns that govern your mind: your worldview, your beliefs about what you deserve and about what's possible. That's the zone of fundamental change, strength, and energy—and the true meaning of courage. (LaBarre, 2000, p. 222)

As Peter Block (1987) describes the choices we make,

> "We choose between Maintenance and Greatness.
> "We choose between Caution and Courage.
> "We choose between Dependency and Autonomy." (p. 11)

We tend to choose maintenance, caution, and dependency, even when that is not at all what we intend.

Facilitation is the leadership secret. No one seriously expects leaders to know everything. But we certainly do expect them, with their colleagues, to push their organizations to make intelligent and courageous choices.

A great deal of attention is being paid today to what the facilitative leader does, to the role of ethics in business, to the need for hard choices. Some facilitators are concerned with issues such as self-mastery, ethics, and meaning of facilitation. The International Association of Facilitators (IAF) has articulated a set of values for the profession that are often discussed at IAF conferences. The conferences provide a forum for discussion about values applied in facilitation.

Although there are any number of suggestions about the sort of courage a leader needs, not so much is said about how one keeps on the path of courage. For many people, it is more difficult to be courageous in front of the many dissenting voices of any diverse organization than it is to make courageous decisions alone. This book is for you if, like so many, you find it hard to keep on day in and day out, standing before declining margins, disaffected colleagues, and demanding customers, choosing again and again an appropriate way to move.

THE DEVELOPMENTAL PATHS AND THE DISCIPLINES

In this book we are concerned with three developmental paths, each of which has three disciplines.

The first developmental path relates to the facilitative leader's internal relationship with *others,* which includes the disciplines of Detachment, Engagement, and Focus. The second developmental path of disciplines is about the inward relationship with *myself,* which includes Interior Council, Intentionality, and Sense of Wonder. The third path is about the internal relationship with *life* itself, which includes Awareness, Action, and Presence.

A model for the developmental paths and disciplines appears as Figure I.1.

In Figure I.1, there is a special relationship among the three disciplines in each row. The left and right disciplines are in tension with one another. The middle discipline encompasses the art of standing in tension between the other two.

FIGURE I.1. THE DEVELOPMENTAL PATHS AND THE DISCIPLINES

Developmental Path			
Regarding Others	Detachment	Focus	Engagement
Regarding Myself	Interior Council	Sense of Wonder	Intentionality
Regarding Life	Awareness	Presence	Action

DISCIPLINES REGARDING OTHERS

In his book *Good to Great,* Jim Collins (2001) introduces what he calls the "Stockdale Paradox," to "retain faith that you will prevail in the end, regardless of difficulties, AND at the same time confront the most brutal facts of your current reality, whatever they might be" (p. 86).

Collins derived this paradox from an interview with Admiral Jim Stockdale, the highest-ranking American prisoner in the Hanoi prisoner of war camp from 1965 to 1973. In describing the years of leading his fellow prisoners of war while all were exposed to continual torture, Admiral Stockdale pointed out that he never lost hope that he would be free in the end. The men who did not survive the camp were the optimists, he said, those who carried on in the belief that they would be freed within a specific time frame. Retaining faith that you will be freed, without holding onto a time, is *Detachment* in practice.

Detachment
Detachment is maintaining one's autonomy in the face of the desire to be comforted in one certitude or another. Not only is it a leader choosing her own autonomy, but helping colleagues to choose their own autonomy as well.

Authentic group decision making, innovation, and the implementation of those decisions require a free flow of ideas. To achieve that, an atmosphere of suspended judgment—detachment—has to be created. This puts the power to make decisions into the hands of the group. The facilitative leader starts with detachment from things, ideas, need for control, power, and recognition. The leader needs to be able to separate the leadership role from his or her ego.

Engagement

The discipline of Engagement is developing the capacity to care, to commit, and to be generous with who and what you are, without knowing what the outcome may be. *Engagement* involves confronting all the facts of your situation.

The facilitative leader intends that optimal decisions will be made. These are the most effective decisions, the most innovative, and those that the group has the will to carry out. While Detachment enables the free flow of ideas among the group, Engagement by the leader sparks willingness and enthusiasm on the part of the group to select and carry out a new direction and to keep going in the face of adversity.

Focus

The discipline of *Focus* is standing in the tension between Detachment and Engagement. Focus is the only place where you can hold these two together.

Focus increases the capacity to choose autonomy and commitment simultaneously. It is concentrating the will so that the moment is fulfilled and the future is also fulfilled, like two lenses that merge into one clear image. Focus is the result of the combination of attention to both immediate and future issues.

In any group interaction, there are all sorts of dynamics at play—short and long term, things not related to the issue on the table, politics, cultural differences, personalities, and so on. In order for the group to achieve its purpose, the facilitative leader needs to continuously balance the conflicting dynamics, and understand without thinking about it where things need to go next. It is here that building the discipline of Focus becomes critical.

DISCIPLINES REGARDING MYSELF

Nelson Mandela was asked whether he didn't in fact despise those jailers who kept him in prison on Robben Island for twenty-seven years. He replied:

> Of course I did, for many years. They took the best years of my life. They abused me physically and mentally. I didn't get to see my children grow up. I hated them. Then one day when I was working in the quarry, hammering the rocks, I realized that they had already taken everything from me except my mind and my heart. Those they could not take without my permission. I decided not to give them away. (Nelson Mandela, quoted in Clinton, 2004, p. 877)

This second developmental path of disciplines has to do with how you relate to yourself. On the one side is *Interior Council,* the practice of forcing yourself to choose self-talk that helps you, as Mandela demonstrated in his responses to his jailers. On the other side is the discipline of *Intentionality,* continually willing what you want to accomplish; as Mandela says, *he* chooses what he does with his heart and his mind—no one else can. What enables an ordinary individual to do something like that? What is the source of such a leader's personal inspiration on the one hand and steely resolve on the other? We believe this has to do with the discipline of maintaining a *Sense of Wonder.* In his autobiography, Bill Clinton (2004) describes a rock on display in the Oval Office, brought back by Neil Armstrong from the surface of the moon and reputed to be 3.6 billion years old. Holding that rock reminded Clinton that, "We're all just passing through" (p. 1065).

Interior Council

Our minds are filled with ideas, sayings, advice, images, and many other voices that guide our thoughts and actions. Some of these mental advisors are helpful and some are not. Interior Council is the discipline of paying attention to and choosing the most creative and enabling from among the voices that guide your day-to-day life.

Leadership is a profoundly draining activity. Inspiration and sources of new ideas are continually needed to keep going. There are moments when the only resources you have are the ones you carry in your head. Another dimension of the need for effective Internal Council is that in working with internal mentors, you have the opportunity to work through issues that you will have to manage in public. It gives you confidence to go ahead and do it, and deeper appreciation for the issues involved.

Intentionality

Intentionality is developing the capacity to manage your desires, to increase control over what you want. Standing as the facilitative leader is standing in a position in which every aspect of your own dark side and your own greatness is magnified. Intentionality is learning to harness both of these energies.

As a facilitative leader, you hold an obligation to achieve what the group intends. This can be exhausting. Building intentionality is needed so that you can keep on wanting and wanting again what needs to be done.

Wonder

A Sense of Wonder results when you are carrying out your best and most authentic understanding in the service of your most powerful resolve for what is needed. It is only when you are working on an arena for which you have forceful resolve and commitment that you feel pressed to push your resources to the limit, to really listen for the wisdom your Interior Council has to offer. In most everyday activities we tend to go with what we already know. But when you are working at your creative edge regarding both commitment and know-how, you really are in unfamiliar territory, on a sort of personal frontier. It is here that the Sense of Wonder is called for, being prepared for the encounter with the unknown, be it in the world, in your colleagues or in yourself.

By maintaining a Sense of Wonder the facilitative leader evokes drive, commitment, and creativity. Having a Sense of Wonder is a choice that one makes. It is looking at reality with all of its warts and deciding it is worth the excitement. It brings together your own best self and the greatness of the people you are working with.

DISCIPLINES REGARDING LIFE

The third developmental path of disciplines is about the way you relate to inventing your life. These are the disciplines of Awareness, Action, and Presence. The joke is told of a newly rich Muscovite who drives his new Mercedes into a tram and loses his arm. He leaps from the car dripping blood, and passers-by ask if he needs help. All he can do is scream, "Oh my car, my car!" "But sir," says one, "what about your arm?" The man looks at the bloody stump at his shoulder and screams, "Oh, my Rolex, my Rolex!"

The humor is that the guy's story about what is happening is completely out of sync with the events themselves. The value framework he has been applying to life before the accident does not support the present in which he is living, with a very serious injury, and he is so out of sync as to be ridiculous.

The struggle with *Awareness* is building your understanding of what is going on around you in a way that helps you live effectively what is really happening. We joke about whether the glass is half-full or half-empty, but everyone knows someone who has taken a reasonable set of life circumstances and believed that it was inadequate and unfair. At the same time, anyone who watches the business news hears day in and day out the effort of business leaders to create *Action* that balances events in their companies with an understanding of the situation that frees everyone to move ahead. The central development path for the leader is here. How you present yourself—your *Presence*—has to do with how you explore the life you have been given to live and how you understand and tell about what is happening to you.

Awareness

Awareness is developing the capacity to confront the truth of a situation in all of its relevant dimensions. Being aware is having the courage to be wise, sophisticated, and subtle. In the same moment one holds a respect—even reverence—for others.

For a group to function effectively, all of the relevant information about the situation needs to be on the table. Because of her commitment to the truth, the facilitative leader pushes the group to ensure that every bit of information needed is brought to bear on their decisions. Just as a leader can permit a group to compromise its integrity, so also a leader can insist that a group bases its decisions on the best truth it can muster.

Action

The discipline of Action is exercising the self-control needed to be effective while assuming only the power to influence. This has to do with finding the locus point at which the action is most effective. Action is discovering those things to do that transform the situation so that you can carry out your convictions.

The facilitative leader enables people to act in such a way that the potential inherent in the moment is realized.

Presence

The final discipline of this developmental path is Presence. Presence is charisma, inspiring and evoking spirit in others. Presence is the unique manifestation of spirit at a particular point of history. At this moment in society's journey, facilitation—enabling collective direct decision-making—is part of the spirit of the times, just as nonviolent resistance was part of the spirit of the civil rights movement in the United States in the 1950s and 1960s. An impending future is sensed and its birth is assisted.

The discipline of Presence is when an individual stands between a profound understanding of what is going on in life, what we call here the discipline of Awareness, and effectively acting out that understanding with courage and creativity, as we call here the discipline of Action. Awareness is challenged and refined in the real world, and Action is informed and corrected by profound understanding and reflection. Martin Luther King Jr., for example, was first a clergyman steeped in Christian theology. He then studied nonviolent conflict for years both in the United States and in India and coupled that with careful analysis of the American racial situation until he developed with colleagues a very sensitive view of what the country needed to be able to change. He worked with civil rights groups across the country, and as strategies succeeded and failed, his understanding grew and his effectiveness improved. Standing in that intersection, avoiding both irresponsible action and paralysis by analysis, he was a figure to be reckoned with, whether you agreed with him or not. This is where the discipline of Presence lies.

USING THIS BOOK

The 9 Disciplines of a Facilitator is divided into two parts. Part One, "The Context," contains four chapters about the spirit of facilitative leadership, the employees' perspective, the skills of a facilitative leader, and some thoughts about what leaders can expect in the future. Part Two, "The Disciplines," contains one chapter for each of the nine disciplines.

The chapters in Part Two each follow a similar structure:

- The discipline is described.
- Issues of the discipline for facilitative leaders are explored: What are the concerns for facilitative leaders? How do people experience this discipline? Why can this discipline be difficult?
- The four levels of each discipline are discussed: What are the four ways people encounter this discipline?
- Practices and exercises for the discipline are suggested at the end of the chapter: What practices and exercises can a leader engage in to build his or her strength in this discipline?

To get the overall story, the book can be read straight through from front to back. However, it can also be considered a catalog of nine different developmental options. You may wish to find the one discipline or trio of disciplines that intrigues you the most, or intrigues the group you are working with the most, and focus on that. The practical folks among you may wish to go directly to the end of each of the chapters and try out the practices and exercises you find there.

These exercises and practices are not intended to be guidelines or techniques that you can use without further preparation. If you want to use the practices, we recommend finding a coach or colleague to assist you. Alternatively, try working through exercises and practices with a team, support group, or book club. The reason for this is that all of this work calls for reflection, something for which two or more people working together can stimulate one another. This is not to say that you cannot enjoy and effectively take things from the book as an individual reader—you certainly can, but you can probably do better with a partner or two.

You may also notice that some activities are intended as individual life practices, such as meditation, whereas other activities, such as the assessment of your personal values or building a life timeline, could better be done with a group and reflected on together.

GETTING STARTED

If you'd like to work on one discipline, here are some suggestions for getting started.

You can approach your selection either by assessing your interest in the nine disciplines or else by your interest in the various exercises and practices. To decide which of the disciplines you would like to work on, look through each of the disciplines and note down your experiences with them. Go back through your list of nine kinds of experience and rank the disciplines one to nine by difficulty for you. If you have the hardest time with Awareness, put that as number one, and so on. Then go through the list and choose one toward the middle of the list that will be a challenge without being overwhelming. You can work on this one first, and then move on to one that you find more difficult.

Alternatively, you may prefer to work with practices and exercises. Look through the suggested practices, such as meditation or journal-writing, at the ends of the chapters. Some of them work with more than one discipline. Select a practice you would like to try out and make a decision to go for it. If you wish, find a coach or class to help you. Try it for one to three months. Any work with the Disciplines requires regular practice. All of these practices should be done on a daily basis, which is a pretty hefty time commitment. As with art or physical fitness, you are always either improving or declining, never standing still.

IF YOU'RE HAVING TROUBLE

You may not have gotten very far at the end of three months, but you will have gotten over any initial resistance to the practice. Discuss your progress with your coach to determine if this is useful for you.

If you fail one day (and it's likely that you *will* fail on some day!), just start again the next day. It is easy to stop doing your practice; the issue is starting again when you stop. Do not convince yourself that the objective is to have a perfect record—after all, who is watching but you? It may take many starts and stops to get into the rhythm of the doing of the practice. Somewhere it is said that it takes three years three months and three days to learn to meditate. You want to practice, so practice.

If you still have difficulty keeping going, you might look at the conditions surrounding the practice. Is the time of the day appropriate? Do you do it regularly and at the same time? Are the conditions under which you are doing it supportive of the practice? For example, if you are meditating, are you physically comfortable enough without putting yourself to sleep?

If after three months the practice is not right for you, try a new one. If you don't find a practice to your liking, try a different discipline. If you can't settle on one, then you might reexamine why you are doing the practice.

However you choose to use the book, we wish you a fine journey.

PART ONE

THE CONTEXT

CHAPTER ONE

LEADERSHIP:
A MATTER OF SPIRIT

A great deal of literature has been dedicated to the questions of leadership. What does leadership do? What are its characteristics? What are its dynamics? Who are leaders? How can I be a better leader?

For us, the key issue on which leadership centers is spirit. Spirit is nothing strange and mystical; it's that spark that makes life worthwhile, the "wow" factor, a force we encounter every day. "Inspiration" is based on spirit. Spirit cannot be controlled or manipulated. It can be evoked, but it does not necessarily or automatically appear. It can appear for a while and then disappear. It seems always to be present, but we don't always discern it. Sometimes it is overwhelming, and sometimes it is like antique lace that crumbles the moment it is touched.

Spirit can be seen in organizations, teams, and individuals. Walk into a company's headquarters, and you can experience the spirit of the place. Watch the Los Angeles Lakers basketball team on court when being coached by Phil Jackson, when that certain spark happens and you see it. Watch Serena Williams or Andre Agassi raise their game when on the verge of defeat and you see it.

A great many books on leadership focus on how to do things, how to communicate, how to lead, how to give feedback, and how to motivate. This book is not about "how to." It is about what happens inside the leader—what and how the leader thinks and decides, and how he or she is a whole person. When leaders take charge of their own interior they are working in the area of spirit.

In this chapter we look at some of the challenges of leadership in today's environment, comparing the old and new approaches. We briefly review some of the failures of leadership and look at the necessity of strengthening the internal state of leaders as a way of improving performance. Finally, we look at the facilitative leader and what such a leader does.

Traditional Versus New Leadership

The difficulties with leadership in our times has several causes, the most important of which is the fact that we are going through radical shifts in our thinking (a new paradigm), social relationships (globalization), and the sources of meaning (values).

The Shift in Thinking: A New Paradigm

The first of the three shifts—the shift in our thinking—can be described as a change in paradigm. A new paradigm is coming into being and an old one is dying.

To understand what is happening to facilitators and leaders, one needs to understand the differences between the old paradigm and the new one. A paradigm defines how we think and act. Being in this transition period means that some of us function largely in the old paradigm and some largely in the new paradigm. Individually, we find ourselves shuttling back and forth from one paradigm to the other.

The structure of the universe in the old paradigm was dualistic. It is difficult to determine when this change in paradigm began. We think a good beginning time is between 1900, when Max Planck published his work on the emission spectrum of black bodies followed by Albert Einstein publishing his work on the special theory of relativity in 1905, and the end of World War I. During these twenty or so years much of the basis of the new paradigm was established. We perceived things as good/bad, us/them, individual/society. In the new paradigm, we perceive things as united. In the new paradigm, there is still good and bad, us and them, and the individual and society, but there is *difference*. Good and bad is a single unity. Good is defined by bad, not by a rigid, unchanging definition of *good*. We know who we are not by some abstract definition but by understanding the many ways in which we are not the "others." We need those relationships with others to understand ourselves.

In the old paradigm from at least the sixth century, when Hindu, Buddhist, and Jain thinkers developed the concept of atoms, until our age, things were composed of "stuff"—of substance. All matter was seen to be composed of natural elements—fire, earth, metal, water, and wood in the Chinese scheme, or water, earth, air, and fire in the Greek version. The scientific paradigm became more sophisticated with the development of modern scientific methods in the sixteenth and seventeenth centuries, the discovery of oxygen by Antoine Lavoisier in 1778, and Gregor Mendel's laws of inheritance, to name but a few. In the new paradigm as it began to emerge in the early twentieth century, however, it is no longer the substance but rather the relations that are important. Understanding the microcosm as a set of interrelated relationships today explains more than does the substance paradigm.

In the old paradigm, things were static, everything had its season, and the seasons repeated themselves over and over. History was seen as a wheel in which reincarnation followed reincarnation. History was sometimes seen as predestined. It was all written in the stars. In the new paradigm, history is dynamic. Nothing is fixed—neither the future nor the past. Change is constant, and nothing is ever repeated exactly the same way twice. The meaning of past events is reexamined, recontexted, and reinterpreted.

The old paradigm was a mechanical one: the clockwork universe. Everything was built to purpose with engineer-like precision. Parts were replaceable. Businesses were also seen as machines. Work processes and the people who performed them could be understood from the point of view of input, throughput, and output. If you do *this,* then *that* would happen every time. The new paradigm is based on probability. If you do this, it is *likely* that this will happen, but these other three things are also possible.

While this mechanical notion of organizations is changing, it remains ubiquitous. Margaret Wheatley (1992) describes how businesses are viewed as machines:

> Organizations-as-machines is a 17th century notion, from a time when scientists began to describe the universe as a great clock. Our modern belief in prediction and control originated in these

clockwork images. Cause and effect were simple relationships; everything could be known; organizations and people could be engineered into efficient solutions. Three hundred years later, we still search for "tools and techniques" and "change levers"; we attempt to "drive" change through our organizations; we want to "build" solutions and "reengineer" for peak efficiencies.

COMMAND AND CONTROL

In the command-and-control model, the company is imaged as a machine, the operator of the machine is the leader, and management provide ongoing maintenance and repair. Acceptable standards were defined and communicated; the various units were required to conform to them. The rules were fixed and enforced. Any sort of change was relatively slow. The organization was designed to bring information to the central command site and distribute and enforce the decisions back to the edges of the enterprise. As enterprises became larger and more complex, the number of intermediate steps increased, as did the amount of information needing to be processed. While electronic media have sped the passage of information through these steps, and even allowed us to eliminate steps, it has not decreased the amount of information that must be processed or the number of decisions that must be made. Even with the new technology, the central command-and-control paradigm appears stretched to its limits (Telleen, 1996).

The control side of the paradigm results in more policing and less negotiating between management and employees. Behavior is monitored; e-mail is structured; and the use of the Internet is controlled. Compliance is required. Rights and responsibilities are given from the center to the members. Are the employees performing per the annual targets? Are the volunteers doing what the board wants them to do? Are the teachers delivering the curriculum as it is intended?

Command-and-control systems centralize power so that decisions regarding influence and benefits are centralized. In multi-stakeholder agreements or projects, this approach becomes even more complex. Stakeholders expect to be consulted and to exercise relatively equal influence on the decisions and to receive equitable benefit from the results. In multi-stakeholder situations, then, the decisions about the way the central organ will operate are very complex indeed, and can often lead to the breakup of the relationship. The struggles within various alliances in European industries are evidence of these dynamics.

> The assumption of the command and control paradigm of leadership is that leaders are responsible for planning, organizing, and coordinating other people's performance and solving their problems. B&S [Sic Belasco & Stayer] claim this is a formula for failure that breeds distrustful workforce and slow change. B&S propose an "intellectual capitalism paradigm" where leaders get people to be responsible for their own performance and solving their own problems. (Boje, 2000)

There are a growing number of situations in which the command-and-control paradigm simply does not work. These situations occur when independence of thought, use of intuition, and high-risk activities are required. In a highly competitive and complex environment, more than compliance is needed. When a problem that is new or unexpected is faced, employees who are personally committed to the goals of the department and company respond differently. When difficulties arise, they tend to deal with them, and if they can't they will check with colleagues and create solutions independent of management input.

SELF-ORGANIZING SYSTEMS

One of the consequences of the new leadership operating in the new paradigm is the emergence of new ways of understanding how organizations work. One understanding is that of self-organizing systems, a term that was created in 1947 by W. Toss Ashby, a psychologist and engineer. The concept came into general use in the scientific community in the 1970s and 1980s.

A self-organizing system is one whose internal organization increases in complexity without being managed or guided from outside. Normally, there are four components of these systems, positive feedback, negative feedback, a balance between exploration and exploitation of the environment, and multiple interactions between components of the system.

You can experiment with one in a simple way, using a group of from eight to fifty people. Give each person the following instructions:

1. Choose two people to be your reference points, but don't say who they are.
2. When I say go, move so that you are an equal distance from each of the two. You don't need to be in a straight line.
3. Pay attention to what happens to the group while you are finding your place in relation to your references. There should be a great deal of movement. After a while the movement should settle down. It may not be stable and it could flex back and forth. This is a simple self-organizing system.

To manage these systems as they appear in organizations requires a new kind of leadership. There is a move from the social engineering of the old paradigm to the use of self-organizing systems.

Self-organizing systems are being developed in a number of interesting ways. Dee Hock's (1999) creation of Visa, the credit card company, as a self-organizing system is an obvious example. Every participating company inside of the Visa organization is bound by the same few rules, and how they fulfill their obligations is up to the members themselves.

Even traffic is being directed by this same principle. An innovative traffic manager responsible for traffic had a vision of using self-organization principles in traffic control. In villages and small cities in the northern part of the Netherlands, traffic that organizes itself has been running as a very successful experiment. All traffic signs and lights have been removed from the roadways. Cars, trucks, bicycles, and pedestrians all share the same pavement. People pay attention because they are not being told what to do by the signs. By paying attention, they are acting more safely (Lyall, 2005). The concept is beginning to move to the United States. "In West Palm Beach, Florida, planners have redesigned several major streets, removing traffic signals and turn lanes, narrowing the roadbed, and bringing people and cars into much closer contact. The result: slower traffic, fewer accidents, shorter trip times" (Hugh, 2004).

A number of approaches to facilitating meetings are based on self-organizing principles. Harrison Owen's (1997) planning process, called Open Space Technology, is based on self-organizing principles. Jim Rough's Dynamic Facilitation is also based on self-organizing values (Rough, n.d.).

ADVERSARIAL RELATIONSHIPS

An effect of the command-and-control way of operating is that institutions jealously guard the people they control and resist the influence of other organizations. Businesses may see themselves in an adversarial relationship with workers, government agencies, suppliers, and customers. Churches are concerned that other congregations will "poach" their members. Associations worry that their membership will lose interest and go to other groups. In today's networked world, this adversarial stance can result in lost opportunities.

Organizations and organization consultants are experimenting with new forms that more closely reflect the new paradigm. The emphasis on teams is one example developed by Katzenbach and Smith in *The Wisdom of Teams* (1992). An effective team is not a machine but more a set of interrelated dynamics that evolve as they interact with one other.

The development of projects and project management processes is also more suited to working with the new paradigm than the old one. Virtual companies that come together to reach a specific goal and then disband are more and more common. Construction projects are often done this way, where a consortium of companies forms a temporary organization for the length of the job. Teams, projects, and virtual companies are more easily created, run, and abolished than are entire organizations. A few simple factors have to be set in motion, such as clearly defining the goal, setting milestones, assigning responsibility, and performing periodic checks on progress. The project teams go out of existence when their work is done, making way for a new configuration.

In the old paradigm, objectivity was an important concept. The scientist had to stand back and observe. In the new paradigm, the very act of observing changes what is happening in the experiment. How the question is formulated determines what will be observed.

When Harrison Owen (1987) began his work in change processes in very large organizations and communities, he recognized that as soon as he started asking questions, he was changing these organizations and communities.

SOCIAL RELATIONSHIPS: GLOBALIZATION

As our way of thinking and conceiving the universe has changed, so also have our relationships with others and with global society. The space we occupy, the way we interact with time, the way we care for others, and even our sense of destiny are changing.

Technology and urbanization are changing the way we relate to one another. We are in instant contact with even the remotest parts of the world. We communicate via the Internet, e-mail, sms messaging, voice mail, conference calls, videoconferences, and dozens of additional ways. New ways of communicating emerge every month as third generation telecommunication adds to the possibilities.

Transportation that is faster and more readily available is also changing the way we act. Some years ago, in Hong Kong, Maureen worked for HSBC. "The HSBC Group is named after its founding member, The Hong Kong and Shanghai Banking Corporation Limited, which was established in 1865 to finance the growing trade between Europe, India and China" (*HSBC Group History 1865–1899*, n.d.).

One of the traditions within the company was to have the Scottish and English employees working in the Far East take "home leave" every two years to recover from the rigors of tropical life. The trip back to the United Kingdom took three months. The employees stayed in their home country for months. Another three months were spent on the return to the Far East. It took months to prepare for each trip: packing, selecting the right food, corresponding with the people back home. These people lived wholly separate lives in separate worlds, and it took a very long time to move from one to the other.

Today, there is only one world to live in, and it is directly linked together. Recently a plane powered by a scramjet (supersonic combustion ramjet engine) was successfully flown at nearly ten times the speed of sound, two miles per second. The SR-71 of the U.S.

Air Force flies at 3.2 times the speed of sound. When a scramjet engine is put into a commercial airplane, the 8,400-mile flight from San Francisco to Hong Kong could be made in seventy minutes, less time than the drive from San Francisco to San Jose during rush hour.

In the old relationships, we lived in a parochial world. For most of us, the physical world we lived in could be walked across in a day. During that walk it was possible that we might not see anyone. In a real sense, our external world was huge. We had space to roam. Our internal world was small. We had few acquaintances and were exposed to few new ideas. There was lots of physical space to live in, but we lived in a very small inner space.

In the new relationships, this situation is reversed. We are crowded together in metropolises, in more than 290 cities with populations of more than one million people. In the past one hundred years, much of the world has become urbanized—there are more people in cities than in rural areas. In the 1920s, more people lived in cities than on farms in the United States and most of the developed world. By 2030, most of the inhabitants of the world will live in urban areas (Hodgson, n.d.).

More important than population density is the question, "Who are these people, who live so close to us?" We are in contact in our cities with the people of the world. Like it or not, our cities are microcosms of the globe. The food, entertainment, social groupings, customs, values, and even the languages of the world are present to some degree in all of our cities. The city of Los Angeles provides translation services in more than 150 languages (Abbassi, n.d.). Places of worship are being set up in small apartments, and when the religious community is large enough and rich enough, buildings are constructed. In Brussels—and we assume this is true in most big cities—you can find a traditional African healer who proffers all of the requisite herbs and spells. The University School of Medicine in the small European city where we live offers degrees in Chinese acupuncture, and the local cable service delivers a choice of channels, including all European languages but also Chinese, Hindi, and Arabic. The university hospital is a leading international medical center.

In the new world, time is frenetic and the rhythms are complex at the best. We—Jon and Maureen—live in a city of two hundred thousand people, and the choices of what to do for an evening's entertainment are nearly overwhelming. There are three cinemas showing twenty to thirty different films, a theatre, an opera house, jazz clubs, rock clubs, tango clubs, salsa clubs. Some 250 restaurants serving Thai, Cuban, Japanese, Moroccan, Turkish, and many more cuisines are available. Our colleagues ask if it isn't boring living in such a small place!

The external space seems reduced, while our interior space has become huge. We live in the globe, not in a village. When oil workers in Nigeria go on strike, the price of oil increases. When you call a toll-free number for information, you could be talking to a service center staffed by people of almost any nationality and located nearly anywhere. Understanding the world time clock, mastering foreign customs, corresponding in a diversity of languages, keeping abreast of diverse currencies and exchange rates, are no longer specialist fields for exotic experts. For a growing number of us, these are everyday business requirements. When we worked in Brussels, our administrative assistant spoke Dutch, French, English, and Spanish. The first three languages are required to work at McDonald's.

Selecting work is a continuing process in today's world. The list of potential jobs is nearly the length of a telephone directory, and few of us expect to stay in one profession for life. Many people take jobs that did not exist when they started their careers. For many people, a career is most interesting in a new technology for which the real applications are not clear yet.

The rhythm of our lives has also changed. In the old world, time was slow and contained simple rhythms. Choices were few and clear cut. There was the choice of what work to do, whom to marry, and where to live. These choices were pretty limited. If you were a boy, work usually was what your father did. If you were a girl, you could expect to do what your mother did, be it housewife or farm wife. Single ladies tended to be teachers, and there were acceptable alternatives for second and third sons, like the ministry or the military. Whom to marry was limited to a few potential partners, and where to live was limited to a few locations.

Choosing marriage partners is difficult now. While there are thousands of potential spouses, it is a challenge to meet and get to know someone suitable. New industries for partner seekers try to meet these growing needs with dating agencies, speed dating, and online dating. It is necessary these days to explicitly discuss values with a potential partner. In former generations, there was nothing to discuss—marriage and children was pretty much a known quantity. Today, each one is a unique creation.

In the old paradigm, our relationships were few but intimate. We lived in the same village or farm our whole lives. Our neighbors knew nearly everything about us. We had an extensive support network that we could call on if we were ill or just needed a little pep talk. When we visited the general store, long conversations would be held about community activities. Extended families took care of the children if parents were away. Orphans were put in the care of an aunt or grandmother, and children cared for their aged parents. These forms of care were not professional in today's sense, but they were available for everyone. Everyone participated in public works, helped one another, and even built one another's barns. The church or mosque or temple was built and maintained by its members. This is not intended to sound idyllic; there were many downsides to all of these traditional community relationships.

In our postmodern society, we live much more anonymously. We often don't even know our neighbors except to nod "Good morning" to. Our support network is to a large degree professionally structured and controlled. We hire baby-sitters sometimes without knowing them personally. Orphans are placed with foster parents or put into orphanages by the state. Professionals care for the aged. The state may determine with whom children will stay. A municipal agency cleans the streets. We hire professional contractors to build our homes and places of worship.

SOURCES OF MEANING: VALUES

Our worldviews and the ways we relate to others are changing, and so are where and how we find meaning in our lives.

In the old world, in order to understand how things worked, we looked for patterns that were repeated over and over in exactly the same way. These patterns, once discovered, were expected to be eternal. The whole basis of science was being able to repeat experiments that "proved" a hypothesis or theory. The truth could be found empirically, and once it was discovered, it never changed.

As the Industrial Age emerged, work was designed as repeating patterns in a mirror image of the giant clockwork.

In the new world we use temporary models, knowing that better ones will emerge. Most if not all problems have more than one solution, and no one of them is best except from a limited objective or bias. Science still repeats experiments, but exactly the same results are not expected. Results are tested against statistical probability. We are moving from knowing for sure to knowing what is likely.

Certitude in the old paradigm was found in authority. Leaders had authority because of their position in a company, community, or family. They had authority because they had the right parents or because they had acquired status—say, a university degree. Of course these were interrelated. People got high positions in companies by having the right relatives and friends. People got into a university because they had the right father or mother. The law, the scriptures, tradition all had authority. Today all of this is being challenged.

Authority has given way to authenticity. People seen to operate out of a high degree of integrity are seen as trustworthy. Work in high-performance teams is being designed so that it is interdependent rather than authority-lead (Katzenbach & Smith, 1992). Specialists exist in these teams, and one individual may be designated the team leader. Some teams have rotating leadership. Other teams change leaders when the work changes for optimal team effectiveness. Who does what work is flexible and fluid according to the project, the client requirements, or the personnel.

Authority has also changed the way companies describe themselves to the public and to potential employees. Companies that treat people well and are transparent in their dealings are growing in authority. There still exists a Fortune 500 for American companies and similar lists in almost every country in the world, but today there are also innumerable lists of the best companies to work for, the most woman-friendly companies to work for, the most admired companies for knowledge management, and so forth. What was once a framework of authority is now a diversified range of values for companies, including worker satisfaction, consistency between public image and internal reality, and the success of clients.

In the old paradigm, we looked to the past, and in the new we look to the future. Today a person's vision is often as important as his or her track record.

FAILURES OF TRADITIONAL LEADERSHIP

The failure to develop effective leadership in the public, private, and even voluntary sectors has been well documented. We briefly review some of these failures, so that we can look at the necessity of strengthening the *internal state* of leaders as a way to strengthen their performance.

ETHICAL LAPSES

Are business and political leaders generally immoral and criminal? Most are not. Some are, and the environment in which they work seems to encourage this behavior. Leaders are often pressured to produce short-term results or face the threat of losing their jobs and in some cases their careers. They often feel they need to avoid being candid when a remark about a shortfall in profits will result in the loss of millions of dollars in the company's value on the stock market. Greed and power affect others.

It is not just a problem of business. There are scandals in sports: the Olympic selection of venues, drug use, game fixing in soccer and cricket, and bribery of officials. Beyond sports, there are corrupt politicians, religious leaders, and artists. Many of those people whom we respect and want to respect seem to behave in questionable ways.

The roots of the problem are clear. Dr. Marilyn Smith (n.d.) summarizes them accurately:

- Companies favor their own interests over the well-being of their customers, employees, or the public.
- Companies reward behaviors that violate ethical standards.
- Individuals are willing to abuse their positions and power to enhance their individual interests.
- Companies and individuals overemphasize short-term gains at the expense of themselves and others in the long run.

- Companies and managers believe their knowledge is infallible and thus miscalculate the true risks and subject themselves and others to excessive risks.

AVOIDING THE TRUTH

Facing the truth has always been socially difficult. Barbara Tuchman (1984) explores this in her book *The March of Folly*. She looks at the fall of Troy, the break-up of the Holy See because of the Renaissance popes, the loss of the American colonies by King George III, and the Vietnam War. In each case the problems were clear and alternative courses of action were known at the time. Groups who were responsible agreed to the actions. They were not individual mistakes or errors of judgment. These policies were seen as counterproductive at the time.

This propensity is in full swing today. In the 9/11 Commission report (National Commission, 2004), several failures are noted. The problems of terrorist attacks were not considered from the perspective of the terrorists. This resulted in what the report called "cultural asymmetry" that blinded the government to the possibility of the threat. The problem for the U.S. government was small, but the desire to strike the United States was very large in the mind of terrorists. Procedures were in place to analyze the information but were not used.

> The methods for detecting and then warning of surprise attack that the U.S. government had so painstakingly developed in the decades after Pearl Harbor did not fail; instead, they were not really tried. They were not employed to analyze the enemy that, as the twentieth century closed, was most likely to launch a surprise attack directly against the United States. (National Commission, 2004)

Leaders and managers seem to want to avoid looking at the worst-case scenarios. Leaders ask their scenario planners for the most likely one, often a continuation of the past, and reject the others. Some organizations trap themselves this way into a culture of the past.

NASA was an organization trapped in a culture of normality. In the shift from lunar exploration to routine shuttle flights, the images of the risks involved changed. When an organization understands that it is experimenting, additional precautions are put in place. By its very nature, experiments have a high likelihood of unpredictable outcomes. They are riskier. Normal operations are considered to be stable and have lower risks. At NASA, the change in thinking from running an experimental project to being a stable operation meant that many of the cautions needed in the higher-risk experimental projects were set aside and the dangers were assumed to be lower.

When the *Columbia* shuttle exploded, it was known that a piece of foam had hit the wing during take-off. That had happened in the past with no difficulty. Engineers requested more detailed photos of the damaged wing to assess whether there was a problem. They were put in the position to prove there was one. "This may sound like mere semantics, but it meant NASA exhibited an overconfident, prove-it-wrong attitude rather than one that demanded engineers prove it right" (McGregor, 2005).

In many organizations that are under high public scrutiny, like NASA, there is a culture of success. Having an unbroken string of successful activities is seen as a way to gain in the world, and admitting that something has gone wrong is seen as a failure. Failures are losers. To maintain a success rate of 100 percent, we report it that way. When we can't report it that way, we create a story about how it was really a success.

BARRIERS TO COMMUNICATIONS

Not only is it difficult to face the truth, it is difficult to communicate it. Another failure of leadership today is the inability to remove the blocks to communications. Many communications problems are recognized but are largely ignored or dealt with in superficial ways. Information is distorted, untimely, wrong, or missing because the social systems inside organizations make it so. The structures through which communications flow are often constricted. The processes filter out important information sent from one part of the organization to another.

Communications is critical to businesses. A growing number of products are intangible. Their very existence depends on the ability to talk, write, and create images about them. Service industries are intangible. You don't know if a stock investment is going to be good until you have made it and made or lost money. We have to find other ways to determine if it is worthwhile. We use indirect ways of evaluating a service, such as the list of clients, the look of the office, or the past track record, even when we know that past records are not a reliable measure of future performance. Response time to changes in the market needs to be quicker and quicker. Both public images and images of the workforce are constructed by what is communicated and how it is communicated by the company. One of the most common problem statements is that there is a "failure of communications." What is the failure?

One component of the failure to understand what is happening throughout an organization is the set of social barriers to communications. Organizations that have a strict hierarchy or a great deal of social distance between the levels make it difficult for disturbing information to reach the top of the company. People lower in the hierarchy exercise self-censorship, and those higher may listen only for information that confirms their own ideas.

As information moves through a hierarchy, filtering takes place and is another cause of information distortion. The filtering often eliminates important information. The top of the organization often has no idea what is actually happening on the shop floor. We (Jon and Maureen) have what we call "the 80-20 rule." Because of misunderstanding or miscommunications, 80 percent of the information a manager receives is passed on accurately to the next person in line. The manager adds 20 percent of his or her own ideas to the information without necessarily differentiating the new ideas from the original information. Within a few layers, the information can lose a great deal of its accuracy.

The values used to interpret information are also a source of problems. Frequently information within an organization is interpreted by a set of values aimed at protecting the managers. We worked with an organization in which the standard practice for the annual and quarterly evaluation of employees was to automatically give them upper middle scores. This meant that everyone got scores high enough to prevent them from being fired and low enough that they would not be promoted or transferred. Any manager who broke the practice was called into question directly by his peers for creating unnecessary disturbance and extra work for everyone.

THE CONFLICT FOR FACILITATIVE LEADERS

The issue facing facilitative leaders is the conflict between the old and new paradigms. This conflict is taking place everywhere—in business, politics, schools, and religious groups. Paradigm change seemed wonderful during the late twentieth century. Joel Barker's training film *Business of Paradigms,* about paradigm change, is said to be the best-selling training video of all time (Advanced Training Sources, n.d.).

Today there is a backlash against the new thinking. Certainly the frightening experience of the terrorist attacks on September 11, 2001, has made many people reconsider whether the new world into which we have moved is such a good thing. Everywhere you see leaders participating in this conflict of change, sometimes longing for the old world and sometimes striving to participate in the new. The paradigm out of which the world operates has changed, however, whether we like it or not. Once you saw that NASA photograph of the earthrise taken from space, taken in December 1968 the maps with all the borders and different colors for countries just never worked the same way again. There is no way back. The challenge today is to learn to live well in the new world. The burden on anyone who dares to take a leadership role today is especially great because the issues that arise are unprecedented.

LEADERSHIP IN THE NEW WORLD

Along with the shift in paradigm, the characteristics of leadership roles are changing. Traditional sources of power, such as access to information, control of resources, and positions of influence, are eroding. Again and again it is clear that leadership today involves consultation with colleagues both inside and outside of the organization. There are always moments when the leader has to stand in front of the group and state the new direction. In today's world, however, those individually focused moments punctuate the more continuous flow of the leader consulting, eliciting motivation, stimulating creativity, and consensus building. Robert Greenleaf (1983, 1996) has spoken of the leader as servant. Jim Collins (1994) researched qualities of leaders in a great number of very successful companies, and described a characteristic called "clock building, not time telling"—leaders build a company that can tick along without them, rather than feeding their ego by becoming indispensable (Chapter Two).

We use the phrase "facilitative" to describe this style of leadership. We also use it to describe facilitators when they are acting in a leadership capacity. What the facilitative leader does is enable groups from within and without the organization to produce their best wisdom and to implement able directions.

The command-and-control paradigm of leadership came down to us from the age of the king and his vassals. The vassals (read senior managers and board members) are offered protection and a degree of security in exchange for loyalty to the crown. Both receive a degree of security. In contrast to this is Robert Greenleaf's "Servant Leader" (1983), in which the leader serves the best interest of the employees rather than the other way around. Harrison Owen's (1990) image is that leaders evoke and nurture spirit. In a similar vain, Dee Hock (1999) suggests that leaders are those who remove obstacles to people's creativity. Many new ways to lead are emerging if we take the trouble to look for them.

WHAT LEADERS DO

Harrison Owen, the creator of Open Space Technology, describes the function of leadership in his book *Leadership Is . . .* (1990). Effective leadership evokes spirit through a vision. It then grows that spirit through storytelling. It channels spirit by creating structure. It comforts spirit when things come to an end. Finally, it reinvigorates spirit when the grief is over.

EVOKE SPIRIT WITH VISION

What is *vision?* It is one of those popular terms that everyone assumes they know what it means. Companies write vision statements and mission and vision statements.

Vision has three qualities. It is big, attractive, and do-able (Owen, 1990). Jim Collins calls these "Big Hairy Audacious Goals" (1994, Chapter Five).

By *big* Owen means there is space within the vision for all of those potentially involved in it to share their points of view, perspectives, skills, and competencies. It has enough room for all of the necessary spirit to function effectively. The vision needs to be big enough to enable participants to grow. A great vision is a challenge and an opportunity for participants to fulfill their own deepest desires. It evokes awe in those who accept the invitation to participate. If it is too small, timid, and tame, its power to gather and to set loose all of the necessary spirit will be stunted. Tame visions are boring from the start; they go nowhere.

A great vision is *attractive*. It generates enthusiasm and commitment, which cannot be coerced, legislated, or achieved through deception. People must be invited, and that invitation must be an exciting and attractive one. It offers the possibility of fulfillment of the dreams of participants. Perhaps people only come to realize what their dreams are when the invitation of the vision happens. These dreams offer an opportunity for growth. If people are to grow, the direction of growth needs to be striking and understandable.

A great vision is also *do-able*. It is in the first place technically feasible, perhaps not at the moment of the first statement of the vision, but realizable within the time frame of the vision. It must also be do-able in the sense of being historically possible. The vision must be appropriate for the circumstances and capacities of the people being addressed.

John F. Kennedy's vision of putting a man on the moon by the end of the 1960s had these qualities. The idea was bold and inspiring to millions of people. It was a continuation of the pioneer myth of the United States. While not all of the technology was available at the time, it was clear that it would likely be so over the next ten years. It also was a Cold War statement to the Soviet Union in response to the United States having lost the race to space. Kennedy's vision was an affirmation and continuation of the exploring new frontiers aspect of the American myth.

There are two type of vision: one is evolutionary and the other is revolutionary. Evolutionary vision reenergizes the existing vision and revolutionary evokes a new vision.

Evolutionary Vision

In the evolutionary form of vision, leadership taps into the hopes and dreams for the company or organization of the people they lead. This is done by asking the right questions, listening to the responses, recording what is being said, and checking to see if what they have recorded is an honest reflection of the group's thinking. In essence, evolutionary vision asks, What does the old spirit mean in today's situation?

We led or participated in a number of community development planning consultations for the Institute of Cultural Affairs, a research, training, and demonstration not-for-profit organization created out of the Ecumenical Institute in Chicago. The consultations were in a variety of cultures and countries; the United States, Canada, Italy, India, The Philippines, The Republic of Korea, Jamaica, Venezuela, and Peru. They were in urban neighborhoods, small towns, and rural villages. Everyone in the community was invited to participate in the workshop, and most came to the evening sessions. People were visited in their homes and places of work during the afternoons, and in the mornings a plenary was held.

The first day of the weeklong planning workshop asked in various forms, "What would you like to see in your community in the next four years?" The assumption is that there was a latent vision of the future of the community. It was mostly unconscious and mostly needed only to be unleashed.

Several things surprised us in the process of leading these workshops. This unconscious vision was common to an extraordinary degree among the residents. If someone said they wanted a voluntary fire department, many others mentioned it also without knowing that the other person had suggested it. At the same time these visions were inclusive of most aspects of the community. Visions included health, education, commerce, infrastructure, plazas, new churches or temples, among many other things. It was striking how diverse the desires of a single community could be. Generally, they were quite achievable. These visions were practical, even when they verged on the overly ambitious. They were truly evolutionary.

In these situations, the old spirit was present. It was alive, perhaps dormant and only needed awakening. Sometimes, however, the old spirit is gone or never existed. When that is the case, something more revolutionary is required.

Revolutionary Vision

Revolutionary vision taps into the emerging future, and asks others to participate in it. It asks, What tomorrow is being born today?

Claus Otto Scharmer (2000) and others at MIT have been working on what happens when leaders tap the future.

> Leaders from around the world are facing a new kind of challenge: coping with the various waves of disruptive, revolutionary change that redefine the context of business. One wave has to do with the rise of the Internet based "new" economy and its driving force, the process of *digitization* (Castells, 1998; Kelly, 1998). A second has to do with the rise of new relational patterns and their underlying driving forces: the processes of *globalization* (of markets, institutions, products), *individualization* (of products, people, and their careers), and increasingly *networked structures* and web-shaped relationship patterns (Castells, 1996). For example, the "war for talent" that most companies deal with is a typical challenge that arises from the interplay of the above four driving forces.

> A third and more subtle dimension of change has to do with the increasing relevance of experience, awareness and consciousness and their underlying driving force, the process of *spiritualization* (Conlin, 1999) or, to use a less distracting term, the process of becoming aware of one's more subtle experiences (Depraz, Varela, and Vermersch, 1999). An example is the recent growth in interest in topics like "flow" (Csikszentmihalyi, 1990) or personal mastery (Senge, 1990) both inside and outside the world of business.

> These three contextual changes present today's leaders with a fundamentally new world in which they must be innovators and radical revolutionaries rather than agents of improving the status quo (Hamel, 1997, 2000). The more the world of business moves into environments of increasing returns, the more the primary challenge for business leaders becomes developing a "precognition" for emerging business opportunities before they become manifest in the market place (Arthur, 1996). (Scharmer, 2000, pp. 3–4)

Both hope and dreams of the future and sensing the future are fundamental to tapping into the enthusiasm, the inspiration of a group. It is the collective vision that is important, not only that of the individual leaders.

GROW SPIRIT BY COLLECTIVE STORYTELLING

The usual understandings of the word *myth* involve ancient stories about the supernatural like the Greek gods and goddesses, or modern people like Elvis Presley who are so well regarded that they are "a myth in their own time," or something that is untrue—the myth of instant weight loss. A new understanding of myth is becoming part of contemporary organizational theory.

Organizational myths in this understanding are, first, usually rooted in historical events. Second, they are rooted in the meaning and values of being a member of the organization. Third, a myth is a symbol of the organization. It tells of the beginnings and endings. It is a stylized narrative of the struggles and successes in the development of the organization. Heroes and heroines are remembered. Stories about times of difficulty are shared. Icons and rituals support stories.

Companies have rituals of many kinds. Some celebrate the amount of time one has spent with the organization, such as marking twenty-year anniversaries. Others celebrate promotions or birthdays. Sales conferences take on a ritualistic tone at times. Day-to-day events like colleagues greeting one another on arrival at work are rituals. A weekly team meeting, a coffee machine conversation, the smokers going outside together for a cigarette, going to a pub with colleagues on Friday afternoon—all of these have some ritual aspects.

Icons, such as organizational logos and house styles, are a bit more obvious. The displays of products or trophies are corporate icons. When you walk into the Nike European headquarters, you see lots of symbols. Pictures of the founders and of sports stars speak to the visitor and staff. The architecture itself is designed to bring to mind a rural college campus.

These stories, rituals, and icons are critical to sustaining the spirit of an organization. Leaders who ignore this dimension of people management do so at their own risk. Stories enable leaders to communicate effectively, to build collective intelligence, to imagine alternate futures, and to successfully introduce new ideas (Kahan, n.d.; Denning, 2004).

Stories and storytelling enable a leader to communicate effectively at many levels. Complex ideas are best communicated through the use of stories. The story asks the listener to imagine himself or herself as a part of the story. When they do, the story becomes their own. It becomes part of their identity and not something imposed from outside.

Stories are being recognized by the world of knowledge management. Until recently, knowledge management has focused on explicit knowledge, those things that can be documented. This kind of knowledge can be stored in computers; it can be retrieved by anyone who has access. It is convenient to manage. The problem is that most knowledge is not explicit. It is tacit knowledge, embedded in the way things are done. Tacit knowledge is also communicated by stories.

Imagine reading a manual about how to ride a bicycle. This manual would describe balance and how to achieve it. It would diagram the inner ear and how it helps a sense of balance. This pretend manual would describe gyroscopic forces when the wheels go around and how they help balance and stability. It would describe how to steer and to peddle. Imagine now getting on a bicycle and riding it. The way most of us learn to ride a bike is to get on and try. Someone might help hold it up and run alongside. They might make suggestions about how to improve. This might speed up the learning process, but the learning is getting on and riding.

More and more knowledge management is about creating communities of people who have this "knowledge in action" and tell stories that capture in some degree this tacit knowledge. The collective wisdom is stored in the memories of these people, captured by their experiences, and shared in stories.

Stories also enable people to imagine new futures. In a sense, any planning is about storytelling. It is not often narrative in nature but it is a construction about what the future could look like or, given enough commitment, will look like. Some of the processes of using stories to create future plans are formalized in strategic planning techniques such as scenarios and appreciative inquiry.

New ideas can be introduced through the use of stories. In complex systems, people need to understand the connections between things and events. Stories help us understand what has brought an organization to a particular place in its development, why things need to change, how they are going to change, and how the organization will benefit. New thoughts and ideas are connected to the existing images and understandings of people. They then become more acceptable.

We worked in a village in Peru for two years doing community development work. Houses were constructed of brick or adobe or plastic sheets on bamboo frames. Everyone was improving on the places where they lived. They were either just finishing an improvement project, planning one, or in the midst of doing one. When we first arrived we thought construction was going on all the time. As we lived there for some months, we noticed that a lot of the construction was not really going anywhere. A few hundred bricks would be stacked against a one-third completed wall, the only one in the new house. They stayed there over the months and years. These incomplete and perhaps never completed structures seemed more symbols of failure than of hope in the future.

The project received a grant to build a new schoolhouse. The village had to supply the labor and expertise, and the organization would supply the building materials, reinforcing rod, bricks, cement, and so on. One of the conditions of the grant was that the building had to be completed in six weeks. The village decided that it would conduct a series of workdays every Saturday. About a hundred volunteers showed up the first day. We dug foundations and cemented in the foundations. At the end of the day the women of the village prepared a feast, and lots of the local brandy and beer flowed. It was great. The next week we had about fifty-five people. The third week we had three or four teenagers. We discussed it as a staff and realized that we were in the process of producing another symbol of failure. The next Monday our staff went to the site and began work. After a while one of the informal leaders came and asked what we were doing. We said we promised to complete the school in six weeks, and we felt that we needed to put in an extra effort to get it done in time. Slowly, more and more people joined us over the next few days until on Saturday we had more than fifty people working. The village did complete the school on time, and it became a symbol of success and one of the stories that villagers told about how they had transformed the community.

SUSTAIN SPIRIT WITH STRUCTURE

Unless spirit is given a pathway to express itself, it will dissipate. That pathway is the structure of the organization, but structure can stifle and kill spirit just as easily as conducting it. Most organizations have the process backward. They create an organization and then try to kindle spirit in the thing, like bringing a robot to life.

An entire industry of motivational efforts has developed to assist this largely misguided process.

The sequence is to evoke spirit, enable it to grow strong, and then create a structure to hold it in being. Structure is more likely to be grown like a plant than to be built like a freeway. To understand how the spirit is moving in an organization, a leader listens to the stories that are being told and watches the way people interact with each other and with their work. His or her work is to create structures that support what is working in the organization.

The setup and style of an organization's space effects spirit. It is not only the architecture but also the décor and furniture. When an organization moves its offices or a manufacturing plant, the spirit can be dramatically affected.

This doesn't necessarily mean anything so *chichi* as a Feng Shui study. When the Navy commissions a new ship, careful consideration is given to the first crew. Not only do they need to be highly professional, but they also need to have the appropriate team and working spirit. The Navy has learned that the experiences of this initial crew can affect the culture of the ship for decades into the future. Would that other organizations were so careful of their newly commissioned spaces!

The space of an organization, in this approach, is created to support the spirit. To do this a leader must be able to know where the spirit is moving and to respond to it with some sensitivity. Paying attention to where the excitement is is the key to discerning spirit. What do people talk about? Where is their energy for doing things? These things will give indications of where the spirit is moving. Too often managers ask questions in a way that indicates what employees should value, and employees too often give what is expected of them. The spirit dies.

The same things are true for the way time is structured in the organization. The rhythms, the paces of work and changes in it, the events that mark time all affect the spirit of the group.

We worked for a small company of about ten consultants in Brussels. Most of the week we had little time to see each other, exchange ideas or report what was happening. Every Friday at 4 P.M. everyone who could would meet at the Pax, a quiet neighborhood café/bar. We had a few drinks, socialized, and told each other about our week. If there were any special issues, they could be brought up and solutions found. Sometimes people would drift home around 5 P.M., and sometimes family and friends would turn up and we would go on until late in the evening. The event marked the end of the week and enabled a transition from the workweek to the weekend.

Leaders who need to control will tend to kill the spirit. They have a hard time understanding spirit and how it moves. When the vision is clear and the collective story is grounded in reality and well told, then the structures will coalesce easily and quickly. By letting space, time, and relationships organize themselves as the spirit moves them, they will reflect and support the most creative and effective dimensions of the company. This process of letting the spirit shape the structure requires some sensitivity. If the structures are fixed too soon, the spirit will be wounded. If the structures are fixed too late, the spirit will dissipate. It is perhaps better to err on the side of too late than on the side of too soon.

Organizations as Containers of Spirit

Scharmer (2000) discusses four archetypes of organization: centralized, decentralized, networks, and communities. All of these can and do at one time in their lives act as containers of spirit. Yet, spirit in our time seems to be moving away from centralized forms toward community forms.

Centralized organizations are the typical hierarchical, pyramid structures. They are relatively simple. They tend to operate out of a machine metaphor and function as bureaucracies. Professional bureaucrats manage them, and oligarchies lead them.

Decentralized organizations are a step away from centralization but have most of the same attributes. They are simple in structure, with several miniature versions of the centralized structure. They are hierarchical and pyramid. They are somewhat independent machines run by decentralized professional managers.

Organizations as networks are a significant shift in operations. They consist of networks of thinkers, brokers, and makers. These networks activate when a task is required. They shift as the task changes. Imagine the design and construction of a complex structure such as a harbor, a long suspension bridge, or a deep water oil platform. Different functions come and go as progress is made in the construction: the architect, the general contractor, the subcontractors. The makers would come and go depending on their specialty, steelworkers in this phase, electricians in that one, and plumbers in another.

Organizations as communities are rare, but more are coming into being. They are communities of reflection, commitment, and practice. Communities of reflection are not simply discussion groups. They reflect on shared experience and operate at a sophisticated dimension of dialogue. Communities of commitment are based on a shared will. It is not common plans, as any group can have these. These communities are built from the subjective nature of shared experience; they care about the same things. They discover connections between members and build on those connections. The common connections then lead to connections to the larger whole. Finally, objectives are discovered and moved toward a shared body of collective will. Communities of practice are just that, communities that practice. They may be groups who play music together or trainers sharing teaching methods by trying them out (Scharmer, 2000).

COMFORT SPIRIT AT THE END

All things come to an end. For some time, American society has tended to avoid dealing with death, although there is some evidence that this is changing. We sanitize the burial and grieving process. Bodies are made up to look like the people are still alive. Coffins are constructed so that they will last for centuries. Funeral homes isolate those who are grieving to protect them from embarrassment and the others from having to deal with the pain being expressed. The language we use softens the experience.

Departments come to an end, and much of the same grief and pain is present. Companies fail. People are let go. Real leaders help people through these ending times. The grieving process in all of these situations needs to be supported. Unfortunately, the norm seems to be avoidance of the human aspects of dying.

> When a human system, particularly a business, or part of a business, shows the unmistakable signs of ending, the sequence of behavior at the top is unfortunately fairly predictable: (one) ignore it, perhaps it will go away; (two) deny it, perhaps it isn't so; (three) find

somebody else to blame, so at least you do not get tagged with the
failure; and (four) bail out as quickly as possible with the largest
parachute available. (Owen, 1990, p. 122)

Of course, this is understandable in a culture of success that de-
nies death. It is precisely at these moments when spirit needs support. True leaders take on the unpleasant task of being there for
colleagues when this happens. It is at these moments that the greatest insights and learnings can be gleaned.

The Grief Work

Much of the work on grief has been done for individuals, but it applies equally to organizations. Harrison Owen (1990) suggests six
stages of the grieving process. Stage 1 is shock and anger. This is a
manifestation of the organization's own need to survive. Stage 2 is
denial and "if only." Denial is pretending that nothing is happening. It is the belief that the organization won't survive without our
contribution. Time spent discussing the "if only's": If we had done
this or if they had done that, it would all be different. This stage is
important because it is building the distance needed to be able to
move into stage 3, which is memories. Here stories are told about
heroes and heroines, the great things we did, the contracts we won
and so on. The fourth stage Owen calls "Open Space." There is silence, a time of reconciliation, not necessarily of a thoughtful sort.
It is like the moment between breathing in and breathing out. It
seems that nothing can be done. The interesting thing about
human beings is that it is precisely in this situation, in which they finally realize that nothing can be done to continue the old situation, that new notions about what can be done begin to stir, and
the fifth stage, "Imagination," begins. These stirrings are not sweeping strategies but rather initial forays in wholly new directions. This
possibility comes from the freedom found in the open space.
Choices are not yet made, but new possibilities are being seen.
From those possibilities a new vision starts to emerge, the sixth
stage, "vision." The vision stage is both the end and the beginning.
It is the end of the old and the beginning of the new.

Obviously no leader conducts an organization through these
stages, but the leader can be supportive of those individuals involved when an organization or department comes to an end. This

is the process of an organization coming to terms with the death of its previous way of being. Effective leadership is able to be present for the organization throughout the process and to support what is, in fact, a fresh development of the new future.

What can a leader do? Attempts to intervene and redirect this process can abort the process. These efforts often come out of the image of the leader as a parent or a master, protecting people from the pain of grief at exactly the moment when in fact they need to experience it fully and take responsibility for their own futures, to be able to move on. Leaders who assume that the organization is incapable of healing itself often create a self-fulfilling prophecy.

Top management may leave the middle manager to carry out the ugly work of downsizing, saving their own reputations for the eventual rebuilding process with the survivors. The struggle to stand with colleagues during the grieving process is much more difficult for those who have to carry out the procedures that cause the grief. The leader has to create his or her own way. Those who are present and authentically care will contribute to the next phase. It is a time of trial, which colleagues will remember—for good or ill—for a long time to come.

Sometimes the grieving process works, and sometimes it doesn't. When it does not, spirit is not revived. When the spirit is dead, a hollow organization continues without ever functioning effectively, like a factory in which a caretaker maintains the facility but production capability rusts away. Alternately, the organization dissipates. There may be remnants that remain.

When the grieving process works, the possibility of something new is created. The vision evokes spirit. Equally, spirit inspires vision. Leaders are attuned and present to spirit, and when the time is appropriate enable the creation of vision.

CONCLUSION

A great deal has been written about leadership. How-to manuals, ethics, qualities, characteristics, and more have been developed in response to the problems of the leaders we seem to be inflicted with.

Leadership is about spirit; caring for others' spirit and your own. As Dee Hock (1999) says, the first person you need to manage, as a leader, is yourself. Taking care of yourself is not just the occasional massage; it is an essential component of being a leader. Traditionally, a leader has had time to step aside to think through a decision and to reflect on what is needed, but that option is less and less available today.

The former mayor of New York City, Rudolf Giuliani, was in a meeting when someone walked in and said, "There's a fire at the World Trade Center. They think a twin-engine plane hit the building . . ." (Giuliani, 2002, p. 4). He had no time to go aside and reflect. He had to act immediately even though many of the emergency plans were of no use. Giuliani acted, as we all do, out of the character that he had developed over all of his years of experience up until then. Caring for yourself is preparing the character you want to have when difficulty arises. It will take more than an occasional massage to do that.

Leadership is also about interacting with groups. The old decision-making processes are dying. Frontline employees are necessarily involved in the decision-making processes because only they have some of the critical aspects of the information needed to make these decisions. They are also expecting to be involved in the decisions. You hear the occasional complaint that they don't want the responsibility for these decisions. "Managers are paid to make decisions, not us." The longer-term and stronger trend is toward participation.

Decision-making processes are becoming more transparent. Smoked-filled rooms are out, not only for health reasons. Increased transparency is being required legally and socially.

CHAPTER TWO

TRENDS IN EMPLOYEE PARTICIPATION

Leadership today must take into consideration some dimension of participation by those who are being led. While this has been the case for some time, we live in an historical moment in which participation is no longer one philosophical or cultural option among many, but is a given, in some form or other, in every society and in every organization. The involvement of participants in their own decision making is part of the fabric of today's world.

The facilitative leader is that leader who understands and applies in her or his situation the skills necessary to gather the best information possible from colleagues and employees, to generate the best ideas, to develop optimal decisions, to enable commitment from the group, and to organize effective implementation and evaluation.

We are convinced that there are two major reasons for this development of a greater understanding of group dynamics and participation in decision-making processes. One is historical, and the other has to do with the changing circumstances of organizations today. As a result, organizations themselves have begun to make changes toward greater employee participation.

HISTORICAL PRECEDENTS TO GREATER PARTICIPATION

The American and French Revolutions mark some of the earliest inclusions of "the many" in the decision-making process. Until these two revolutions, the prosperity of a country depended to a large degree on the quality of its king or queen.

The ending of slave trade and the abolition of slavery created a legal framework of equality for nonwhite men. The right to vote was granted to women in New Zealand in 1893, spread across North America (the United States in 1920 through a constitutional amendment), most of Europe (the United Kingdom in 1928), and finally the greater part of the world, although women are still not allowed to vote in some countries.

These developments increased the numbers of those individuals who could participate in formal decision-making processes. One result of their institution was the spread of individual responsibility and freedom of choice. Another is a doubling of the number of those eligible to vote, dramatically changing the dynamics of elections throughout much of the world.

The civil rights movement in the United States took concepts like the right to vote, equal access to public services, and other legal rights and turned them into realities.

While the political world was shifting in the nineteenth and twentieth centuries, the world of economics was changing as well. The Industrial Revolution dramatically changed interaction in the workplace. A key consequence was that workers were no longer individuals, but were now a collective body, part of the production process. Individuals were replicable parts of a machine. During this period there was enough surplus labor that finding replacements was relatively easy. This gave a great deal of power and control to the management of industries. In response to potential and often real exploitation of workers through the use of this power, a movement centered on the rights of workers emerged. This took a number of forms, from anarchism at the end of the nineteenth and beginning of the twentieth centuries to socialist political parties, especially in Europe and to a lesser degree in the United States. The individual worker had to surrender workplace freedoms for the sake of the collective labor effort. This powerful new social entity—workplace labor—needed organization of its shared interests and goals, resulting in increased participation in decision making by the collective labor force. Karl Marx and other socialist intellectuals developed the theoretical basis, and the implementation was done by labor organizations such as unions and political parties. Not only did collective labor increase the power of the working class but it also developed skills in participation in decision-making processes.

The right to participate is growing in other ways also. Children have gained rights and even at times influence in decision-making processes. The right to participate, while not a reality everywhere, is recognized as something that should be allowed.

Changes Facing Today's Organizations

Three characteristics mark the circumstances of modern organizations and their functioning. First, organizations are becoming more complex in content, processes, and dynamics. Second, they are required to be more attentive and responsive in order to achieve their goals, whether social or business. Third, organizations today need to be increasingly creative and innovative in order to survive in the competitive and rapidly changing environment.

Organizational Complexity

Complexity is part of our age. The amount of information necessary to operate even a simple business is massive. The blueprints required for constructing an offshore oil rig run into a million or more drawings, each one of which requires that decisions be made. Some of these decisions may require inputs from three or four different companies and any number of specialists. Added to this huge technical complexity are things like stakeholder relations, management of suppliers and subcontractors, government agency coordination, and human relations issues. And this is just a construction example; think of a school district reconsidering its curriculum; an association adapting its bylaws; a hospital trying to improve its service delivery.

The accepted wisdom in these complex situations is that the situation must be broken down into manageable pieces. Decisions in each arena are typically taken independently of each other, resulting in less than optimal interfaces between the units. Doing your bit well, tossing it over the silo wall, and letting those on the other side deal with it as they will is a typical result of this approach.

While breaking tasks down simplifies each of the tasks, independent specialist teams can increase the cost and complexity of a job. Automobile designers, for example, might create dozens of different specifications for various nuts and bolts, when in fact only five or six more generalized ones may be needed. The teams designing the chassis, interior, suspension, drive train, and engine all need bolts and nuts. Teams left on their own tend to create specifications that meet their needs, without reference to the needs of other teams. This makes manufacturing the car more complex and more costly.

Organizations, realizing that this "silo behavior" is less than helpful, look for ways to include people from the whole process in their planning. The idea is that people working in each phase of a project can develop a clearer idea of the issues, constraints, and expectations of the rest of the process. In principle, pickup by the next phase of workers is smoother and more trouble free, and this saves time and money.

DYNAMIC COMPLEXITY

Peter Senge (1990, pp. 71–72, 364–365) describes "dynamic complexity," where the relationship between cause and effect is subtle and the effects over time and distance are not obvious. Many organizations today work routinely with this type of problem. This is especially true any time an organization works internationally. When the effects in the short term are different from those over the long term, or when the effects of a change in one part of a system are dramatically different from those in another part of the system, dynamic complexity is operating. A problem may take years, even decades to work its way to the surface and become visible as an issue that needs attention. Traditional planning, forecasting, and analytical techniques are not designed to deal with this kind of intricacy. "Balancing market growth and capacity expansion is a dynamic problem. Developing a profitable mix of price, product (or service) quality, design, and availability that make a strong market position is a dynamic problem. Improving quality, lowering total costs, and satisfying customers in a sustainable manner is a dynamic problem" (Lyneis, 1980). International organizations find that a policy that is much appreciated among one segment of their membership may be despised in another segment.

An example of actions having one effect in the short term and another over the long term is the emergence of hyper-virulent infections that reside in hospitals. They have evolved from normal infectious bacteria. As patients were treated with antibiotics for their infections, some of the bacteria survived and evolved so that the antibiotic became ineffective. Hospitals then switched to new antibiotics, resulting in the bacteria evolving further. The bacteria began evolving faster than new antibiotics could be developed. The short-term consequence is saving lives, and the long-term is the development of virtually untreatable infections.

Gathering and understanding information across different teams and over time are not typical command-and-control activities. This sort of complexity calls for a maximum of effort by all involved, not only to deliver their own input, but also to understand and adapt to the input of the others.

Organizations are also awakening to the fact that information and knowledge is distributed throughout the organization, a radical shift from the belief that all relevant information resided in management. For everyone to have access to distributed information, new channels of communications and processes of decision making are necessary. Facilitative leadership is an effective way to deal with complexity that calls for a diversity of inputs, perspectives, and experience to be understood and managed.

Organizational Responsiveness

One nagging issue for organizations today is how to respond quickly to ever-present challenges and demands. For businesses, the capacity to discern and respond to a wide range of changes in the marketplace, business environment, customer expectations, and supplier information is a critical competitive advantage. In the area of social services, there is the need to be ready to provide care immediately, keeping bureaucracy and paperwork for recipients to a minimum. Similar circumstances apply in many other fields.

In order to ensure increased adaptability, organizations have tended to move their decision making closer to their corporate interfaces: service recipients, customers, suppliers, and other stakeholders. Greater decision-making responsibility is being given to caregivers, salespeople, repair people, and service representatives, so that whatever services are delivered, they are provided in the most effective manner possible.

We worked with the U.K. sales office of a large European paper manufacturer. There were inside and outside sales representatives. Inside sales reps took orders over the phone based on contracts the outside reps had generated by visiting clients in person. Most of the negotiations for price, delivery time, quality, and so on was taking place in the phone conversations between the purchasing agents of clients and the inside sales reps. When the inside reps were given a limited band within which they could negotiate without needing permission from supervisors, sales were completed much faster, clients were better served, and the reps were more satisfied with their jobs.

The development of new products and processes in response to customer requests is being institutionalized. Product improvements are closely tied to complaints and suggestions when the customer interfaces with the company. Repairmen and women, service desk operators, and sales people often have a better understanding of customer needs and expectations than do the product designers.

For companies whose competitive advantage depends on minimal length of supply chains, the distance between companies and their suppliers is so close that at times it is difficult to distinguish the two organizations. The core suppliers of Dell Computers receive communications every twenty seconds. Deliveries to their Austin plant from suppliers are within ninety minutes of order. In another example, when selecting a new supplier, a Japanese car manufacturer will send a manager to work inside the new supplier for two years to learn the supplier's strengths and weaknesses. Both companies adjust to the needs of the other.

Responsiveness is a function of a number of strategic, tactical, and operational systems, all of them based on continuous communication across functional and sometimes organizational boundaries. Leadership is not confined to delivering quality in one's own field, but it includes the ability to gather relevant information from a diversity of sources and enable them to arrive at mutually satisfactory ways of working together. Here again, the skills of group facilitation are a critical component of leadership in today's world.

ORGANIZATIONAL CREATIVITY AND INNOVATION

In addition to coping with complexity and responding quickly and accurately, organizations today also need to be creative and innovative. Certain conditions need to be in place to do that: dissatisfaction with the current situation, perception that there are or could be acceptable alternatives, confidence in the ability to change, supportive and challenging environment, independent thinkers, free-flowing ideas, information, and time.

It seems obvious that for innovation to happen people need to see the need for change. To generate creative solutions, people need to believe that a solution can be found and that they can find it. Leadership that supports creative thinking takes responsibility for supporting this belief across the organization. If the situation is seen as hopeless, it will be hopeless. Belief in the ability of the existing organization to solve its problems turns an insurmountable obstacle into a challenge to be taken on. Leadership can support this belief by listening to and providing help as ideas emerge. Not all ideas need to be supported forever, but the process of generating ideas does need support all the time.

Creative thinking begins with a quantity of ideas, not with quality ideas. It may be that 99 percent of what is proposed is not much use, but without that 99 percent, the one good idea would have never made it to the top. It is a little like panning for gold. You put a shovel full of sand in the pan, slowly swirl it around in water, and the last few grains may be gold. Leadership appreciates the 99 percent for that golden 1 percent that it produces.

The right balance between supporting creativity and challenging people to be creative is necessary. Creativity takes place in situations where the organization is challenged and there is no easily perceived solution. Leadership needs to encourage, express, and explore new ideas and take risks.

In 1997, the Central New York Regional Transportation Authority (Centro) lost one-sixth of its operating income from national and local government cuts and a generally depressed local economy. No new sources of income were obvious. The new general manager, Joe Calabrese, stated:

"The job of leadership is to take people where they ordinarily would not go." Hence, he encouraged his employees to "Take a chill pill" and not worry so much about the consequences of new techniques. He backed that up by assuring them that there would be no penalty for first time failures of new attempts to improve service and agency efficiency. Mr. Calabrese believed that providing his staff with a certain amount of "cover" was one of his primary responsibilities as General Manager. He always wanted to test new ideas. "Let's try—it could be fun," was one of his mottos. (National Center for Transit Research, n.d.)

Centro reduced costs, increased revenues, and received a three-year emergency supplemental grant from the New York State Legislature.

Creativity requires that organizations have independent thinkers. The processes of combining ideas in new ways, of seeing things from new perspectives, and developing new applications need minds that are unburdened by fixed ideas. Creative thinkers live simultaneously in both the worlds of fantasy and of reality. Many also have a wide range of peculiar, seemingly irrelevant interests that may contribute nothing obvious to the creative process. These interests, however, can be a rich source of metaphor, parallel thought processes, and associations that lead to creative ideas.

People need to be stimulated if they are to think creatively. They need access to ideas and information. Without some clear understanding of what the actual situation is, even the most creative people cannot solve the real problem. One of the prerequisites for a creative environment is an ongoing flow of ideas and information. The effective leader in a creative organization is not expected to come up with solutions to all of the problems alone. Rather, the leader needs to build an environment that encourages open dialogue in which people can risk sharing new ideas and thoughts.

ORGANIZATIONAL MOVEMENTS TOWARD PARTICIPATION

At the same time that historical trends have been moving toward increased participation in decision making, and organizations have sought more creative solutions to the challenges facing them, organizations themselves have developed ways of increasing employee participation.

In the 1930s, social psychologists in Europe and later in the United States began researching the functioning of groups by observing their workings. Kurt Lewin (1951) pioneered this work and influenced millions of managers over the world. Lewin and his followers "developed a concept that became central to organizational reform: You cannot know an institution until you try to change it, and you cannot change it without reflecting on its purpose. This meant studying companies with full immersion in their cultures, in partnership with those managers who wanted to make change— typically managers of some pilot project within the firm" (Kleiner, 1996, pp. 30–31).

By the middle of the twentieth century, group methods as such began to emerge. Many of these were influenced by the work that had come to be known as *Robert's Rules of Order* (*A Short History*, n.d.), one of the early works on group decision making, originally published by Henry Martyn Robert.

> In 1941 Alex Osborn, an advertising executive, found that con-
> ventional business meetings were inhibiting the creation of new
> ideas and proposed some rules designed to help stimulate them.
> He was looking for rules, which would give people the freedom of
> mind and action to spark off and reveal new ideas. To "think up"
> was originally the term he used to describe the process he devel-
> oped, and that in turn came to be known as "brainstorming. . . ."
> He described brainstorming as "a conference technique by which
> a group attempts to find a solution for a specific problem by
> amassing all the ideas spontaneously by its members." The rules
> he came up with are the following:
>
> • No criticism of ideas
> • Go for large quantities of ideas
> • Build on each other's ideas
> • Encourage wild and exaggerated ideas. (Infinite Innovations,
>   2003)

Such research and practical developments enabled social sci-entists and managers to become more aware and more sophisti-cated in their understanding of the way groups worked.

With the emergence of the computer-based workplace and em-ployees working individually on networked personal computers, organizations needed more than the command-and-control model's simple compliance by employees to a job description and routine. A more powerful employer-employee contract became necessary. Commitment cannot be ordered; it has to be freely given. As knowledge workers have emerged as a significant force in organizations across the world, structured, measurable tasks have become increasingly difficult to design and implement. Creative problem solving has become a required competency for employees well below the management level. Judgment, responsiveness, and the need for the employee to "embody" organizational goals, values, and work processes calls for a new type of relationship between manager and employee, among managers, and among employees themselves.

WHY FACILITATIVE LEADERSHIP?

Facilitative leadership enables all of the relevant ideas to get onto the table and creates an environment in which constructive dialogue can lead to innovative breakthroughs.

Facilitative leaders recognize that new ideas develop in stages. Ideas don't emerge fully matured. In the very early stages of development, ideas are fragile and need to be encouraged. At a later stage ideas need challenges or they will not have the strength needed to survive in the long term. Later, when the idea has matured a little, it needs both challenges and testing in the real world.

In the next chapter, we discuss types of facilitative leadership skills and how they can be applied to specific organizational challenges.

CHAPTER THREE

THE SKILLS OF A FACILITATIVE LEADER

The skills of a facilitator can be divided into three types: facilitating the environment, facilitating diagnosis, and facilitating resolution. Environmental skills are aimed at the question, "What social/psychological atmosphere is needed to get this job done?" Diagnostic skill is applied to answer the question, "What is going on here?" Skill in collective resolution answers the question, "What can be done to improve the situation?"

FACILITATING THE ENVIRONMENT

Facilitation creates a place and time of mutual trust. The reason for this is not just that trust is a nice thing, but that a degree of social comfort is necessary for people in a group to interact effectively. Being creative requires risk, and the right environment helps people find the willingness to take risks.

At an organizational level, the facilitative leader puts into place policies that ensure employees that they can expect justice and corporate support when they deliver their best efforts to the shared enterprise of the organization. This means allowing enough time and budget for people within the organization to know one another. They need to be comfortable dialoguing outside of their daily work groups.

When preparing to cope with a project or problem-solving situation, the facilitative leader creates a suitable environment. Here "creating an environment" means building trust in the management or project team. There is no group, no matter how senior or professional, that can ignore attention to personal relationships. The facilitative leader ensures that the team learns to know and respect one another even as they begin the important work of initiating their project.

When working in a specific meeting, the leader as facilitator is careful to create personal respect among group members. The participants need to believe that they will be listened to and that their ideas will be taken seriously. The facilitative leader is responsible for creating such a place and time. In order for that to happen, the leader needs to be committed to an enabling environment, to model appropriate behaviors, to use group process techniques effectively, and to intervene in ways that promote helpful group dynamics.

FACILITATING DIAGNOSIS

At the organizational level, the leader, facilitator, or manager simply asks, "What is the challenge, opportunity, or issue the organization is facing? What should be done about it?" The ways these questions are answered depend on the models, methods, and experiences of the people answering them.

To discern the situation in an organization, the facilitative leader begins with some model of what an organization is and how it works. These models typically operate as unconscious underlying assumptions. It can be less important what the model is than that the manager or leader becomes aware of the model he or she is using, so that he or she has the option of changing it.

A classic set of models or metaphors of organizations is provided by Gareth Morgan (1986). He describes eight different metaphors of an organization: a machine, an organism, a brain, a culture, a political system, a psychological reality, a system of flux and transformation, and an instrument of domination. His analysis can be helpful in clarifying one's own assumptions as a leader and the assumptions operating within an organization.

Many facilitative leaders use more than one model or image to understand the organizations they are working with. In fact, a single organization may be operating with several different metaphors in different departments or divisions. Morgan (1986) describes McDonald's outlets as machines. Very specific sets of processes that are to be precisely followed are taught to every employee at every McDonald's restaurant. Even behaviors such as "Smile at the customer," "Count the change out loud," and so forth are regulated. On the other hand, McDonald's headquarters are creative and innovative. The atmosphere is more like an advertising agency. Whiteboards on the hallway walls encourage people to put up ideas. A quiet room is available for people to meditate.

In preparing for any project or problem-solving activity in the organization, the facilitative leader is concerned with similar diagnostic questions about the challenge, opportunity, or issue facing the organization and what should be done about it. In this case, standard project management and needs assessment tools come in handy. Concern with deliverables, budget, time required, and processes to be followed are important.

For leading a meeting, the facilitative leader needs to be ready for the specific realities of the day. No two meetings, even those with the same agenda, are alike. The leader first needs to have an understanding of the content of the meeting, not as the expert in it, but to consider what the important discussion points will be, and what information may be required to make needed decisions. Second, the leader needs to have a process in mind for how to proceed, step by step in the meeting. Third, the leader needs to consider the individuals who will attend, thinking through how to approach the various issues on the table in light of the personalities and values of those anticipated around the table.

FACILITATING RESOLUTION

Resolution is a combination of the promise of a situation, the solution reached by the group, and the commitment to see these first two brought to fruition. Enabling resolution of a group is the most common form of facilitation—the ongoing decision making, implementation, and discussion with colleagues. Flexibility is the hallmark of the effective interaction. Of course, that flexibility is the result of having thought through very clearly both the objectives and the human dynamics of the organization, the project, and the meeting.

At the organizational level, *interaction skill* means that the facilitative leader is prepared to deal with the details surrounding any new direction. This means thinking through and managing not only the big picture, but being prepared to work through the ways that the big picture gets communicated and interpreted across the organization.

In preparation for a new project or initiative, the facilitative leader is prepared not only to present one approach, but to proceed with the numerous iterations and negotiations needed before a shared approach can be agreed upon.

In a specific meeting, the facilitative leader is concerned to effectively manage content, process, and people.

MANAGING CONTENT

In dealing with the content of the meeting, the facilitative leader is concerned that the group has all of the information they need to make the decision or have the discussion that is intended. In the first instance, this means that the group is clear on what the topic really is. We recently led a workshop with a new department that combined four aspects of information management. While the participants were interested in their separate fields and emerging technologies, the issue at hand was the future organization of these functions within the company. The content of the meeting was the various issues the new department faced as it reorganized. Important discussion topics were milestones for the new organization, next steps for the four teams, and who should be responsible for what. Preparation for the workshop focused on devising ways to allow the teams enough time to discuss their own technologies and interests, while also arriving at the needed departmental conclusions.

The facilitator should never underestimate the importance of definitions of terms, abbreviations, and key points of understanding in discussion. A little point of information can make a big difference in what is going on. Maureen had a harrowing workshop with a group who thought they were working on the same budget until she happened to ask for clarification on what currency was being used, only to discover that different segments of the group were using the same numbers, but in different currencies!

Content-level interaction is most often made in the form of clarifying questions. "How many people are regularly involved in that work?" "Can you give an example of that process?" "What would be the consequences of that kind of action?" They allow the group to look at the content from a different perspective or in a more detailed way. A facilitator may simplify complex situations by restating something someone said in simpler terms and check with the person presenting the idea if the restatement is correct.

MANAGING PROCESS

Processes are the activities of the event, the way information is dealt with, and the steps by which the group works. The difference between process and content is a bit like painting a wall—the content is the paint itself and the process is the method by which the paint is applied, be it brushing, rolling, or spraying. Facilitation as process means continually checking the extent to which the agreed process is delivering the results the group intends. Process interactions are the most common actions done by facilitators. They ask the group to manage the content in some way. When, for example, a group has discussed a list of options in such a way that the options are already prioritized, the facilitative leader may well state what the priorities are, ask if the group agrees, and suggest that the prioritization step is done and that the group may move on. Alternately, when a whole-group discussion seems stilted, a facilitative leader may suggest that people discuss the topic in pairs or trios to warm up a bit.

The International Association of Facilitators Methods Database (www.iaf-methods.org) describes three levels of process interactions: Applications, Methods and Models, and Interventions.

> An application is a facilitated process that is complete in itself. The process produces a complete product, no other process is required except using the results. Examples of this are scenarios, the critical path method and the ICA's project planning. . . .

> Methods and Models are standardized processes that produce a product but are usually used in conjunction with other Methods and Models to create a final product. Examples of this are brainstorming, paired comparisons, and gap analysis. . . .

> Interventions are methods or techniques that are usually not planned in the design and development of a group process event but are used when specific situations present themselves. ("Level of Process," 2005)

Interventions include things like techniques for dealing with difficult people or situations, with a group that is avoiding making decisions, or with a group that is prone to discuss interesting but
irrelevant topics. For example, if a group cannot stay focused on
the topic, the facilitator might remind the group about the purpose of the meeting, the process that is being used, and where they
are in that process. The facilitator then might say that it is important to stay focused in order to achieve the goal of the meeting. If
that is not successful, the facilitator might lead a discussion about
the intent of the meeting.

Managing People

Interacting with content and with processes deals with the group
as a group and not so specifically with separate individuals in the
group. For this reason, anyone working with a large meeting, something over thirty people, for example, tends to use more interaction with content and process than with the individuals. With
smaller groups and with those coming together for the purpose of
personal interaction, attention to the people as individuals is critical. Here is where sensitivity to people interaction comes into play.

   The facilitative leader needs to develop an understanding of
the group he or she is working with. If the facilitator knows the
group already, some additional thought is wise. We would ask ourselves about a group we knew, "What concerns do they bring to the
meeting? What might they be interested in that is on the agenda?
What might their opinion be?" We are not really interested in coming to a conclusion about the group but to have a sense of where
they are coming from so that we can enable the meeting to work
more effectively.

   If the facilitator is not familiar with the group, more time might
be spent on understanding the group. Normally, the most that can
be expected is a conversation with the manager or the person organizing the event. We would ask such questions as

- How many people will be in the meeting?
- What is their average level of education?
- What is their age range?
- What is the ratio of men to women?

- How much experience do they have in the topic?
- What is your reason for asking them?
- What is their reason for coming?
- What do they expect from the session?

The best way of developing an understanding of the group is to work with them. We find that a series of conversations about the topic with as many members of the group as possible is a start. When we need to have cofacilitators from the group, we would either train them as facilitators or, if they have some experience, have them help design the session.

At its most cognitive, sensitivity to people has to do with attention to inferences. Also important is attention to emotions. Spirit of the group is often overlooked in dealing with the people part of facilitation.

THE LADDER OF INFERENCES

The Ladder of Inference was developed by Chris Argyris, Robert Putnam, and Diana McLain Smith (1985) and described in an operational form by Rick Ross in Peter Senge's *The Fifth Discipline Fieldbook* (Senge et al., 1994). The Ladder of Inference is "a common mental pathway of increasing abstraction, often leading to misguided beliefs" (Senge et al., 1994, p. 243). Different versions of the ladder exist, and the one we use goes something like this from bottom to top:

1. There exist observable "data" and experiences (as a videotape recorder might capture them).
2. I select "data" from what I observe.
3. I add meanings of my own based on the culture around me.
4. I make assumptions about what is happening.
5. I draw conclusions.
6. I take actions based on my conclusions.

This is how an individual processes information. The processing takes place instantly and largely unconsciously. One important way for the facilitative leader to manage the personal interactions in the group is by asking people to clarify their assumptions, moving "down the ladder" of inference. Group dialogue can ensure that assumptions are brought to light in a systematic way. Of course, no amount of pressure can get a person to reveal assumptions of which they are wholly unconscious, but the discussion can be useful at reaching new perspectives on the discussion.

ATTENTION TO EMOTIONS

A second point where the facilitative leader may interact with individuals in a group is with their emotions. Emotions are always present and need to be dealt with, if for no other reason than that emotions have such a powerful impact on the group. The issue for the leader here is that groups and individuals differ greatly in how comfortable they are with emotional expression. What would comprise normal dialogue in one group would include raised voices and interrupting one another with emotional language ("I am appalled at . . ." "Oh, wow, we were just so delighted when . . ."). Another group, feeling exactly the same way, might speak quietly and take turns, using different language altogether ("It seemed interesting that you . . ." "One wondered why . . ."). A third group with the same strong feelings might insist on a break to discuss things privately with their friends or just clam up altogether.

Expressing feelings of any kind in a meeting embarrasses some groups. ("We are here to talk business, not all this fuzzy stuff.") This may call for permission to talk about the feelings themselves by the facilitator. In another case, shouting and strong expression is wholly appropriate, it gets expressed what needs to be expressed, and the meeting moves on. ("Some of us are really committed to this association, and by God, we're not afraid to show it!") How groups handle emotions is a particular point of attention in culturally mixed groups, be those national or organizational cultures. What is normal dialogue for more emotionally expressive cultures may be scandalous to members of another group. Culturally expressive members may block out participation from their less expressive colleagues; the facilitator needs to be attentive to this risk.

For some facilitators, agreements on group behaviors are a way of managing this arena. They are a good way of managing a group that requires little risk or personal engagement. It is a different situation, however, when a group requires strong trust in each other and/or when very different cultures work together. Too often lists of dos and don'ts take no consideration whatsoever for the styles and cultures around the table. A rule, for example, about speaking one at a time is perceived by many as a call to talk like an Anglo-Saxon, not much welcome for Latin participants, especially when it is linked to another rule about "participating fully."

There may be cases where as leader you find that specific emotional issues need to be brought to the group's consideration. For instance, when one individual seems to be persistently disrupting another, the facilitator might say something like, "Bob, when you snort like that when Fred makes a comment, I have the impression that you are belittling him. Is that your intention or have I misunderstood?" There is any number of formulae for such interventions; the key question is when and whether to do it.

There is no doubt that this sort of question will put Bob on the spot, and that beginning a group dialogue about personal relations with one another will take considerable time. You should do this when you decide that three conditions are in place: first, it is clear to you that dealing with Bob publicly is necessary for the group (otherwise you may want to talk to him outside at the break); second, the meeting is aimed—however tangentially—at dealing with personal relationships; and third, you as facilitator have whatever permission may be needed in the organization to raise issue with Bob's behavior. If those three are not in place, you may want to deal with Bob more indirectly.

Any work done in understanding the group before the session will pay off here. By the time the meeting has heated up, the facilitative leader understands the group dynamics.

A further consideration in very severe conflicts is whether you as the facilitative leader are capable of dealing with what is being done. You may not be up to managing some things, no matter how gifted, committed, and well intentioned you are!

When the facilitator lacks the ability to deal with a situation, it is often best to explain the problem to the group, suggest alternative actions, and ask the group what they recommend. We led a session in which none of the participants wanted to be there. They felt that it was a waste of time and the only reason they were there was that their boss had forced them to come. When this became clear to us, we explained what we were hired to do and why we thought it was important. We told the group that if they want to go they could.

Quite apart from individual confrontations, there are many moments in the life of any group that require that the group members look at their feelings. Even when no direct attention is paid to the emotional dynamics in the group, the important thing is to remember that emotions are always there. Building a budget, evaluating construction of a freeway, selecting a new secretary—all are emotional processes; the question is how expressive the group is and how relevant the emotional dynamics are to the process. In every session, no matter how technical and goal oriented, a reflection here and there on the emotional tone of the work can help the quality of people's input without necessarily making the discussion intrusively personal. Questions such as, "What went well for you today?" "What do you regret about this past year's performance?" "What can we celebrate at the end of this day?" "What can we be grateful for?" can be welcome in many different group situations.

OCCURRENCE OF SPIRIT

The last form of interaction that a facilitative leader deals with is spirit. Spirit in a group is their capacity to will success, the degree of passion and commitment in the group. Spirit results in what Mihaly Csikszentmihalyi (1991) calls "flow." It is what motivates people to take serious risks and to overcome difficult situations.

Spirit cannot be managed in any traditional sense of the word. Spirit happens when it happens. It cannot be controlled. A person can be open to it, but it usually appears when it is unexpected. It can be evoked, but there is no guarantee that it will respond. Spirit can be experienced. You know when it is present.

It is present when awe is experienced. Rudolf Otto, in his book *The Idea of the Holy* (1958), describes the occurrence of awe as an event during which there is a precognitive experience of fear and fascination. In other words, something happens, and before we think about it, we feel both fear and fascination at the same time. It can happen in groups when a remarkable idea is expressed and a kind of chill passes through the room. When that happens, spirit is present.

Conditions can be set that will maximize the chances of spirit emerging in a group. Stress is one. Many people will argue that there should be as little stress as possible in order for spirit to emerge. But our experience is that one of the conditions of spirit is a seriously challenging task. Csikszentmihalyi (1991) describes *flow* as what happens when a person's or a team's peak ability meets *a challenge that is equal to that ability.* If the challenge is too far above or below the group's ability, flow does not happen. Challenge someone to fly or to pick up a piece of paper on the floor, and there is certainly no flow—and no spirit.

Spirit happens when the group is connected to things that they find deeply meaningful, even profound. It happens when the group sees or experiences a connection to a meaningful purpose, such as John F. Kennedy's challenge to go to the moon. It happens when a group experiences being connected to a powerful past. Martin Luther King Jr.'s "I have a dream" speech connected people to the past and to the future. Expanding the context in which people see themselves working increases the possibility of spirit emerging. Nike evokes spirit by having new employees visit the places of significance of the company's founders. Leaders also can use their own setbacks as sources of inspiration. In Steve Jobs's commencement address to Stanford University graduating students in 2005 he said, "I'm pretty sure none of this would have happened if I hadn't been fired from Apple. It was awful-tasting medicine, but I guess the patient needed it. Sometimes life hits you in the head with a brick. Don't lose faith. I'm convinced that the only thing that kept me going was that I loved what I did. You've got to find what you love"(Jobs, 2005).

Spirit emerges in a special atmosphere, in which nothing is "business as usual." Facilitative leaders create this atmosphere by paying attention to the significance of what people are doing. Leaders take risks and ask that others do also. Greatness is demonstrated, asked for and given. Trust is carefully maintained. Results, even bad ones, are communicated with employees. When a failure happens, lessons are learned and applied in the next attempt. Goals are clear to everyone, and individuals are reminded regularly how they contribute to those goals. Facilitative leaders take responsibility for failures and give credit to the team.

CONCLUSION

Facilitation is often described as making group processes easy, but facilitative leadership is anything but easy. Watching Venus Williams serve a tennis ball at 125 miles per hour may look easy, but no woman had ever done it before she did. A great facilitative leader makes leading look easy, but she is in fact applying a great deal of knowledge, skill, sensitivity, and responsiveness to the work she is doing.

In the next chapter we look at several issues that facilitative leaders will be faced with in the future (and in some cases today). Then, in Part Two, we look at each of the nine disciplines.

CHAPTER FOUR

THE FUTURE OF FACILITATION

Before beginning our discussion of the individual disciplines, we want to draw attention to current changes in the workplace that put stress on facilitative leadership. These are online meetings, communication through art, multicultural groups, and complex systems. Each of these developments demands of the facilitator new kinds of self-mastery.

ONLINE MEETINGS

More and more meetings are taking place online. Advances in technology are making it possible to hold meetings that span several time zones and include people in many locations. In May 2001, IBM held WorldJam, an online meeting of fifty thousand of its employees, in a four-day workshop that generated more than six thousand proposals.

A growing number of organizations use online communications as the medium of choice for conducting meetings of employees from diverse locations and for providing training. Shell's new learning center in the Netherlands has online facilities built in to all of its meeting rooms and classrooms. Shell has discovered that online learning is no less expensive than face-to-face classes, but for its far-flung international employees, the effectiveness of lessons that can be applied immediately in the home workplace is a major advantage. For many international associations, e-mail and free software like Skype make international communications that were once prohibitive affordable.

New technologies emerge every day, from video conferencing, teleconferencing, chat, and video chat to online presentation systems and online decision-making software. Participants can hear and see each other. They can read the same documents. They can write or draw on a shared electronic whiteboard. They can watch the same presentation. Employees can participant synchronously (everyone online at the same time) or asynchronously (individuals participate when they have the time).

This is a wholly new environment for leadership. As in any situation, a facilitative leader wants to enable the group to make effective decisions, to develop as a community or team, and to share learning. However, these processes are an unfamiliar terrain, both for leaders and participants. The difficulty is that we try to apply the same processes as in a face-to-face meeting, and find that they are strangely off-kilter. Different dynamics exist. Less information is available to the group and to the facilitator because of the limits of technology. As one colleague put it, "You can't smell the anxiety online." It is not only the lack of the "cues" of face-to-face communication. Online work demands much more frequent and articulate communication than face-to-face processes do. Many excellent face-to-face leaders find this requirement of the online environment irritating and daunting. Self mastery is called for here in the form of humility—even with decades of experience, one needs to learn some things all over to develop the new skills called for in the new world of technology in which we operate. It can be a tough challenge indeed to risk looking foolish and incompetent among colleagues who have come otherwise to respect you for your wisdom and experience.

Another problem with the online relationship is the ease of tuning out. Many of us continue to attend team meetings, continue to join group discussion, continue to work through a project to its end long after we have lost interest in the content because we feel obligated to meet the expectations of friends and colleagues. In a face-to-face team, we turn up even after the thrill is gone. Social bonds are much weaker online. The rate of dropout from online training is more than 50 percent, largely for this reason. How does an online leader create sufficient excitement and commitment among a team to keep colleagues involved? For those of us who intend to continue leading into the future ahead, disciplining ourselves to hear, see, and respond in the virtual world is a major challenge. The limited number of visual clues, even in a video-conference, makes managing discussions much more difficult on-line than face-to-face. In the videoconference, one tends to speak not to one or another individual as in a face-to-face discussion but rather to the whole group. The facilitative leader has to clarify which messages are meant for individuals, which messages are for part of the group and which are for everyone. Sometimes one lo-cation is really having a meeting among themselves, witnessed by other locations. Sometimes a teleconference is best run with one speaker per location reporting what that location has already de-cided among themselves in previous local gatherings. The online facilitative leader has to think through a meeting structure for these matters and be ready with a backup plan should technology fail for some of the participants at the last minute. This work can be more complex than the simple agenda that might serve for a face-to-face meeting.

When the dialogue is by teleconference, the facilitator needs to be much more explicit than in a face-to-face environment as to what the structure of the dialogue is, because there are no visual clues at all. A printed roundtable with names or pictures of participants can be a great help in creating an image of who sits where at the virtual table and who might follow whom for a roundtable discussion. A list of discussion questions sent out beforehand can help. During the meeting the facilitative leader needs to be quite active, to state what the question is, how people can respond, actively summarize, raise the next question, ask individuals for their contributions, and then to move the group to a conclusion. Ground rules can help. People may be asked to give their names at the beginning of each comment. Controlling the number of teleconference participants can help. A group over twelve can simply be too large to suitably manage in a teleconference, especially if they are using what for some people is a second language. It is better to hold regional sub-group meetings and pull the results together. The lack of visual clues means that the teleconference facilitator needs to ask specif-ically for input, perhaps even to individual contributors, much more frequently than would be the case in a face-to-face discussion.

When dialogue takes place through written, threaded discus-sion, the group knows more easily than in the teleconference who is saying what but the tone of voice is missing. Some participants are more fluent in spoken language, and some are more fluent in writing. This is true both for native speakers and for those working in a second language. Consider also that written dialogue has the advantage of reflection time. Some of us like to be able to think and edit before we join a dialogue. The online written dialogue is in fact a more comfortable medium for these folks than is a face-to-face discussion, because there is time to think your responses through, check your responses with colleagues, edit, and then submit a well-reflected comment. For those who like the passion of off-the-cuff exchange, this may be irritating. The facilitative leader has to be ready to return often to the discussion to clarify and summarize points and move the dialogue further. We do this easily in spoken face-to-face dialogue, but it is more time-consuming for the online facilitator, and written fluency is an important skill.

COMMUNICATION THROUGH ART

There is a trend today among facilitators and managers alike to use art in meetings, planning, and problem-solving processes. These applications include graphic and visual facilitation in meetings, storytelling about individual and social situations, and the use of poetry and music. Some facilitators use art as a source of ideas or inspiration. Others use art as a way of capturing not only the ideas being presented but also the context and feelings connected with the ideas. This can include images produced by the group leader, images drawn by the participants, or even images chosen by participants from photographs and postcards. Accelerated learning facilitators make powerful use of different tempos of music for creating different learning environments in groups. "Appreciative Inquiry," first developed by David Cooperrider (1999), is a method used in workshops that involves people telling stories about their best experiences with the area of the question. Another use of stories includes story-telling exercises as energizers. The Institute of Cultural Affairs has a myth-creating exercise used in their strategic planning workshops.

Some planning processes have participants give poetic titles to the strategies developed in addition to the more traditional titles. Songwriting workshops can capture the enthusiasm of a team newly committed to a plan and also encapsulate learnings in a way that the team can remember. A participant in a workshop in Italy spontaneously wrote an aria for the closing of the four-year planning session.

The use of art in group discussion can add dimensions to the process that are not available otherwise. John Seely Brown, the former chief scientist at Xerox Park, describes the use of stories in solving problems that couldn't be dealt with in standard ways. His research was with photocopy machine repair people.

When the repairmen have a machine that they can't figure out, "they call their buddies, and together they . . . socially construct an understanding of that machine. How do they socially construct an understanding of that machine"? They walk around it, and "they start to spin a story. . . . Finally they are able to explain every piece of data, every piece of this complex machine. When they have constructed the narrative that explains [the problem], they have actually figured out the machine. And now they can fix the machine" (Brown, 2001).

In all of these situations, art is used to contribute richness to the dialogue, to increase understanding among a group. For the leader this means willingness to risk encountering more detail than he or she may be prepared to manage. This means accepting dialogue that may touch upon deeper levels of awareness than a group has discussed before. An individual who has to be in charge of the direction of the discussion will find this process uncomfortable. This openness is an issue of internal discipline, not technique or procedure.

Any leader can strengthen his or her work by considering in a given meeting or workshop at least one way in which the task could be strengthened by the addition of an artistic medium. Consider asking a group to draw an image (or choose from pictures you provide) of the past month in the department, or of the material they are working on. Even people who may find the prospect of drawing something quite impossible may well be prepared to choose from among a stack of magazine photographs, art postcards or symbol cards to indicate a choice of images. Questions can be along the lines of, "What have we accomplished this month?" "What is it like to work with this team?" "What would the future of this community be like when we finish the project successfully?" "Draw a machine (or animal or robot) that could solve the problem we have here."

You can see that in all of these cases the art work is a way to begin a dialogue, not an end in itself.

As you conclude a meeting, you might ask people what they might title the meeting if it were a film or a book, or what music the meeting was like.

You can also consider literally playing music as your participants arrive or as they work. Is your meeting or workshop something that needs a peppy, rock and roll feel to it at the beginning, or a reflective event that could benefit from a Mozart start? The feel of the room, and the quality of the group's thinking, changes according to the music you play.

For many leaders, attention to the artistic side of things is a threatening walk into the non-rational. Taking up this challenge can be frightening, but the rewards in increased motivation and commitment from the team can be surprising.

MULTICULTURAL GROUPS

A third pressure on today's facilitative leaders is the increasingly multicultural nature of today's groups. Global businesses, intergovernmental organizations, and nongovernmental organizations have always worked with culturally diverse situations. For many leaders today, however, a local group or a comfortable national organization has become intercultural without the leaders being prepared for it. Globalization in the marketplace, greater ease of international communication, and streams of international migration mean that many of us participate in very diverse cultural groups without ever having planned or intended to do so.

A facilitative leader today may need to develop wholly new skill sets to understand and respond appropriately to their teams. This involves not only attentive communication, but also being prepared to create innovative approaches to decision making and team building. The difficulty with intercultural groups is that everyone has to be prepared to set aside their trusted maps of the universe and open themselves to new approaches. The challenge to the facilitative leader is to find within oneself the generosity of spirit to learn all over again things that you believe you know already.

It takes a great deal of courage to create a discussion in an existing team about *how* decisions should be made, or what group guidelines should be followed. Many of us have used the same approaches for years under the slogan "if it ain't broke, don't fix it," and yet we can be surprised and invigorated to hear new approaches proposed by colleagues.

Many facilitative leaders have been surprised to learn that a new group has a wholly different set of values than they are accustomed to. Task-oriented output of a meeting may be the expectation of the Western manager, who finds that an Eastern team values the personal sociality that takes place between colleagues more than task. Both sorts of groups may well achieve their ends with equal efficiency, but they require very different types of attention and different activities from their leaders.

Even things such as body language can be confusing. During a discussion in the Czech Republic about body language, we were showing different pictures. One was of a young woman wearing jeans, and she had her thumbs in the front of her belt. We thought that she was saying that she was determined and proud. The whole Czech group said no, she was saying that she is a prostitute. Our Polish cofacilitator agreed with the group. It appears that this is true throughout Central Europe.

Complex Systems

Some business and social situations are so complex that it takes days of presentations to simply understand all of the factors at play. A strategic plan may have four or five hundred activity clusters representing thousands of specific actions.

As organizations need to deal with complex situations in some depth and breadth, facilitative leaders will need to develop methods and skills to do the necessary analysis and planning. Leaders will need to develop the tools required for the very complex networks and alliances that are involved. This requires attentiveness to content far beyond what most facilitators are now prepared to deliver. But the old saying, "The devil is in the details" is supremely true in large, complex projects. In complex situations, the devil is also in longer time frames and distant locations. Facilitative leaders who will move with the trends of the future need to be prepared to take on these new intellectual challenges.

In a very complex project, it does not help to scrimp on the time needed for everyone to understand the background. Summary documents sent out beforehand, which in other situations may go unread, can be extremely useful here.

A systematic and methodical approach is important. Frequent reminders of where the group is in the process and what content has been covered are useful. Minimizing distraction is critical. It is easy to reopen discussions that have already been resolved. The facilitator needs to remind the group that the group is beyond these discussions. When things get confusing, stop and summarize what just happened and begin again where the confusion started. Watch for clues of people being lost and ask.

Do not underestimate the importance of specific expertise. One meeting held when all the relevant players can be present can be more useful than three partial meetings in which the participants cannot answer key questions.

Any means by which all players can keep track of progress using a shared tool can help a team working on a complex project, whether that is a timeline, a checklist of deliverables, or a series of shared milestones. Be aware, however, that not everyone has to share everything.

The art of leadership here is determining what level of detail is needed by all and what level is only needed within specialist subgroups. Complexity is a personal intellectual challenge to many leaders, keeping track of more detail than one has ever before had to manage. For many others, the personal challenge is one of renouncing control. In a situation in which no one individual can understand or keep track of all of the details in a project, the leader who is prepared to fully trust his specialist colleagues can accomplish more than the one who has to have his or her hand in every detail.

We have mentioned here a few of the important trends that influence the way leaders work today. New ones are turning up every day. In all of these situations, facilitative leaders are required to achieve ever-greater sophistication and subtlety in their work. Managing the self is the key to these developments.

So how can one maintain greatness in challenging times as well as easy ones? We explore this in Part Two by looking at each of the disciplines. Chapters Five through Seven (Detachment, Engagement, Focus) are about the facilitator's relationship with others. Chapters Eight through Ten (Interior Council, Intentionality, Sense of Wonder) describe the relationships the facilitator takes toward his or her own self. The final three chapters, Eleven through Thirteen (Awareness, Action, and Presence), have to do with the facilitative leader's relationship toward life.

Developing internal disciplines is not a theoretical or intellectual exercise. It is doing the work. The whole process is a journey that has many steps. You will run into detours, plateaus, rocky places, hills and even mountains, beautiful woodlands, and rivers to cross. The journey is one of fresh discovery, even though many have taken it before us.

We believe that these nine disciplines, however they are practiced, create the paths to effective facilitative leadership.

PART TWO

THE DISCIPLINES

CHAPTER FIVE

DETACHMENT: STEPPING BACK

All of us have had the experience of detachment. It is very much a part of the human experience. We learn as small children to accept the fact that we can't always have what we want, and of course learning to accept this continues as adults. We lose jobs or tasks or friends or roles that were important to us as technology or the organization changes. We move to a different part of the country and leave behind friends, favorite places, and familiar surroundings. We find ourselves having to let go and turn our attention to the present and the future. We get a new role or we learn to use our time in other ways. Sometimes when we have had a relationship for a particularly long time and we have put a lot of effort and spirit into that relationship, losing it is extremely painful. We seem to carry it around with us for a very long time. This process is for the most part a combination of grieving and building a new set of relationships. Sometimes the process is difficult, especially if you have little experience with having to give up relationships. When we moved from Peru back to the United States, our oldest son had a difficult time giving up his relationship with the village we lived in. Once, a few months after we had moved to Chicago, our son and we met a Maryknoll priest who had helped us in starting the project in Peru. The priest greeted our son in Spanish, a language he had learned in Peru. Our son ignored the greeting. The priest greeted him again. Our son screamed that he hated Spanish and never wanted to speak it again. His way of detaching himself was to refuse any reminder of the relationship. We could have done a better job of enabling the grieving process that he was going through.

Some years later when we left Rome and closed the office there, we created a ceremony of departure. We acknowledged the great things that had happened there, what we liked about it and what was difficult about living there. We celebrated the fact that we were leaving a place we loved very much and going to a place that we had not yet learned to love in Portugal.

People who move a great deal especially as children cope with these sort of changes in ways different from those who only move occasionally. They tend to have two specific characteristics: they make friends very quickly and move to some depth in their relationships quickly. They also seldom or never have very deep relationships. This is perhaps their way of avoiding the pain of separation from more profound relationships.

Only when we put those things that had meaning for us into perspective can we enjoy the memories without the loss or the desire driving us. This is everyday detachment.

As we mature, we find that we also need to self-consciously step back from something we want and let it go. We might be relaxing at home when our child is seriously hurt. We know that if we give in to the emotions that well up inside of us, our child will not be adequately cared for. We set aside our fear and pain, perform the best first aid we can, and rush the child to the hospital. For that moment, we have self-consciously and deliberately set aside our needs for the sake of the needs of the child. This, too, is everyday detachment.

The capacity to step back, to set aside, to suspend our immediate thinking and emotions is not only an everyday experience, but also a key to facilitative leadership.

WHAT IS DETACHMENT?

This discipline begins with the awareness that everything is transitory, that whatever plans or decisions are coming into existence will also go out of existence. Secondly, one learns the capacity to step back from what's going on, to become detached, disengaged from the situation. Then you realize that you need nothing whatsoever from this group. You then find that you have all the capacity you need to do what is needed. This is an ongoing process, which is rediscovered in every new situation you confront. (Jenkins & Jenkins, 2002)

Elizabeth Harris (1997), in her work on early Buddhism, talks about it this way:

> Non-attachment or non-grasping would therefore flow from the awareness that no possession, no relationship, no achievement is permanent or able to give lasting satisfaction; from the discovery that there is no self which needs to be protected, promoted, or defended; and from the realization that searching for selfish sensual gratification is pointless, since it leads only to craving and obsession. Phrases which overlap with attachment in this context and which can help to clarify its meaning are: possessiveness in relationships, defensiveness, jealousy, covetousness, acquisitiveness, and competitiveness. Through non-attachment, these are attenuated and overcome. There is nothing yet in this description which points to a lack of concern for humanity or the world. The emphasis is rather on inner transformation so that destructive and divisive traits can be destroyed, making way for their opposites to flourish.

Detachment is not doing without, but rather refusing to allow these things to have control over you and your decisions. Detachment is an interior state. The problem is that sometimes we think we are in control but in fact we are not.

THE FOUR DIMENSIONS OF DETACHMENT

Traditionally, people are detached from four things: goods, work, relationships, and self. The following examples point to various aspects of detachment.

Goods

While we were working on a development project south of Lima, we made contact with a number of executives and local managers of multinational companies to ask for support in the project. One of them was the president of Southern Peru Copper, one of the largest copper mining companies in the world. Hanging on the wall of his office in Lima was a picture of a typical junkyard found on the outskirts of Lima. Seagulls were flying above it and rats crawling through it. Men and women were picking through it searching for anything that they could use. The picture seemed out of place and somewhat disturbing.

After we had gotten to know each other a little, we asked why he had the picture in his office. He said that it was too easy to forget the real world of Peruvian life amid the surroundings of a multimillion-dollar company in an office high above the street, where none of the dirt or poverty was visible, and with all of the perks his position provided, including a driver and luxury apartment. The picture was his way of reminding himself of how fleeting these benefits are.

Work

In *The Ronin* (Jennings, 2001), the novelization of a myth from southern Japan, the protagonist digs a tunnel through a mountain. Villagers will then be able to avoid the long trek around the mountain. It is for the Ronin an act of penance for his previously violent and destructive life. At the end of decades of digging by hand, he discovers that he has miscalculated. The only solution is to cut a stairway down the face of the cliff. He walks away. Like the Ronin, leaders must have the capacity to walk away from their own accomplishments and their own failures. Walking away from a failure is different from transferring blame to others. It is both acknowledging the failure and also refusing to let it determine what is done next.

Jim Collins in his book *Good to Great* (2001) suggests that one of the characteristics of great leaders is willingness to share credit with their teams. This is the strength of realizing and admitting that any corporate change is the work of many people and not solely to the credit of any one individual, no matter how powerful. This is one way of maintaining detachment from our own work.

> When CEO Joe Cullman reviewed the decision by his company Philip Morris to buy 7UP in 1978 and sell it 8 years later at a loss, he admitted that it was his mistake and it could have been avoided if he had listened better to the people who challenged the idea at the time.
>
> When they do go well they attribute success of their companies to external factors, their team or luck. (Jenkins & Visser, 2003)

Relationships

In every situation of leadership development, coaching, or training, there is a phase in which the teacher, coach, or trainer moves from directly advising and guiding the learner to having that learner take over the activity himself or herself. This occurs, for instance, when the driving teacher gives the wheel to the student and stops using the auxiliary pedals to control the car. It is the day that the new leader chairs a meeting instead of watching the expert. At this point, both learner and coach are faced with a change—they must both let go of the familiar student-trainee relationship and form something new. No longer can the experience and judgment of the coach take precedence. Here both face the need for detachment from their personal relationship in order to create a new one, in which control moves into the hands of the learner. The same struggle can be seen between parents and children as the children move to become independent adults.

Self

Sometimes the need to be detached is only an interior one. When we become aware of the fact that we are too attached to an idea or a plan, the ability to become detached is needed. Bernie DeKoven put it this way:

> Letting go of a plan that I have invested in, especially if I have already announced it. Getting out of my "planning mind" and just letting things happen or select their own course. My practice is to think of these times as opportunities for sharing the planning mind, getting the group to take on part of the burden and perspective. (discussion with author)

Another way of making the same statement is described by philosopher Peter Koestenbaum in an interview in *FastCompany:*

> Taking personal responsibility for getting others to implement strategy is the leader's key polarity. It's the existential paradox of holding yourself 100% responsible for the fate of your organization, on the one hand, and assuming absolutely no responsibility for the choices made by other people, on the other hand. (LaBarre, 2000, p. 222)

Detachment is not a way of avoiding responsibility. It is operating out of the freedom you have and allowing others to operate out of the same freedom. Another dimension of the discipline of Detachment is not letting your own needs, your status, your plans, or the need to get credit for the quality of the decision control the choices you make.

Lao Tsu (1994) says, "[T]he sage puts his own person last, and yet it is found in the foremost place; he treats his person as if it were foreign to him and yet that person is preserved" (p. 7).

This self-denial is not for the sake of glory. It is not for the sake of the gesture, a sort of "at least I tried" when it was clear to all that failure was the only option. James Kimsey, founding chief executive officer of America Online, has said, "If you have to lay off thousands of people from your company, there's no excuse. You should have seen it coming and done something about it" (Hammonds, 2001, p. 106).

THE ISSUES OF DETACHMENT FOR FACILITATIVE LEADERS

Detachment is not easy to achieve. A number of issues make this so.

Aspects of our self-understanding make it difficult. We invest a huge amount of our selfhood into the roles we play, whether as teacher, steelworker, leader, or whatever. This makes it difficult to separate our role from our self.

The individualism of Western culture in combination with the command-and-control paradigm (discussed in Chapter One) can lead us to believe that decisions are best taken alone. We may fear the loss of power or control in turning decisions over to a group.

The competitive nature of organizational life and the fear of not being recognized or being seen as foolish make it difficult to share ideas, particularly nascent ideas, with others and with groups. The environment of trust in which risks can be taken is lacking in many organizations.

When organizations do invite groups to share in decision-making processes, it is rare that the groups have the opportunity to make mistakes and to grow from their failures. When a decision seems to be going into a dangerous direction, it is not uncommon for leadership to take power back from the group and move the decision in the direction the leaders prefer.

Aspects of the way we think make it difficult to be detached. As we try to understand a problem or generate a solution, we tend to take the first idea that comes to mind as the right one, and stop trying to understand the problem any further. This inability to suspend judgment is a weakness in solving complex issues.

We may believe that what is important in thinking about a topic is the content. It is becoming increasingly clear that *how* we think about a topic is more important than *what* we think about it. Learning to be concerned about group process in place of content alone is difficult.

In the next sections of this chapter, we explore each of these six issues: Separating self from role; transferring power to the group; creating an environment of trust; enabling growth through learning from mistakes; suspending judgment; and focusing on process.

SEPARATING SELF FROM ROLE

In an interview of Harvard's Ronald Heifetz, William Taylor points to the problem of separating self from role.

> I'm working on this question with a Kennedy School colleague, Martin Linsky. We're writing a book for leaders that will be called *Staying Alive.* To sustain yourself over the long term, you must learn how to distinguish role from self. Or, to put it more simply: You can't take things personally. Leaders often take personally what is not personal and then misdiagnose the resistance that's out there.
>
> Remember: It's not you they're after. It may look like a personal attack, it may sound like a personal attack—but it's the issues that you represent that they're after. Distinguishing role from self helps you maintain a diagnostic mind-set during trying times.
>
> There's a second point: Because we get so swept up in our professional roles, it's hard to distinguish role from self on our own. That's why we need partners who can help us stay analytical. And we need two different kinds of partners. We need allies inside the organization—people who share our agenda. And we need confidants inside or outside the organization—people who can keep us from getting lost in our role. (Taylor, 1999, p. 130)

Jon Katzenbach and Douglas Smith (1992) point to a similar problem with what they call "teams at the top," such as boards of directors and executive teams. Such groups can have a great deal of difficulty with separating their mission as a team from the mission of the whole organization.

Many people go through a crisis when they retire. They now have to confront the question of who are they once their role in the working world has finished. Willy Loman in *Death of a Salesman* (Miller, 1998) understood himself as having a single role, that of a traveling salesman whose success depended on his ability to be liked. He could not conceive of himself not being liked. As the play goes on, he is fired; he witnesses his sons' failures. When these things that give his life meaning are gone, Willy can find nothing left of his self and commits suicide.

Everyone knows that the inability to separate self from role is a problem, and yet it remains a very difficult one to deal with.

TRANSFERRING POWER TO THE GROUP

One of the more difficult aspects of detachment for the facilitative leader is found in turning over decision-making power to the group. Most managers and executives are taught that their most important role is that of making decisions. It is hard to see why it is important to renounce this power. The power to decide is seen as the responsibility of the job.

Managers often fear that they are losing power when they transfer responsibility for decisions to groups. They are. Members of the workforce also resist being given influence over decisions. Not infrequently, they don't want this responsibility. They say that decision making is the responsibility of management.

Perhaps even more important for managers is the fear of losing control of decisions, of the direction of the organization, and of their influence. The old paradigm and the command-and-control culture promise control, and while it may not be perfect, it is seen as a lot better than lack of control.

Group decision making has two advantages over the normal command-and-control approach: the view from many perspectives, and easier implementation of the decision.

Multiple Perspectives Bring Better Information

The first advantage is that the decision to be made can be seen from a number of perspectives, many of which are not available to any single individual. Organizations often believe that the more abstract and often more distant view of managers and executives is sufficient to respond effectively when decisions are needed. In today's complex world, the manager is rare who can grasp all of the consequences of a decision. International impact, software impact, operational impact may all be involved in a single simple decision. The management view of the organization is one perspective of many that need to be taken into account to succeed.

By involving people who represent the many different functions of a department, plant, or even a whole company, the work of the whole is present in the process. Managers have an abstract "overview" of their areas of responsibility; they can see the issues the workforce deals with, and yet even then they only see part of the way things are done. The employees bring their own perspective, but not necessarily the view of other parts of the organization or the overview of management.

Any group includes diversity beyond that of job functions. Awareness of the differences in backgrounds, education, lifestyle, religion, culture, and much more can enrich a discussion both in understanding the situation of an organization and in creating solutions.

By involving these perspectives in the dialogue and by encouraging people to share ideas, problems can be discerned earlier. Differences in perspectives can also help an organization to learn what the problems are in a deeper and more inclusive way than when a single viewpoint dominates the analysis.

Differences in perspective can also assist when generating solutions; they offer a rich mix of possible ways of solving the problem. When the diversity of perspective stems from a variety of roles in an organization, differences also offer a better perspective about what is feasible and what is not.

Implementation Is More Successful

The second advantage of group decision making has to do with the implementation of decisions. The problems involved in communicating the decision to the whole organization and gaining commitment to the results are reduced. Because the whole organization is present through the representatives of every function, the lines of communication are shorter. The way the decision is described can be adapted to the audience more readily by those individuals from that audience.

The levels of commitment by participants in the process to the success of the decision are greater than when the decision corresponds to one organizational perspective. By being directly involved in the decisions, participants want it to be successful. When things go wrong, there is a tendency to solve the problem in such a way that the overall goal of the plan is preserved even if the tactic and operational levels are completely reworked by those implementing them.

CREATING AN ENVIRONMENT OF TRUST

The third issue is the problem of developing and maintaining trust in organizations. In order for an organization to function effectively and creatively, a minimal level of trust between management and the workforce and among individuals is mandatory. The same is true in society at large.

A great deal is being written about the need for social trust and the erosion of social capital. D. Cohen and L. Prusak (2001) put it succinctly:

> Social capital thrives on authenticity and withers in the presence of phoniness or manipulation. As many failed experiments in social engineering have shown, even well-intentioned and intelligent plans for model towns and cities and countries founder on people's refusal to do exactly what is expected of them, no matter how healthy or sensible that expected behavior is. In fact, the enormous dangers of social engineering might be considered one of the major themes of the twentieth century. Even efforts driven by noble motives have sometimes had dire results—unintended consequences run amok. "Rational" human engineering frequently seems to kill the life it tries to "improve."

The consequences of a lack of trust are many. Organizations in which social trust is limited tend to block the free flow of ideas. Some have cultures in which contributions by the majority are not expected and naturally are not given. In some organizations, individuals fear being ridiculed, punished, or having ideas stolen by senior people, and so tend to not suggest ideas. Some organizations make it frustratingly difficult to get new ideas heard. Some focus on delivering immediate results to the exclusion of any improvements in quality. Because of these and other situations, employees may choose to channel their creative thinking outside the workplace.

Central to enabling creative thinking at work is developing means by which an atmosphere of trust is created. This might be at a special time and place, such as when Japanese managers take all of their reports out for noodles and a night of drinking together. Criticisms can be freely given without fear of punishment. Some organizations have creativity spaces, "away days," and planning meetings or retreats where ideas can be shared openly and without worry. For these kinds of activities to generate trust, those leading the sessions need to be open to the suggestions and display a willingness to change; that is, they need to be detached from their own ideas and their need to control the situation.

The facilitative leader is responsible for creating such places and times. In order for that to happen, the leader needs to model certain kinds of behavior, use certain kinds of group process techniques, and intervene in certain ways that promote these kinds of dynamics.

Ideas can be compared to seedlings. They need protection while they are germinating and in their early growth stages. As they mature, they need exposure to the rigors of their environment. Without increasingly difficult challenges, they do not prepare themselves adequately for the dangers of life in the world. Ideas need protection early in their development and increasing challenges as they develop.

Not only do people need to trust that their ideas will be taken seriously, but they need to know that their contribution will not jeopardize their position or the work of the organization as a whole. Creativity is sometimes discouraged, and it is often lost through self-censorship.

ENABLING GROWTH THROUGH LEARNING FROM MISTAKES

The quality of the decision is another concern. A leader can be preoccupied with the notion that his or her own decisions are "better" than other people's. That is, after all, what leaders are paid for—making good, successful, effective decisions. Here's where detachment comes in. In this example the detachment is from the "superiority" of their ideas.

"In addition to the content, the direction of the group's decision can be an issue. Facilitators quite often find themselves leading meetings wherein they disagree with the decision they have enabled a group to reach" (Jenkins & Jenkins, 2002). The two questions the facilitative leader has to answer go something like this, "Is the long-term development of the group's decision-making competency worth more than the cost of a decision that I disagree with?" And "Will the enthusiasm and commitment of the group in the implementation recognize and overcome defects in the plan?" This question requires that the leader step back from the immediate and look at the longer-term future. It also requires the maturity to realize that he or she may be wrong about their ideas.

A community in which we worked in Venezuela was convinced during a development planning consultation we helped to lead that the village could become a tourist center for weekenders from Caracas. In preparing for the consultation, we had had no little difficulty in convincing advisors and supporters to drive out into the country as far as the village. Naturally we strongly discounted the idea of this village as a community of weekend homes, when it seemed so very difficult to get people there even for a good cause like a planning consult. We had to reexamine our assumptions a few years later upon seeing a portion of the village redeveloped with holiday homes for weekenders. Once the village had the other facilities that the project developed, weekenders found it a charming place to visit.

"Group decision-making processes are often part of the journey the group is making. Learning to come to better decisions is part of that journey" (Jenkins & Jenkins, 2002).

SUSPENDING JUDGMENT

As Edward de Bono (1973) points out, human beings have a remarkable and necessary capacity to reach conclusions with little information. We discern patterns with surprisingly little data. We see part of a word and recognize it. Two small lights close together, at waist height on a dark road, slowly becoming larger and moving even more slowly apart look like a car coming toward us. It could just as well be two motorcycles or an illusion. This capacity to discern patterns has advantages and disadvantages. One disadvantage is that when considering information or a problem, we tend to stop searching once we see a pattern or a solution. The first conclusion is not necessarily the optimal one, but tends to be the one chosen.

In order to continue searching, we need to be able to suspend judgment. This works at the group level as well as the individual level. Thus, the same thing is true when brainstorming as an individual. We need to shut down our internal critic in order to generate ideas. When our critic is operating, we censor our thinking without even knowing it.

The facilitative leader suspends judgment when new ideas need to be generated and uses critical capacities to evaluate the merit of an idea when it is time to make choices. These are two different intellectual processes, and they do not work well simultaneously. There is a time of creativity and there is a time of evaluation, and both are served when done separately.

The facilitative leader needs the capacity to give up their ideas as better ones emerge from the group. Sometimes they may need to give up their ideas even when better ideas do not emerge.

The facilitator needs to be able to suspend his critical thinking about individuals and groups he is working with. This is part of the process of suspending judgment about ideas. For example, if you are convinced that employee James never comes up with anything worthwhile, then you will never hear the worthwhile ideas that he does come up with.

Facilitators can be external to the organization, hired as independents or from facilitation companies. Internal facilitators come from within the organization. Some companies have facilitation departments and some have networks of facilitators who have other primary jobs. These networks are usually coordinated by one or two individuals.

"Facilitators are hired as neutral parties, to enable group processes, whether that is to arrive at a decision, to create a plan, to build a model, or perhaps to improve the group dynamics or communication skills of the group members. The substance behind the image of neutrality is the discipline of detachment" (Jenkins & Jenkins, 2002).

While all facilitators have the issue of detachment, facilitators from within an organization tend to have a more difficult time with this than those hired from the outside. Detachment is particularly difficult for facilitators leading their own department's sessions. In these cases the facilitative leader is already involved in the decision-making process. He or she often originates the discussion. She is responsible to her bosses for the outcome of the decision-making process. He has definite ideas about what the outcome should look like and how it can be achieved. The facilitator's capacity and willingness to suspend judgment enables the development of creative ideas within the group and enables the capacity to judge ideas at another point in the process.

The external facilitator usually has detachment from the decision because whatever it is it will not affect them in the same way as it will the participants in the workshop. What the external facilitator often needs to develop is commitment to the successful creation of the decision.

FOCUSING ON PROCESS

Another struggle for the facilitative leader related to detachment has to do with the difference between content and process. What is meant by *content* is the topic or ideas being dealt with by the group. The *process* is the way the content is handled. For example, a strategic plan can be done in a number of different ways: scenarios planning and strengths, weaknesses, opportunities, and threats (SWOT) analysis are familiar processes to many managers. What is included in the plan, including the finances, product development, changes in corporate capacity, the way markets are developed, and so on, is all content. The way these are treated and the steps used to reach the plan are process. Different methods have different sequences of steps, different activities the group does together to reach their conclusions. The facilitative leader, while facilitating, must be primarily concerned with process.

Most leaders believe that what is important is the content of the session. This belief is what makes it difficult to focus on the processes. We often do an analysis of meeting dynamics for clients using four categories: content, process, emotion, and group spirit. By far the greatest number of inputs from participants is in the areas of content and emotions. Process and group spirit are less frequently addressed in meetings, and yet it is in these areas that the power of leadership comes into play.

Maintaining content neutrality and process concern is made more difficult by the fact that sometimes issues or ideas come up that the leader feels should not come up. Some issues are irrelevant, some are embarrassing, and some make the decision more complex. Sometimes important issues just don't come up. The need to maintain neutrality in these situations is one of the reasons that the discipline of Detachment is necessary.

The Four Levels of Detachment

Like all disciplines, Detachment has levels of intensity or stages of development. While it is actually a continuous process, it can be divided into four levels. (We use this device of four levels for all of the disciplines.) In the case of detachment it begins with being sensitized to the reality of detachment. Next comes the willingness to sacrifice what you have, who you are, and what you do to some larger good. The third level is renouncing all of these things. Finally, once they are given up, you experience a surge of power, release from all of those things that have taken power from you. At any given moment you can find yourself at any of these levels.

The Sensitivity

This first level is becoming sensitive to the reality of detachment. This seems to be done when you have a close experience with death. We all have experiences with death, but we are often protected from them by our societies. It is not too difficult to avoid dealing with death at all. Things, ideas, people, and organizations end their existence. They die.

When we encounter death, perhaps through a friend's illness or an accident, something happens to most of us. At least for a moment, there comes a new and intensified appreciation for life. Sometimes this appreciation leads to larger changes in the way we behave.

Dee Hock (1999) describes his life-changing event taking place during a hunting accident. While on a duck hunting trip, a boy slipped, and his shotgun went off and killed him. While the other boys went to get help, Hock spent hours waiting with the dead boy. Another example comes from the religious leader Joseph Mathews.

We frequently heard him describe how his experience as a chaplain in the Pacific theater in World War II, burying hundreds of young soldiers, shaped the direction of the rest of his life.

Certainly this sensitivity to the fragility of life can also happen without an encounter with death. Joseph Jaworski (1996) describes a series of soul-shaking events that changed the direction of his life. He was traumatized by discussions with his father, who was the Special Counsel investigating President Nixon's Watergate scandal. His wife divorced him. He left his Houston law firm. He took a trip through Europe to reflect on what he was doing with his life.

Whatever the occasion, the first level of Detachment has to do with being sensitive to the transitoriness of all things. When that happens, you are on the journey of Detachment.

THE SACRIFICE

The second level of Detachment is sacrifice. This sacrifice is the experience of giving things up. Sometimes we seem to be forced to choose. Once you experience that everything goes away, there seems to be a choice that you are confronted with. Do you care? You see the suffering, you know you could do something, but do you have the courage and discipline to do something real? You see fellow workers being treated unfairly. Do you do something about it? Many of us choose to do nothing. This leaves a hollow place at the center of our being. Some of us choose token activities, like donating $10 a month to an AIDS charity. We think that at least we are doing something, but deep down there is a nagging sense that it is insufficient. Our care keeps demanding that we do more.

When you choose Yes, your life is changed. Care is doing something, not feeling something; in fact it is a discipline of doing something. Care might begin as a romantic attachment to a good cause, but it moves to something more.

Jon once led a planning consultation in Central India in the village of Sevagram. It was a complex situation. At the end of a very difficult three weeks, a group of us left on the train to Mumbai. When we got to the city of Mahmad, the train stopped. There had been a train wreck further up the line and the train could go no further. We decided to rent a couple of taxis for our group.

A friend, Bhimrao Tupe, and Jon were walking to the taxi stands and got ahead of the rest of the group. They came out of a little alleyway and saw a girl of thirteen or fourteen years old going through a garbage pile. Her clothes were rags and she had the look of someone who was starving.

Jon was stunned. Every once in a while the girl on the garbage pile in Mahmad comes back to his mind to ask, "What are you doing to care, Jon?" The girl became a symbol for how easy it is to suppress the ability to care. Jon realized that care takes place wherever you are. He recognized that it is easy to forget the innocent suffering that is everywhere. Jon then knew that care was something that had to be worked at, not just experienced. He had to give up the luxury of forgetting others' pain.

Maureen once worked with a very gifted conference organizer, Linda. She was in line to take over the conference section for a large multinational. One day Linda announced that her boyfriend had the chance of a promotion to work in Brazil, but it meant that she would not be able to work. The choice was more than between moving to Brazil and staying in Holland; it affected her whole future and the career she had planned. It meant a change of outlook; it meant giving up the luxury of regret.

The choice is not always forced upon us. Jon met a man in Tokyo who had given up a great deal. He had gone to the best schools in Japan and graduated from Tokyo University. He was a member of the Japanese intellectual elite. He could have joined any of thousands of companies or government agencies. Upon graduation he chose to become a garbage collector in one of the poorest communities in Tokyo.

RENUNCIATION

The third level of Detachment is renunciation. The experience here is that you are nothing; you are a failure. Your wealth, social standing, power, friends, intelligence, and all that you value are meaningless. You desperately want them to have a purpose, but you experience them as having no value whatsoever. At this level you are in the process of giving them up.

In her book, *The Wisdom of No Escape*, Pema Chödrön (2001) talks about the dharma (the way of enlightenment) that is taught and the dharma that is experienced. She begins with the dharma that is taught, saying that it is like a precious jewel that can be covered with dirt. The dirt does not change the jewel. When someone reveals the jewel under the dirt, it resonates in the hearts and minds of those who can see. Sometimes while our hearts and mind resonate, we have a hard time figuring out what that may have to do with everyday life. This is where dharma that is experienced comes in. It is the experiencing dharma and not its philosophy that enables us to live with the suffering and pain of losing a job, having a family member die, or having a spouse leave (pp. 82–83).

The experience of renunciation is described in the parable about the rich man giving up his wealth being like a camel going through the eye of a needle. We think the best perspective for looking at this parable is not as a detached observer or from the perspective of the person trying to push the camel from behind. It is best understood from the perspective of the camel that has gotten partway through the eye of the needle. Imagine the effort that has gone into the process so far. There is no guarantee that the camel will succeed. She could be stuck here forever. Sometimes we choose being stuck rather than face the challenge of getting all the way through. Perhaps this is what Jean-Paul Sartre's play *No Exit* (1949) is about, being trapped in a place in which we choose to stay even if it is self-destructive, because we dare not envision a future.

We sometimes prefer the present pain. Yet the camel continues. On it goes until the camel makes it, stopping to be stuck for a time but with nowhere else to go but through. Pema Chödrön describes this as an in-between state, being homeless, a refugee. "You've left the shore, but you haven't arrived anywhere yet"(Chödrön, 2001, p. 91).

The memories of what you have given up are still with you. They may haunt you, but you know you have done the right thing. They still have power nonetheless. Jon remembers being on a five-day fast taking clear liquids only. On the evening of the fourth day, Jon went to a restaurant and had a hamburger, fries, and a cola, consuming them all. Now he was certain he was an ill-disciplined failure. He went back to his fasting colleagues and ended the fast together with them. Jon knew that he was violating his own integrity, yet he went ahead. He had to diminish and desensitize his self-honesty to do this. He did not know it or at least did not admit it; he was in a dark place in his life. While experiencing quite a dose of guilt, he also knew that there was no point wallowing in guilt about it.

In these dark moments, the camel may break through. To see how this works, let us return to what Pema Chödrön (2001) has to say. She speaks of the Buddhist teaching about four horses. The excellent horse moves even before the whip touches his back, moving at the slightest sound or movement by the rider. The good horse runs at the lightest touch of the whip. The poor horse only moves when it feels pain. The bad horse, however, moves only when he is jarred with pain to the marrow of his bones.

She goes on to recount a story by Dainin Katagini Roshi. When he first came to the United States from Japan as a young monk of twenty-seven to teach Buddhism, he struggled greatly. In Japan all of his colleagues and his surroundings were neat, precise, and clean. His students in the United States, however, were hippies. They had long, unwashed hair, wore sloppy rags for clothes and no shoes. He did not like them. He couldn't help it; he just couldn't stand them. They offended his every sensibility. He said, "So all day I would give talks about compassion, and at night I would go home and weep and cry because I realized I had no compassion at all. Because I didn't like my students, therefore I had to work much harder to develop my heart" (pp. 8–9).

It is in the situation of being the worst horse that one finds oneself working on their heart. It is when working on our heart that the camel can break through. When we see that both failures and successes are not the meaning of who we are, we have renounced all.

THE POWER

Power is the final level of Detachment. It follows the levels of sensitivity, sacrifice, and renunciation. Power occurs when you have relinquished all of the claims upon you of things, accomplishments, relationships, and even your own self-discipline.

The experience is first of all one of having a huge burden lifted from your shoulders. You have everything, and suddenly you are free. Because you can walk away from everything, you control everything. Gains and losses are the same. The joy of work is not in the product but in the work itself. All people are the same. It is from this perspective that it is said that all of humanity are brothers and sisters.

CONCLUSION

We do not mean that detachment is a virtuous thing to do, or even something you should do. It is a state you find yourself in, not something you should be. Trying to be detached is almost contrary to being detached. Practices are helpful in being open to detachment, but there is no automatic result.

It is perfectly normal to experience power over some dimension of your life while at the same moment becoming aware of some other dimension that you are afraid to let go of. This awareness is the beginning. Watch how the fear manifests itself. What and who is supporting the attachment? What is the source of the fear? What is the cost of giving it up? Perhaps awareness coupled with detachment exercises is sufficient.

We are using two terms that need to be clarified: *exercise* and *practice*. What we mean by exercise is an activity that is usually only done once. It is used to bring awareness to the reality of the discipline. A practice is an activity that is done regularly or at special occasions. Meditation or journal writing that is done daily or a weeklong silent retreat done annually are practices. Some practices are done whenever needed, such as the two suggested by Roger Walsh in the following section. Practices are intended to deepen the disciplines; exercises are intended to build awareness of the disciplines.

◆ ◆ ◆

Practices for Detachment

The classic practice for detachment is meditation. There are many forms of meditation to choose from. We share one here called "Centering Prayer."

Centering Prayer

Centering Prayer begins with selection of a sacred word representing your intention to be present to the mystery of existence and to surrender to the inner movement of the spirit. The word should be something that represents your own personal decision to be open, perhaps something like "love," "Lord," or "peace."

Sit comfortably enough not to be distracted by physical discomfort or pain, but not comfortable enough to fall asleep. You can also avoid falling asleep by avoiding practice immediately after eating. The back should be straight but not stiff. Close your eyes and step back from the things surrounding you.

Begin to quiet your mind. When it is relatively quiet, think about your sacred word. Whatever thoughts come to mind, gently turn them aside by returning to the sacred word. If you fall asleep, when you wake up, return to the sacred word. You may experience strong emotions or become aware of powerful images. Gently return to the sacred word. You may experience a kind of wakefulness in which your mind is blank. You have no thoughts or experience anything at all.

The sessions should be about twenty minutes long, once early in the morning and again at night. At the end of each session, sit quietly to bring yourself back to the reality of the room.

Besides meditation, there are a number of other practices that assist in developing the discipline of Detachment.

Fasting

We have mentioned fasting in a variety of forms. Some people go for twenty-four hours once a week without eating and only drinking water. Some people also do a monthly three-day fast. Pre-Vatican Council Catholics practiced meatless Fridays. Buddhist monks and nuns beg for a single meal each day. Muslims practice the fast of Ramadan.

Two practices suggested by Roger Walsh in his book *Essential Spirituality* (1999) are Indulge an Attachment and Frustrate an Addiction.

Indulge an Attachment

The Indulge an Attachment practice describes one of Walsh's meditation teachers who had spent years in spiritual practices. The teacher had one fault, a firm attachment to sweets. He would spend a significant amount of his meager income buying candies and other sweets. One day he went to the market, and going from stall to stall, purchased different sweets until all of his money was gone. He then went home. He placed the box of candies in front of him and meditated until his mind was clear. He then took one candy and placed it in his mouth. He focused his awareness on the experience of eating the sweet. He was aware of the anticipation of the first touch of the candy in his mouth. He paid attention to the flood of pleasure that filled his mind. He savored the taste and smell. He observed as he swallowed and reached for a second piece.

Keeping himself focused on the experience, he ate candy after candy until he noticed a change in the experience. The taste began to be less stimulating, and the pleasure disappeared. He continued to eat and pay attention. The eager anticipation turned to distaste until he found that he had to force himself to eat the next candy. He began to feel ill. Still he continued to eat. He forced another and another until the sight of candy made him feel sick. By the time he was finished, he was cured of the attachment.

This is not a practice for all things, but with care and thought it can be a way to build detachment from some things.

Frustrate an Addiction

Walsh's Frustrate an Addiction exercise is familiar to many who have dealt with addictions. It begins with selecting something that you are attached to, perhaps a favorite food, cigarettes, or TV. Set a realistic goal of doing without whatever you have selected for a specific period of time. This might be a day or a morning. It has to be actually doing without, and it has to be a realistic time frame. It is better to stop smoking for an afternoon and succeed than commit to a lifetime and fail. Bring as much awareness as you can to the period you are doing without. Pay attention to thoughts, feelings, physical reactions, and so on as the time passes. When the period is over, reflect on the experience. What fears did you experience? What new thoughts or ideas did you have about yourself or your addiction?

This practice not only helps in dealing with the addiction, it can help develop understanding of yourself and also strengthen your willpower and your self-esteem.

◆ ◆ ◆

Exercise for Detachment*

Personal Values

We use this exercise in a retreat we do on the Nine Disciplines. We hand out a worksheet and ask the participants to do the first part of the exercise. We then have people gather into small groups and discuss the questions

---

*This exercise is based on a similar one from Peter Senge and others, 1994.

together. Finally, we lead a discussion of the whole group. We ask participants to share what they chose and how they felt while making those decisions. We ask them to reflect on what the meaning of their choices is. We end with a short discussion about what they can do to deepen their ability to be detached.

Look over the following list, and select and circle which of the following are the ten most critical values for you. If there are other important values not shown on the list, write those in on the empty lines at the bottom of the list.

Honesty	Openness	Fair play	Respect	Justice	Gracefulness
Fortitude	Integrity	Balance	Charity	Joyfulness	Understanding
Simplicity	Moderation	Enthusiasm	Wealth	Health	Self-assurance
Status	Empathy	Courage	Dedication	Vision	Imagination
Creativity	Spirit	Curiosity	Power	Zeal	Professionalism
Thrift	Kindness	Good cheer	Humor	Tradition	Forgiveness
Nerve	Energy	Generosity	Sensitivity	Wisdom	Risk-taking
Reliability	Commitment	Logic	Modesty	Charm	Perseverance
Success	Duty	Family	Influence	Peace	Entrepreneurship
_____	_____	_____	_____	_____	_____

Return to your list and remove five of the items, leaving the five top values that you live by.

Return to the list again four times, and remove each time one more value until you arrive finally at the one that you rank the highest. Don't take away the last four in a single sweep, but evaluate them one at a time to make sure you have as honest a ranking as you can.

Now discuss the process with the team:

- What is the value that remained for you?
- What process did you follow—what question did you ask yourself—to remove values from the list?
- What did it feel like to remove values?
- What is the struggle here? What is this about?
- When do you struggle with this process in your work? what are some examples?
- What is important to keep in mind here?

CHAPTER SIX

ENGAGEMENT: COMMITTING TO THE GROUP

The discipline of Engagement is developing the capacity to care, to commit, and to be generous with who and what you are, without knowing what the outcome may be.

The facilitative leader intends that optimal decisions be made. These are the most effective decisions, the most innovative, and those that the group has the will to carry out. While Detachment enables the free flow of ideas, Engagement enables the willingness to select and carry out a new direction.

The discipline of Engagement is, in this time, more difficult than ever before. People are reluctant to engage fully. Before the Vietnam War, the ranks of soldiers with the highest mortality rates were the junior officers, who led their troops into combat. In Vietnam, junior officers tended to remain behind the lines, directing their troops into combat. This marked a profound change in commitment in the U.S. military.

The inability to face difficulties in relationships has become a common societal theme. Men and women struggle with their difficulties with long-term relationships. When things get difficult, embarrassing, or awkward, the relationships can change. Sometimes partners change; sometimes the character or quality of the relationship changes so that the individuals are more distant and less involved.

Perhaps it is our individualism that is driving this. We fear that if we commit, we will lose something of ourselves or lose control of our lives. Perhaps we distrust the societies we live in. The faults are clear. Forces beyond our control manipulate political and economic structures. In order to keep some semblance of control, we retreat to the one place where we think we have control, namely ourselves.

Perhaps we simply fear death. Engagement requires that we expend ourselves; expenditure leads to depletion, and depletion leads to death. The illusion is that if we never engage, we won't become depleted and die. At least we won't experience those moments of failure or incapacity, those little deaths. Perhaps we simply do not want to have to decide, to make choices. To choose, we say No to something in order to say Yes to something else. We feel that we should leave all our options open.

What Is Engagement?

Engagement is a common, everyday kind of experience. We join a sports team or reading club with the idea of spending time participating, adding to, and benefiting from the team or club. We find ourselves faithfully defending a group we belong to because of its traditions. We are loyal to the past, the present, and the aspirations of the group. We are dedicated to and participate in change processes in the belief that things will get better. We work long hours for the community far beyond what is expected.

In the process of joining and becoming more involved in a group, we take on the group's ways and perspectives. We begin to know the people and create bonds with them and the group as a whole. After a period of confusion we pick up the norms, the jargon, the way things are done. Some of us may use these tactics with missionary zeal to demonstrate that we are members of the group. We become more and more committed to the future of the group.

In ancient India, life was seen to have four phases: youth, warrior, householder, and elder. The Institute of Cultural Affairs used a similar understanding. Youth was seen as birth to twenty years old, a time for discovering the world. The Warrior or Young Adult, from twenty to forty, is creating her or his life, family, career, place in society. The Householder is an Established Adult, from forty to sixty, who is maintaining continuity and enabling stability. The Elder, over sixty years of age, brings perspective and wisdom to society. You see these same roles being played out in well-established organizations. New people are eager to learn and ask lots of questions, sometimes to the point of being annoying. Once people know their way around the work and organization they begin to create their place in the organization. They are the real workhorses. As workers become established and have a solid place, they begin to be looked to for continuity and stability. Finally, workers approach retirement. They are in their last assignment. They have "seen it all" and have a unique perspective on the organization. Each of these roles is one aspect of engagement.

In the first phase, getting acquainted with the group, we often are highly enthusiastic; running around like puppies brought home for the first time. We test limits and figure out who the alpha dogs are, and where we fit in the hierarchy. The group will adjust somewhat to us, but by far, we adjust to the group.

In the mid-1960s, Jon interviewed for a position with IBM in San Francisco. He was struck by how much all of the employees looked alike: young, well-manicured men in blue suits. At the end of the interview, the interviewer said that he would like to have Jon join the company, and if Jon wanted to be a member of the IBM team, he should get a haircut. The assimilation process had begun even before employment was agreed to. The interviewer was helping Jon to understand what assimilation at IBM would mean.

The next phase of integration with the group is characterized by the individual wanting to be successful, to make a mark, and to improve things. We are ambitious. As we become more familiar with the boundaries and norms of the group, we begin to settle into its routines. In a combination of finding and creating a place, we create a role for ourselves. We search for the limits of our abilities. Everything seems possible. We can't fail.

The third phase is that of a mature member of the group. At some point, most of us become the establishment. We embody the norms of the group and pass them on to new people. In many ways we are the role models that others look to. At this point we are both the best and the worst of the aspects of the group. We are the journeyperson of the organization. We are depended on to do a good job.

The final stage is that of elder. This role is difficult in the West. The elder is a strange combination of symbol of the past and of the end of a career. The elder is a threat and at the same time offers perspective to a group. He or she often carries the collective memory of the organization. The elder, with the longest experience of the organization's successes and failures, can sometimes be the one most eager for dramatic change.

The Four Dimensions of Engagement

Engagement has to do with the relationship that a leader takes toward an organization. We point to four different dimensions of that relationship: promoting stability, encouraging change, maintaining balance, and caring for spirit. These are not intended to be a sequence of activities but facets of the same reality. These dimensions are internal states of an individual and as such are very difficult to distinguish from externalities.

Promoting Stability

The leader who is engaged is committed to maintaining stability. This stability is not the stability of a clockwork view of the universe where processes and roles are stable. It is the stability found in chaos.

Imagine a fast-running stream high in the mountains. At every moment the flow around the rocks changes a little. Eddies spin on the downhill side of the rocks. The force of the water digs holes in the riverbed. There is no way of predicting exactly what will happen next, yet there is order, the banks contain the stream. The rocks force the water to go around them. The general flow of the water is always downhill. Chaos? Yes. Order? Yes. In organizations, stability is found in maintaining the values, principles, and meaningful purpose of the organization over the long term. These cultural aspects of an organization, once established, are difficult to change. Processes, job descriptions, products, and other organizational aspects can change within this kind of stability.

Leaders' support for stability begins with loyalty to the organization. It is commitment to the present situation. It is the desire and willingness to maintain the status quo. This dimension is essentially conservative. Leadership in this aspect is about enabling order. This is the establishment, and the establishment faces the past.

Some degree of stability is necessary for organizations to survive. A certain comfort comes from knowing that things will be the same tomorrow as they are today and were yesterday. Planning is possible when there is some degree of predictability in an organization.

While it is clear that the saying "Change is the only constant" is relatively true, it has some flaws. The level of change is not as great as this saying seems to imply. Imagine a place of real constant change. Imagine having a new career, with new colleagues you have never met, every time you come to work. Imagine the difficulty of doing any work, in adjusting to each new day, if every day a totally new job awaited you, in a place you had never been. Imagine new processes, products, prices, and possibilities. We do live in a world of continual change, but we also live in a place of stability. What remains stable and what changes are the key questions.

The danger is that organizations become frozen. They crystallize and can't break free from the past. The past, its traditions, while usually idealized, define the meaning of the structure. "Things have always been done this way."

A British military officer was visiting an exercise by the Austrian Army. Part of the demonstration was firing artillery pieces. As the officer watched a squad go through the sequence of firing their weapon, he noticed that one of the men walked to the side and held his arms close to his side and bent at the elbows with his fist clenched in front of him. The British officer asked what the man was doing. Everyone said that they were not sure, but it was part of the manual of operations for these artillery pieces. Finally the officer came upon a very old veteran who explained that in the days when horses moved artillery pieces from place to place, it was necessary for one man to hold the reins of the horse to keep it from bolting when the guns were fired.

Today there are no horses, but the person holding the reins often still remains part of the process. It may well be that traditional practices that have outlived their function, like the man holding the reins of the nonexistent horse or the bearskin hats on British Beefeaters, may remain for ceremonial or symbolic reasons. In these cases a practice or process is kept to fulfill a new and quite different social function from the one for which it was first intended. This is quite a different matter from holding onto outdated processes without any idea why.

Encouraging Change

This second dimension has to do with breaking with the status quo. Engagement in this dimension breaks free from what has been and explores the new. It is not interested in tradition or stability. Promoting stability is about conserving, and encouraging change is about liberating. Leadership in this aspect is about justice. This is the rebel, the disestablishment, facing the uncertain future in search of better ways of living and working.

Aware of the problems in the current organization, the leader explores and introduces new ways of thinking and doing things. With time, ideas are brought into the organization that may have been unthinkable at the beginning. What is paramount here is that change happens in a positive way. Without this dynamic, an organization will not grow or evolve. It will be unable to meet demands from clients, employees, the competition, suppliers, or the social economic environment in which it operates.

Liberation, constantly seeking the new, also has its destructive side. It can lead to forgetting the past, learning nothing. The new can become an end in itself. Change can be sought for the sake of change, rather than for its intrinsic benefit to the organization or its members. Change is always partly inventing and innovating and partly destroying. When liberation dominates, it becomes chaos without order and change without progress.

Change for the sake of change can lead to reorganization efforts that remove all of the people who know how the core processes work. The Dutch telephone company replaced its switching equipment and downsized all of the personnel who managed that equipment. The old equipment nevertheless remained, unused, in place. When ADSL (Asynchronous Digital Switching Language), the next generation of high-speed Internet connections, was introduced shortly thereafter, it could be employed on those old, disused networks. The old switches came back into use for the new technology. Because the people who had maintained the old equipment had been let go, the company had to find and train a new generation of replacements.

Maintaining Balance

This third dimension has to do with managing the distortions brought about when either stability or change dominates. Engagement is the capacity to see the positive and negative aspects of both stability and change. This balance recognizes that when the conservative forces dominate, the forces of liberation need to be called on. When the liberating forces dominate, the forces of conservation need to be called on. The need for the honoring and maintaining continuity with the past is balanced with the demand to face and invent the future.

At times a group is stuck in a thinking pattern that they need to step out of in order to move effectively. This is more common than the reverse, where a chaotic situation needs to be ordered. In the mid-1970s we led a planning consultation with a small village in central Italy. Jon's team was working on commercial and industrial development. The team consisted of twenty residents of the village and four outside consultants plus Jon and a businessman from Milan who was acting as translator. We explained that we were going to do a workshop in which we would share ideas about the village. We would record them on the flipcharts. We asked that we respect each other's opinion and speak one at a time. We asked the first question, "What would you like to see in your village in the next four years?" Both the businessman and Jon were stunned when what seemed like the whole room stood up and began shouting at each other. It was evident that there was no way the workshop could happen in the orderly fashion we had planned. After a minute or two, Jon asked if the businessman could catch some of the points being made. He said Yes, and they began writing them down. After they had about ten points summarized on the board, they tried to calm the group down. Kind requests that people stop resulted in complete failure. Jon asked how to say "Quiet!" and the businessman said "Silencio!" and both shouted it. The chaos abated. We explained once again what we were doing, reviewed the ideas we had captured, and asked if there were more ideas. Pandemonium broke out again, with ideas gathered as quickly as possible. The whole week was spent balancing highly creative mayhem and imposed silence. The group recognized that the order was necessary if their ideas were going to be part of the plan. We recognized that the chaos was necessary if we were going to have the creativity of the villagers in the plan.

Balance in this respect is similar to what Harrison Owen in his book *Leadership Is . . .* (1990) says about love. He talks about the two faces of love as acceptance and challenge, a similar polarity to the balance of conservation and liberation.

Love as acceptance is unconditional acceptance. It is taking others just as they are, in whatever space they are in, and how they are, no questions asked. This aspect of love is nonjudgmental beyond reason, in fact quite unreasonable. It is acceptance without the other needing to justify, rationalize or apologize.

This kind of acceptance is dangerous. Without standards life turns to mush, without rigor thinking becomes sloppy, without judgment anything goes. Pure acceptance leaves you as you are and never urges you to become everything you could be.

Love as challenge is a confrontation in which the other is catapulted into new ways of being. Standards are set, expectations are there, judgment is real, mushy life won't do, sloppy thinking is unacceptable. Challenge is the road to fulfillment, but of course challenge by itself is disastrous, for it creates a life of unmitigated harshness.

Neither face of love will work alone. While we may prefer the comfort of acceptance, we require the stringent slap of challenge. Challenge must always be grounded in acceptance, acceptance excited by challenge. Great love is acceptance and challenge without boundary (Owen, 1990).

One aspect of this balance is the ability to recognize when decisions need to be slowed down for reflection and consideration and when they need to be made quickly and with conviction.

Caring for Spirit

What is spirit? Spirit happens or it doesn't happen. It cannot be forced or tricked into manifesting itself. It is found in the courage to act in freedom. It is found in meeting the obligations of the time in which we live. Spirit is will, not the little will in *willfulness* but the larger will in *willing greatness*. In the old paradigm, caring for spirit was seen as motivation, or getting more out of people. This was understood to be a "carrot and stick" approach, which at its heart is a belief in the mechanistic, cause-and-effect world of the eternal clock. "Do this, and there will be spirit in the business." In the new paradigm, things are much more messy. Spirit is evoked or enabled, not switched on and off like a light bulb.

Bill Russell (1979) describes his experience of the release of spirit in *Second Wind: The Memoirs of an Opinionated Man:*

> Every so often a Celtics game would heat up so that it became more than a physical or even mental game, and would be magical. That feeling is difficult to describe, and I certainly never talked about it when I was playing. When it happened I could feel my play rise

to a new level. It came rarely, and would last anywhere from five minutes to a whole quarter or more. Three or four plays were not enough to get it going. It would surround not only me and the other Celtics but also the players on the other team, and even the referees. To me, the key was that *both* teams had to be playing at their peaks, and they had to be competitive. The Celtics could not do it alone. I remember the fifth and final game of the 1965 championship series, when we opened the fourth quarter ahead of the Lakers by sixteen points, playing beautifully together, and then we simply took off into unknown peaks and ran off twenty straight points to go up by thirty-six points, an astounding margin for a championship series. We were on fire, intimidating, making shots, running the break, and the Lakers just couldn't score. As much as I wanted to win that championship, I remember being disappointed that the Lakers were not playing better. We were playing well enough to attain that special level, but we couldn't do it without them. (Russell, 1979, pp. 155–156)

Engagement is the capacity of a leader to evoke this state in all of their followers. For Russell and others who describe this state, it does not happen very often. Conditions have to be right, and many of those conditions are outside their influence. Mihaly Csikszentmihalyi (1991) describes this condition as being found at the point where your ability is exactly matched by the challenge you face.

Spirit is found in special circumstances. It manifests itself at the end of something, in dying. It is found in the moment between the end of the old and the beginning of the new. It appears when the new is a helpless infant that needs nurture. It can be found once the new is strong enough and structure has been created that embodies it. These moments are when leadership is required. Caring for spirit is enabling people to make these transitions. It is also enabling people to connect to a higher purpose, to care for others and the greater Other, to take risks, and to balance liberation with conservation.

THE ISSUES OF ENGAGEMENT FOR FACILITATIVE LEADERS

Engagement for leaders goes further than for members of the group. It is sustained commitment, a covenant. It is care for the organization or the group. It is taking responsibility for norms of behavior.

"For the facilitator, engagement begins with a simple act of agreement to do a job, and as such the facilitator is committed to the success of the group. This kind of leadership models what it means to be a good participant. They are responsible for the implementation of the process" (Jenkins & Jenkins, 2002). As such they commit to the quality of the group's actions.

Engagement is also sustained commitment. To be engaged is to act in an ever-changing environment and relationship. In these circumstances actions are responses to what is happening. Engagement as response is based on taking responsibility over the long term for those actions. It is caring as action even when frustrated or continually blocked. It is taking necessary risks. It is responsibility for standards. In the next sections of this chapter, we explore each of these issues.

SUSTAINED COMMITMENT

Commitment, in our use of the word, operates at two levels: to a larger meaningful purpose for the organization and to a business or organizational goal.

At the level of larger purpose, Engagement is commitment to a meaningful reason for the existence of the organization and keeping that reason consistently in view. This purpose answers the question, "What is the social function of the company I work for?" A social purpose is not making money per se. The social function has to support the capacity to make money if the organization is a business, or to acquire donations and volunteers if it is a nongovernmental organization (NGO), or to receive funding if it is a government agency.

Many mission statements and advertising slogans are good statements of meaningful purpose. A well-crafted mission statement can be a driving force in the life of an organization. Ackoff (n.d.) states it this way:

> A mission statement should be exciting and inspiring. It should motivate all those whose participation in its pursuit is sought; for example, one Latin American company committed itself to being

"an active force for economic and social development, fostering economic integration of Latin America and, within each country, collaboration between government, industry, labor and the public." A mission should play the same role in a company that the Holy Grail did in the Crusades. It does not have to appear to be feasible; it only has to be desirable. (Ackoff, n.d.)

A great deal of information is available about how mission and vision statements are created, how they differ from each other and what they are not, so we will not go into the practices here. Rather we point to their importance in connecting work to a larger purpose.

We led a workshop for the London sales office of a major paper manufacturer. The mission statement was fairly long and had three parts. Part one was about customer satisfaction. Part two was about maintaining the highest standards of paper. Part three was about minimizing environmental impact in manufacturing and delivering paper. After the introductions, we went around the room and asked each person to read out loud part of the company's mission statement. We then discussed each part of the statement. The employees were very positive about the overall mission of the company and how they could contribute to it. They came up with suggestions for using environmentally sustainable manufacturing processes, contributing to the customer's ability to be an effective business, improving the character of the office, and providing improved market information.

Stories of why it is important to do the day-to-day work of the company sustain the larger purpose. These stories reflect the past and present and point toward a better future. They invite people to commit to that future even if it cannot be completed in a single lifetime. They result in a sense of urgency and of participating in destiny. However, more than just story is needed. The story must reflect the activities of the company, its employees, and its management. If the management does not live the story, it will die. Employees cannot be forced or tricked into buying a false story. They can only choose freely to make the larger purpose their own.

Here is a story that we heard in the 1970s while developing a strategic planning method.

Davy Wood was the teenage son of a prominent lawyer in a prestigious Chicago law firm. The family was wealthy, and Davy needed little materially. Nevertheless, he decided to take a summer job in a factory manufacturing seat belts.

The work was tedious. Put the webbing and buckle into a press. Activate the press. Remove the belt. Put the webbing and the buckle into . . . Hour after hour, day after day, the same thing repeated over and over.

After some weeks, Davy's mother began to notice that he was working later and later. Instead of coming home at 5:30, he arrived at 6:00, then 6:30, then 7:00. She thought that there must be a girl involved. She decided to take dinner to work for Davy. She could then see what was going on.

She arrived at 6:00. There was Davy, standing in front of his machine making one seat belt after another. She asked what he was doing and why he was staying so late. The work was boring and didn't make much money.

Davy replied, "I am saving twenty thousand lives a year."

On Davy's first day on the job his boss had taken him around the plant, shown him the different operations, and told him how seat belts saved lives. Company literature showed precisely how seat belts reduced injury. Employees used the company's seat belts in their own cars. Unlike many young workers, Davy understood clearly why it was important to work at the plant.

What was needed for Davy next was that this relationship to his work be maintained. We do not mean the number of hours he is spending; that may in fact make the relationship unsustainable. We mean the perspective that the work is important far beyond Davy and even beyond the company he works for.

It was equally important that Davy have specific goals for the day or hour. The larger reason for working becomes meaningless if it is not attached in some concrete and visible way to real accomplishments. Davy had quotas for the number of seat belts he produced a day. Let's say he was expected to produce 450 a day. In the old mechanical universe, what was important was that he meet the target of 450. In the new universe, what is important is that he makes the connection between the 450 belts a day and the twenty thousand lives saved. This connection needs to be made not once, but often and honestly.

The leader enables the emergence of a sustained and sustainable central reason for the organization's existence, and enables people to make the connection between their day-to-day work and the larger purpose of the company.

CARING AS ACTION

Everyday living is connected to a larger purpose, a contribution to society. That connection is created and sustained by care. The word *care* has several definitions, and for our purposes there are two. First, care is an emotion, the sense of having affection for someone or being attracted toward them. Second, care is an act, in the sense of treating, supporting, enabling, or serving someone. While the emotion may precede the action, it is this second meaning that we are concerned with.

> Engagement is . . . service. A facilitator is a servant of the group's processes to make creative and meaningful decisions. Engagement is the discipline of caring about the quality of people's decisions and their capacity to enact them. Caring in this sense is not the emotion but the act. (Jenkins & Jenkins, 2002).

Robert Greenleaf, the late AT&T executive, used the term *Servant Leader* in his attempt to describe the role of the leader as caring for others.

> Servant-Leadership is a practical philosophy which supports people who choose to serve first, and then lead as a way of expanding service to individuals and institutions. Servant-leaders may or may not hold formal leadership positions. Servant-leadership encourages collaboration, trust, foresight, listening, and the ethical use of power and empowerment. (Greenleaf Center, 2002)

Robert Greenleaf suggests the difference between those who put being a servant first and those who put leadership first:

> The difference manifests itself in the care taken by the servant— first to make sure that other people's highest priority needs are being served. The best test, and difficult to administer, is: do those served grow as persons; do they, while being served, become healthier, wiser, freer, more autonomous, more likely themselves

to become servants? And, what is the effect on the least privileged in society; will they benefit, or, at least, will they not be further deprived? (Greenleaf, 1970)

Taking Risks

Having a larger purpose and caring for others is not easy. Engagement is also taking risks. It may mean challenging the status quo, taking on unpopular positions, or doing things that are unproven or never attempted before. It means making choices. In order for risks to be taken, one needs to have choice or at least perceived choice. Choice implies taking responsibility for decisions and their consequences.

In his book *Real Change Leaders,* Jon R. Katzenbach (1995) describes the process leaders go through, as they become real change leaders.

> Change leaders gain the self-confidence—as well as the credibility—they will need for change by taking a series of connected actions that, once started, play out in series. Some may not seem inherently courageous, but each requires additional levels of risk and boldness on their part. These actions do not necessarily represent one big leap of faith, but rather a set of ongoing and interconnected choices that often appear in retrospect to have been one leap. (Katzenbach, 1995, p. 106)

The steps of becoming real change leaders are (1) "making the initial commitment"; (2) acting on that commitment which results in building conviction and confidence in themselves and credibility and stature among colleagues; (3) becoming a vocal advocate of important aspects of change; and (4) creating a number of successes by removing blocks or putting in place innovations (Katzenbach, 1995).

Sun Tzu, a Chinese general and writer on war who lived sometime between 400 and 320 B.C., suggests that people stop worrying about the risks they are taking when they experience themselves overcoming difficulties (Sun Tzu, 1963). Such steps not only increase the self-confidence of the change leader but also demonstrate to others that risks can be taken.

Responsibility for Standards

For the facilitative leader, standards are important not for the sake of control but for the sake of providing the best the organization has to offer. The leader is strongly committed to a set of values against which the work of the organization is tested. If the work is found wanting, it changes. The leaders are models of what is expected of everyone in the organization.

Sun Tzu is studied in Asia by millions of people as a metaphor guide to running a business. His thinking has since the 1970s moved into the business world of the West. He says that war (read "business") must be appraised by five factors. "The first of these factors is moral influence; the second, weather; the third, terrain; the fourth, command; and the fifth, doctrine" (Sun Tzu, 1963, p. 63). What he means by moral influence is the cause of people being in harmony with their leaders. One of his commentators, Chang Yü, puts it this way: "When one treats people with benevolence, justice, and righteousness, and reposes confidence in them the army will be united in mind and all will be happy to serve their leaders" (p. 64). Those leaders with high moral influence will be more able as leaders; they will have followers who can take advantage of situations they find themselves in, can act more in line with the values of the organization and be more effective in what they do.

The Four Levels of Engagement

Engagement has different levels of intensity, and they are sequential. What we describe in the next four sections takes place internally. It may not be noticed by anyone but the person experiencing and developing the discipline. Like any discipline, Engagement requires practice, and in this case, the commitment becomes steadily deeper and more profound. The four levels are covenant, submission, responsibility, and freedom. Developing skills and attitudes to achieve some mastery of engagement means going through these stages or levels. In some cases the stage is achieved quickly and perhaps without being conscious of it, while other stages may require a great deal of time.

Engagement is about a larger purpose. It is bringing into being something of greater meaning, like Davy Wood does. While it is possible to reduce commitment to small things, leaders expand it to encompass the whole organization.

THE COVENANT

The initial level of Engagement is that of covenant (commitment). At the simplest level, we have all experienced the feeling of longing to have a lifelong relationship with someone or something. It can be a potential partner, music or art, a cause or a community. Leadership involves making a lifelong decision to be of that company, that spouse, that place, or that task.

In order to understand covenant we need to understand commitments. We live in an age of failed commitments. We have a great ability to be detached in a negative way. We can leave things easily. We are able to leave our spouses, homes, jobs, and friends. We divorce. We not only change jobs, but we change careers. We move from city to city, leaving friends and sometimes family behind. Naturally, the historical moment we live in contributes to this by making change easier.

Traditionally, one was given a place in life—a profession, a social class, a spouse, an extended family, a religious life, a place to live. Today all of these things are choices most of us have to make, not once but again and again. Few people expect to follow for life the career they studied at school, to live in the same town for life as the one they grew up in, and so on. It is easy to forget in today's world how difficult these choices are. The rate of job change, of moves from place to place, of divorce, all bear testimony to the fact that we change our minds, we make mistakes, we change over the years.

We have become "tourists" in jobs, in relationships, in communities. Civil society organizations note that without commitment to the community, the quality of life declines for everyone. We relativize our commitments so that when we fail to meet one, it is not really important. We can say to ourselves that it was not a big failure; all of us have little failures, and little failures are okay.

Contract Versus Covenant

Failure of commitment is at its heart found in the difference between *contract* and *covenant*. In a contract, the two parties agree to exchange one thing for another. In addition, they agree that if one of them fails to deliver, then the contract is void and the other party does not have to deliver what they had agreed to. The manager is paid by a company to lead a department. If the manager fails to manage or the company fails to pay, the contract is violated. Key to a contract is that it is a legal agreement.

In a covenant, the two parties also agree to exchange one thing for another. In a covenant, however, if one party fails to deliver what they agreed to, the other party is still under an obligation to deliver what they had promised. Key to a covenant is that it is morally and spiritually binding. It is not necessarily legally binding. In this perspective, a manager who is not paid by the company is still morally obligated to manage the department. In our modern, commercial society this seems crazy. We will be taken advantage of. We feel we really do need a prenuptial agreement.

The great diversity of approaches to ethical questions adds to the difficulty of operating out of a covenant. We have one ethic for work and another for home. We have one ethic when making choices about a supplier and another about selecting an employee. To make it even more difficult to operate out of a covenant, we have a tendency to substitute the law for morality. We seem to believe that if something is not illegal, then it is okay. If we can't agree to what is right, we can pass a law to make it illegal.

Multiple Commitments

In today's world, we all struggle with multiple commitments, all of which are clamouring for more and more attention. Our families, our jobs, our friends, and our own quiet time demand our time. Mostly we hop from one commitment to the next, hoping that we achieve balance. None is satisfied, and neither are we. Our hopping becomes more frenetic as the different voices become more effective in attracting our attention, whether by being louder or offering more satisfaction or power or money.

Making a covenant is an unconditional declaration of intent. It is bringing integrity to a new level. It is manifesting to the world what you truly value. The covenant becomes an anchor and definition for all your relationships, in fact, all relationships. It enables all other relationships to be defined. It is saying to those who you are in covenant with that they are so special, so central that no matter how they change or the circumstances change, or you change, you will maintain the relationship. It is de-relativizing your relationships.

Covenant is experienced as wanting to spend one's whole life doing the thing you are engaged in or to. At this level, consequences are unimportant. In fact, it is important to avoid thinking about consequences at this point. Enjoy the thrill of being involved. Savor the taste of finding a true direction for your life. The necessary checks with reality will come, but now is the moment to engage, to appreciate.

THE SUBMISSION

The second level of Engagement is submission. It is the experience of turning your life over to the person, group, or cause you are engaged in. At first it can seem quite exciting. You are in love! The happiness of the other person is all-important. Your cause is the end-all and be-all of your existence. The organization or effort defines who you are. At the same time it is frightening. You are surrendering your will to something else. Deep down we know that that something else is always flawed, and yet the risk is worth it.

In part, submission is learning the jargon, taking on the habits, food, and dress of the group, getting inside of the assumptions of those people, participating in the activities of the group, accepting the obligations of the group as one's own, telling the story of oneself as someone who's part of the group, whose fortunes are connected with the group's success.

This level involves creating the story of "us"—the story of how we met as a couple, the story of how I came to work for this company, the story of how I left my home and came to be part of this society. This is even as simple as the story of how I came to be assigned to this project. In creating this story of meaning, submission has begun. At this level, consequences become important, not in their entirety, but as to how the "other," that something else, views you. You are surrendering yourself, and you are very concerned that the sacrifice is worthy, and that you are up to the job. Doubts are present, as they should be, but you decide to go ahead anyway. In fact, you feel compelled to go ahead.

Jon was meeting regularly with the chairman of the board of an electronic purse company, an interesting combination of the "wow" factor of high tech and the conservative perspective of banking. During one of the meetings they discussed motivation. The chairman told of a marathon that he had run a few years earlier.

He described the training process. The first twenty weeks was spent just building up mileage so that he was averaging twenty-five miles per week. At this point he began a maintenance schedule of running of eight to ten miles a day, four or five days a week, and resting two or three days a week. Some three months before the marathon, the schedule picked up until he was running up to forty-six miles per week.

Not only did he have to put in the miles, he had to avoid injury. He consistently trained to a schedule and steadily built up miles. He engaged in cross training such as swimming, cycling, walking, and rowing to help develop stamina and cardiovascular strength while allowing running muscles to rest. He developed upper body strength through weight training or cross-training to help hill climbs and late in the marathon as neck and shoulder muscles tire. Diet was important, as was the right choice of shoes.

He described the trauma of the race itself, especially toward the end. He was exhausted. His legs seemed on the verge of losing control of themselves. His mind kept saying, "Quit, Quit, Quit. All you have to do is quit." At twenty miles, he stopped to rest and discovered that he could not start again. Jon asked how he kept going. The chairman said "You have to keep doing the rituals. . . . like saying 'just one more step, one more step, one more step.'"

Engagement as submission is to surrender all to the chosen task. It is making other parts of your life subservient to that task. Other interests and responsibilities either become a part of your engagement or become lesser priorities.

THE RESPONSIBILITY

This third level of Engagement is being responsible. This involves both the fact and the experience of responsibility. You are responsible for what you do. Finally, you are *only* responsible for the things you do and don't do.

Another way of looking at responsibility is to see its meaning as "able to respond." While it is true that you are only responsible for what you do, and how that influences the relationships that you are part of, these relationships each have their own circles of influence. Like a pebble dropped into a pond, the ripples spread out far beyond where they began. The facilitative leader assumes responsibility for the consequences of his or her actions. By changing the way you respond in a relationship, you change the relationship.

Dietrich Bonhoeffer (1965) describes responsibility as the tension between freedom and obedience. He contrasts the two by pointing to the extremes.

At one extreme is the individual who acts outside the constraint of obedience, in a kind of complete freedom. This Bonhoeffer calls an "irresponsible genius." This individual without regard for the world around them finds the justification for his or her actions within themselves. This kind of freedom operates in the illusion that a person is ultimately independent of all others. Like a child, the irresponsible genius says, "I did it because I felt like it."

At the other extreme, the person who justifies their actions because of obedience is equally irresponsible. In this case they transfer their own responsibility to an external authority. It is the "I was just following orders" justification. Kant's ethic of duty is the result. Again the justification is found within themselves, as it is the obedient one who chooses to follow the dictates of the state, the boss, or even one's partner.

In Bonhoeffer's view, responsibility is found in realizing both obedience and freedom. There is no justification except the deed itself. Transferring responsibility either internally, such as to one's own feelings or beliefs, or externally, to some authority or law, are equally ways of escaping from responsibility (Bonhoeffer, 1965).

This kind of responsibility is a huge burden. The leader who takes this kind of responsibility no longer has the luxury of saying that someone else is at fault. With assumption of this kind of responsibility, a new deep integrity is realized. The consequences of the actions of the facilitative leader are of great importance, as they provide clues to future actions.

THE FREEDOM

The fourth and final level of Engagement is that of realizing freedom. This is a common experience, and yet it can be the most frightening of all.

It is common for a person to struggle with a job he dislikes. Perhaps he is not good at it. He keeps the job for various reasons. It may be that he needs the money and doesn't see a way to get it otherwise. It may be that he wants to demonstrate loyalty to colleagues or to the company. Perhaps he is hoping for a promotion. He is unhappy. His colleagues feel the self-destructiveness of his behavior. One day the person decides to leave the company. With that decision he is transformed. His work improves. He is happy while doing it. He is acting in a positive, creative way. By taking responsibility and making this decision, he finds himself free from what are now obvious as self-imposed limitations.

Knowing that you have taken on the responsibility for your own life as well as that of your organization, self-consciously and without being coerced, you then are free. You have no one to blame, no excuse, no justification except that of having made an informed and free choice. You can't even blame inner drives or desires. They are there, but they are not the reason you made this commitment. Freedom is found in your connection with others and with the larger society.

Like playing a piece of music or reading a poem, life can be a duty or a free act. The music can be played with great skill and feeling, or it can be played mechanically and with little sense of the real meaning under the notes. It can be different each time it is played. The score of the music limits the player to the notes on the sheet. Freedom is found not in changing the notes but in playing them with abandon.

In an interview with Larry King of CNN, Nelson Mandela discussed Mandela's years in prison. Mandela explained being able to make free choices in the service of a larger purpose, without letting anger or the need for revenge control him.

King: But, logically, you should have been angry. Logically, you should have wanted revenge. Why not?

Mandela: Well, you have to understand the thinking of the men around me in prison, especially those who spent long terms of imprisonment. They lost an opportunity to serve their people during those years, and they were, therefore, determined to catch up. They could only catch up if they were properly focused and concentrating on both things, which will help out the liberation of their people. I am not the only one who did not want revenge. Almost all my colleagues in prison did not want revenge, because there is no time to do anything else except to try and save your people.

King: Didn't you hate your white captors?

Mandela: No, because one has to take into account that many people in the situation in which we were—a promotion to higher position depended on the extent to which you supported apartheid and, therefore, good people would have the attitude—had the attitude—a forced attitude of saying, "I want promotion. Therefore, I must do what my superiors want me to do." (King, 2000)

CONCLUSION

The journey from covenant, to submission, to responsibility, and finally to freedom is one that great leaders make. We all experience this journey in different ways and with different intensities. A facilitative leader brings discipline into maintaining and deepening their capacity—whatever that may be—to be engaged. Engagement is easy when there are no distractions, nothing else demanding your attention, and none of the internal anchors preventing us from committing. Of course, it is precisely in those moments of distraction and difficulty that the discipline is required.

◆ ◆ ◆

Practices for Engagement

The most common practices of Engagement are symbolic and ritualistic in nature.

Levels of Contribution

Create a diagram by drawing a line horizontally across a sheet of paper. From the ends of the line draw concentric semi-circles within semi-circles, like a rainbow, with at least six concentric arches. The outermost one is the world, then the continent, the nation, the city, down to your family and finally yourself. In each circle, write your contribution to that level of reality. Start at the top and answer the question, "What am I contributing to the world?" Work your way down the diagram until you have reached the self. The trick here is to find an authentic balance between bragging and being self-depreciating.

Preparing the Space

Another Engagement ritual is to remind yourself of your commitment to a group you work with by caring for the space in which you will spend your time together. A tea master begins the tea ceremony by physically sweeping and scrubbing the tearoom. In the same way, you can try to arrive early at the site where a meeting or workshop is taking place to prepare the space. You may not have to clean the *tatami* mats like a tea master, but do look at the room where the event is going to take place, and arrange it to your satisfaction. Open or close the curtains, set up the tables and chairs, move the plants, place the equipment where it will work best. You may set the places of the participants with paper, pencils, and workbooks. You may see to adding and removing pictures from the walls or adding flowers, charts, toys, or whatever suits.

Of course you could do all of this by phone to the maintenance staff, and never waste your valuable time. However, being there for even a few minutes beforehand is a discipline that performs two important functions, one practical and one symbolic.

On the practical side, you are rehearsing the flow of the session ahead in a spatial sense. Just as you "know" the process ahead from your notes, you "feel" the process ahead by organizing the space and equipment, in the same way that a dancer rehearses choreography. For those of us whose energy is more physical than cognitive, this can be more useful preparation for a meeting than anything else you do. It is amazing how often, in the midst of looking at the room or moving a chair, you realize a better way of running part of the discussion ahead, or think of an individual who may need some special attention.

On the symbolic side, this is a ritual of taking responsibility for the group. It calms you by putting your focus physically on what is ahead rather than on your own concerns or issues. A group can recognize immediately a space that has been prepared for their own event as opposed to a space—

however beautifully set up by efficient hotel staff—that has not been personally cared or.

Walking in Bombay

A final practice of Engagement is something we did during our first assignment outside of the United States. We were sent to work in a slum neighborhood in Bombay, India. Everything there was strange, fascinating and terrifying at the same time. It was astoundingly hot and dusty; there were people everywhere, staring, touching, rubbing past, saying things we couldn't understand. There were magnificently, elaborately dressed, gorgeous men and women, side by side with appalling cases of disfigurement, disease, and malnutrition. Spending five minutes on the street was completely overwhelming. How could you ever find any place in all of this? What would you ever do here?

One of the other expatriate colleagues there said he made it a rule to go out every day and just walk around for a half-hour, just keep soaking it in. At the time this sounded like a scandal, but we just did it. Sure enough, even that street started to lose its terrors. We met people and became part of that place. We've used that rule for every place we have ever lived and worked since, walking out the door on a regular basis, talking to people and finding out what is happening.

We have given here a few practices we use to rehearse Engagement. You may try out our practices, but it is more important to choose your own practices personally, in dialogue with the communities you are leading.

◆ ◆ ◆

Exercise for Engagement

Behavior Modeling

To consider Engagement, bring to mind a workshop, presentation, or meeting in which you participated in which a leader inspired you. It may not have been intended as a formal, capital L leadership role, but whatever the context, you were inspired or impressed in some way. Close your eyes and recall the things you remember that leader doing that you found inspiring or admirable. Now fill in the following boxes:

About the Leader I Admire	About Myself as a Leader
List the behaviors that the leader you saw was modeling—in other words, what ways of communicating was she or he demonstrating for the group?	What are the values that I cherish as a leader—what do I want any group I work with to experience?
List here the values you believe the admired leader was being faithful to.	What behaviors can I model to embody the values listed?

When you have finished filling in your boxes, discuss the following together:

• What are some of the values you listed for yourself?
• What are some behaviors you listed for yourself?
• What did you have to think about to translate values into behaviors?
• How can you help yourself make this translation more readily?

CHAPTER SEVEN

FOCUS: WILLING ONE THING

Focus is the balance between Detachment and Engagement. It is increasing the capacity to choose autonomy and commitment simultaneously. It is concentrating the will so that the moment is fulfilled and the future is also fulfilled, like two eyes that merge into one clear image. Focus is the result of the combination of attention to both immediate and future issues.

In any project in which people work together, all sorts of dynamics come into play—short and long term, trivial distractions, politics, cultural differences, personalities, and so on. In order for the group to achieve its purpose, the facilitative leader needs continuously to balance the conflicting dynamics, and to understand without thinking about it where things need to go next. It is here that building the self-discipline of Focus becomes critical.

Peter Senge, in his book, *The Fifth Discipline* (1990), looks at what he calls "self-mastery." This is at least in part what focus is about. Self-mastery has two parts. The first is having a personal vision of a significantly better future. This is a better future for the organization you are leading and for the world. The second is being brutally honest about the present situation. There are three things that make this difficult. First, it takes a fair amount of imagination and courage to envision a better world that is conceived out of neither naiveté nor cynicism. While a vision of an organization may be somewhat easier, articulating that vision to yourself and others with some honesty requires courage. Second, being honest about the current situation is equally difficult. We would rather look at the bright side and deny the darker places. The negative dimensions are often seen as reflections of our own failures, which are difficult to admit. The third issue is holding the tension between the hoped-for future and the real present situation. It is easier to lower our expectations to the point that there is no appreciable difference between the two.

Maintaining both a personal vision and a clear understanding of the current situation produces a tension between the two that is a potential source of great creativity. Standing in this tension is the discipline of Focus.

WHAT IS FOCUS?

Focus is the central discipline of the developmental path regarding others: the trio of Detachment-Focus-Engagement. Detachment and Engagement stand in tension with one another. Focus, however, is the standing place from which one can hold this tension in an appropriate balance. It is only from a stance of real commitment to the job in the moment that Detachment and Engagement make any sense. It is only there that a suitable balance can be found. Trainee managers and facilitators alike always ask how involved or how detached they should be in the life of the group. All sorts of rules and conditions can be offered for deciding what is and is not appropriate—how much hands-on or -off, how much process and content, and yet, when the right balance exists, it's obvious.

Compare all this struggling for balance with making love. Lovers are certainly following a process, aiming for a relatively specific outcome. And yet the question of detachment, watching how the process is going, or engagement, being personally involved, just aren't relevant at all. The lovers are one with what they are doing, managing the process in complete detachment and enjoying the experience in complete involvement. In fact, if they are spending their time worrying about whether they are too engaged—"Hmm, am I enjoying this too much?"—or whether they are too detached—"Is this really the best way to be doing this?"—one might wonder if something foundational is not amiss in the relationship. This concentrating the will so that you are one with what you are doing is focus. It goes today often under the name of "single-mindedness." Too often focus gets used for trivial things, however—commitment to a brand of sports shoes or to a TV series. That's not it. The discipline of Focus is about an exclusive, living relationship.

The holding of both Detachment and Engagement together is not a matter of living in some artful balance but rather of responding to the needs of the situation from the perspective of radical commitment to the situation. Mihaly Csikszentmihalyi (1991) describes the state of *flow*, in which the difficulty of a task is exactly matched by one's capability to do it. This is Focus.

THE THREE AREAS OF FOCUS

We next look at three areas of Focus: focus on this moment, focus on this situation, and focus on the whole being.

Focus on This Moment

Focus has first of all to do with time. Just as the lovers referred to earlier are watching anything but the clock, you can recognize focus by the way an individual uses this given moment. Focus is living in the now. All of history has conspired to bring us to this moment. Likewise, what we do in this project is the thing that will make the difference in all of our futures. There is really nothing special about this. When else would anything happen if not now? And yet most of us spend most of our time convinced that it's either too soon—I need more experience, preparation, contacts, or whatever—or else it's too late. This would have been a terrific idea in 1987, or before the reorganization, or when I was thirty or when I worked in that other team. Focus is simple in this respect. It's now, period. This is the best possible time to do whatever has to happen.

Acting in the now is not just doing whatever may feel appropriate for you at the moment. The now is what the past has created, and it is the potential future. The now has the right thing embedded in it. Acting in the now requires finding that right thing, depending on our refined intuitions. Using your intuitions and watching what they do and do not deliver is the route to refining them.

The movie *Patton* illustrates bringing the past to bear on the present moment. The general, along with a driver and General Bradley, took a turn into the North African desert where Patton said, "It was here. The battlefield was here. The Carthaginians defending the city were attacked by three Roman Legions. Carthaginians were proud and brave but they couldn't hold. They were massacred. Arab women stripped them of their tunics and their swords and lances. The soldiers lay naked in the sun, two thousand years ago; and I was here" (Caffey & Schaffner, 1970).

Bringing the future into the present can be illustrated by the book *Built to Last* by Collins and Porras (1994), in which they point out that great companies are constructed to last past the lifetime of the founder or any other of the executives that run them. These kinds of leaders keep the long view, looking decades and sometimes longer into the future.

Bringing this huge context into the present moment can be found in many places. In Frank Herbert's *Dune* series (1965–1985), the transformation of the planet Dune was expected to last six hundred generations. John Wesley, the founder of Methodism, declared the world as his parish (1951, p. 42). In Martin Luther King Jr.'s "I have a dream!" speech, he looked back over the past hundred years and looks to a future of justice.

Focus on This Situation

Focus is not only about the now; it is also about this specific situation. Albert Einstein was quoted as saying he wasn't really a genius, he just stuck with problems longer than most people. This is focus, keeping at the issue until it finally yields. As Auntie Mame said in the film of the same name, "Life is a banquet, but most poor fools are starving to death." You can recognize focus when you see someone really grabbing that new project or client or product, and working it to the hilt. This is taking on the circumstantial situations of your life to such a degree that they become transparent to life itself—you can see through the everyday actions of your own life to existence itself.

There is an amazing phenomenon with graduates of behavior courses—dialogue, sales skills, consultancy skills, and facilitation skills. Although someone may understand the theory completely and have applied it in a practice session, there is always a threshold to practicing new skills. The graduate returns to work and watches him- or herself in horror, falling right back into the same counterproductive, defensive routines that the course was supposed to correct. What is happening here is that the graduate may have a new repertoire of behaviors, but her underlying assumptions about the situation and her personal relationships with colleagues have remained the same. Only when she lets go of the old assumptions and embraces a new approach to those existing relationships can she effectively take on the new behaviors. This discipline is Focus.

In Dietrich Bonhoeffer's (1954) writings about Christian community life, he notes the terrible shock, disappointment, and guilt that community members feel when they find quite un-Christian behavior among themselves, in groups where Christian fellowship was the intent. Although contemporary business groups would never call themselves communities, you often see desperate guilt and despair among members of supposed high-performing teams who find themselves reliving their nonproductive, dysfunctional relationships over and over again, like a dreadful nightmare that won't go away. Bonhoeffer speaks of the danger of the "ideal" group. He says that nothing is more dangerous to authentic community than our dreams of community. Today we could speak of the danger to our work teams of our dreams of high performing teams. For we will always love our dreams more than the people we are being given.

Focus on the Whole Being

Finally, focus is bringing your whole being to bear on the present. At the same time it is making your whole life a single act of will. This is not a moral obligation but an act of discovery.

Focus is bringing our conscious and unconscious minds into alignment. We watched an acrobat pilot preparing for his stunt program. He checked the plane by walking around it and looking for potential problems. He touched it here and there like a horseman might pat his horse as he walked by. He then went some ways away from the plane. He put his hands together with the backs of the thumbs touching, fingers spread the way you would if you were making a bird shadow puppet. His hands went up and rolled over, they went parallel to the ground. They rolled a quarter of a turn, stopped, rolled another quarter. His hands flew as high as he could reach, stopped and slid backwards, tilted and then they rolled upright and recovered from the stall. He was moving his hands around following the sequence of his stunts. He was practicing. He was aligning his unconscious and conscious minds by mentally and physically rehearsing the program.

He was focusing his whole self for the next thirty minutes so that the performance would be flawless. This is the art of the facilitative leader as well, preparing for a meeting, initiating a project, or just starting a new day.

DIFFCULTIES OF FOCUS

Focus is difficult in our moment of history for a variety of reasons. Reasons include conflicting demands, expectations of endless accessibility, and uncertainty about one's life purpose. We look at these issues next.

Conflicting Demands

We face an overwhelming set of conflicting demands, all of which seem to be of equal importance. There are family, friends, work, community, and world affairs, to name a few.

Jon and Maureen once coached four teams of university professors regarding their time management. Many complained that the teaching load coupled with the demands of student care and administrative tasks was infringing on their home lives and threatening relations with their families. We discussed various approaches to prioritizing their work. Two things emerged. First, some of the professors found it very difficult to say No to any request, especially to an immediate demand. Second, some made it clear that they preferred being victim to conflicting demands rather than taking charge of their own time. As they chose to see it, responsibility for their inability to accomplish one thing or another lay not with themselves, but with those who were making the demands.

A study of British men ages twenty-five to forty-four found that 70 percent of them suffer very high levels of stress. One reason mentioned was the attempt to accommodate the growing number of demands that society places on them. The men studied are anxious about their jobs and relationships, of course. But there are also many new issues, such as financial security (Will I have a pension left when I need it?) and roles in the family (Should I be staying home more with the children to enable my spouse's career?). In many cases, there are few role models or guidelines for how to respond to new demands.

Traditionally, people faced new demands with the help of so-cial support structures. The extended family, while restrictive, of-fered social and physical support, and could be counted on in times of need. No more. The village or neighborhood offered many of the same kinds of help. There were workmates, the church, synagogue, or mosque, all of which provided ways of cop-ing with difficult demands. Today those supports are very often un-available; for people who need to move frequently there is not the time to build the roots that past generations had. There are efforts to compensate for this lack, with religious groups, community as-sociations, and support groups of many kinds. Nevertheless, many of us face unprecedented levels of stress, whereby focus becomes difficult.

Expectations of Accessibility

Another aspect of the difficulty of maintaining focus today has to do with our increasing accessibility. Accessibility has two dimensions to it. The first is related to the variety of communication modes we live with. There is voice mail and call waiting, text messaging, photo and video transmission. The computer collects e-mail, possibly into multiple accounts, and there may be telephone or video conferenc-ing. The fax and the mail complete the picture. We are accessible to an unprecedented degree, which makes simple concentration on one task or one message something that needs to be planned and defended.

The second dimension is that of our own personal and social expectations. We expect to be accessible, and we expect others to be also.

Uncertainty About Life Purpose

All of this has a more fundamental underlying issue: choosing what your life is to be about. In an earlier era, many of the practical as-pects of our lives were chosen for us. We now have to make these decisions ourselves. We are not especially psychologically or spiri-tually prepared to do this. Our societies are not helping much.

The issue is not just preparing for and retiring from a job. It is what might be called choosing a *vocation*. Søren Kierkegaard (1969) used the term "purity of heart"; he called focus "willing one thing" with your life. The multitude of choices today makes this seem impossible. Things change so much and so quickly. Choosing what your life is about seems so final and frightening. Why not float along and let whatever comes along determine your destiny? As is commonly said, If you don't know where you are headed, then any path will take you there.

When you look back at your life, much of which you seemed to have little control over, and say, "This is what I am about," you assume responsibility for who you have become and how you became who you are. Looking into the future and saying, "This is what my life is about" assumes responsibility for what you will become. Of course there are fate, luck both good and bad, and random acts of nature. Your decision about who you are will determine how you will respond to whatever life throws at you.

THE ISSUES OF FOCUS
FOR FACILITATIVE LEADERS

For the facilitative leader, Focus is where Detachment and Engagement come together. It is the ability to stand back and observe what is going on while throwing yourself fully into the situation. It is holding your hopes and dreams in creative tension with an honest understanding of present reality. It is the capacity to bring all the strands of your life into a single weave.

The facilitative leader struggles to maintain his or her own focus. Focus at one level requires two dimensions that are in tension with each other. One is being focused on the group. This is about willingly embracing the problems and blocks the group experiences as the only issue, the only agenda, one is dealing with. Focus has to do with being mindful of and acting at the level of the group's operating images—who does this group see itself to be, and what are they doing? The facilitative leader is realistic about the boundaries in which a group has to operate. He or she has the capacity to focus both on the long term and on the immediate need.

The facilitative leader may not be the manager or the expert on the team, but he or she surely is the one whose commitment to the team's direction is unquestioned. The issue for the facilitative leader is communicating to others the critical importance of this moment, this task and their role in it. "The crucial challenge," says

Steven Covey in his latest book, ". . . is to find our voice and inspire others to find theirs" (Covey, 2004, p. 5). For a command-and-control leader, it is enough to tell people that their role is important. For the facilitative leader, the message has to be communicated through deeds and approaches to working together.

Issues discussed next are leading the group, taking risks, and holding the vision for the group.

LEADING THE GROUP

The outstanding characteristic of a focused meeting or workshop is that the facilitator does nothing that is superfluous to what the group needs. It is this direct alignment of who and what the facilitator is with the will of the group that is focus. The facilitator helps the group to align their unconscious and conscious selves. Some of this has to do with the quality of the leader's preparation. Preparation has to do with embodying what you intend to do and why, understanding who the group is and what they bring to the discussion, and awareness of who you are and what you are bringing to this group. The facilitative leader milks the given situation for all it's worth.

Here is how one leader talked about it:

> Maybe that's [listening] more a part of something else, like "being engaged." Truly listening and being full engaged, and doing that well, to me is a critical component of facilitation. I also would use the term "focus" to describe what I do (or perhaps rather what I am or my state of being) during a facilitated session. As the facilitator, I am totally focused on everything going on in the session. I am constantly listening, watching, and evaluating whether there is something I, as the facilitator, need to be doing (or need to be doing differently) to address issues, direct or re-direct the discussion, or guide/assist the group. By the end of a session, I am often totally exhausted, due to the level of the "focus" workout I have had. (Soper, 1999)

TAKING RISKS

One of Maureen's favorite exercises in working with people who design large drilling projects is having the team come up with as many options for drilling as they can for a project. For each option, they list all of the risks they face in taking that approach and then devise mitigations for each of those risks. The group becomes increasingly committed to the project and simultaneously more aligned with one another, even as they are doing a very structured exercise.

There is a lot of talk today about people who have commitment phobia, who are terrified of taking the risks involved in focusing on one thing or another. In this situation, the facilitative leader enables his or her people to move by insisting on a decision one way or the other. In the case of the workshop just mentioned, thinking through risks and mitigations allows the group to wholeheartedly embrace a decision and take action.

HOLDING THE VISION

This is a serious challenge for facilitative leadership. One cannot do anything without a vision, and yet those same visionary ideals easily become a dream that seems infinitely more desirable than the situation and the team we have. Consider all of the teams you have met who spent their days regretting the fact that their membership or their reporting structure, their leadership or their style of meetings didn't measure up to the way "real" high-performing teams are supposed to work. A focused leader smokes out these untested assumptions and gives people a chance to appreciate and celebrate the greatness of what they have been given.

Focus, as we have said before, also has to do with having your own personal vision of who you are and what your life is about, independent of the group.

Focus is holding many dimensions of work together at the same time. The short-term goals and the long-term vision need to be held together in balance. The complexities of the real world need to be held also. Having a vision of responsibility often adds to the complexity.

Some leaders simply have social responsibility on their minds all the time, even while they are delivering a good product and making a profit. An example of this is two very successful brewers from Fort Collins, Colorado.

Jeff Lebesch, an electrical engineer, and Kim Jordan, a social worker, the founders of New Belgium, are an example of this kind of leadership. New Belgium is a beer company located in Fort Collins. They offer a range of "Belgian" style beers including a triple, framboise (raspberry), a pilsner, and various ales. From its beginning, the company has looked for ways of being more socially responsible. They recognize the fact that the business has to be sustainable if their efforts are going to have an impact. "Don't be fooled by the crunchy image, though. 'We're very clear that the first thing that we have to be here is profitable,' says Jordan" (Koudsi, 2003).

They are the first U.S. brewer to be 100 percent wind-powered. Their employees voted to do this and offered part of their bonuses to help finance the conversion. They reduced the consumption of water, a key issue in the western United States, by nearly 50 percent of the national average of eight barrels of water to produce one barrel of beer. A water treatment plant cleans water used in brewing and cleaning, reducing the burden on the city plant. The treatment plant also produces methane that is used to produce heat and electricity. They use sun tubes to provide some of the light for the whole facility. Heat is reused from the brew house. They also reuse cleaning chemicals and water. Spent grain is converted to cattle feed. Keg caps are turned into table surfaces. Paper and office furniture are recycled. Motion sensors on the lights reduce the use of electricity. Induction fans pull in winter air to chill the beer.

Jeff and Kim are a demonstration of the discipline of continually looking for ways of being more socially responsible while having a profitable business.

The Four Levels of Focus

Just as with the other disciplines, we talk about four levels for Focus. The levels are vision, promise, greatness, and the absurd. Becoming more proficient at being focused is to experience these levels. Again it is not that you *should* experience them, but that you will. If you don't, it is not worth worrying about. You may well have experienced them in some other fashion than what we are able to describe here.

The Vision

The vision is being in control of your own thinking. This began early in life, when you first noticed that "I" was something different than "they." As adulthood approached, you began to have control over more and more of who you were. You may have discovered that if you went to bed at night thinking about something important, you were likely to dream about it, or wake up from time to time still thinking about it. You may have woken up in the morning with some new ideas about your concern. You may have begun to use this sort of process intentionally, bringing a problem to mind to "work on" as you retire at night and finding new insights in the morning.

You understand that you have your own biases. You have a "dark side"—a destructive dimension to who you are. You begin to recognize what your sensitivities are—what things can get you interested and engaged, what you find boring, what upsets you. These discoveries are scary, a lot of hard work to deal with. As soon as you learn to deal with one aspect of your dark side, another arises.

More than once we act in a way that moves us away from our vision and things go wrong. Maintaining a vision means not giving in to the setback but reengaging in making the vision happen.

A few months after our oldest son was born, Jon was out of town. Maureen was very busy. She was working full time, had a young baby to take care of, and needed to leave the following morning to deliver a difficult new presentation. She sat down in the rocking chair to feed Jean-Paul, intending afterward to finish the presentation and pack for early departure. The next thing Maureen knew, it was late the next morning, Jean-Paul was wet and hungry in her lap, and nothing was ready. Like with many a working mother, exhaustion had won. As she dashed to get organized, the thought came to her mind, "At least I'm not bored." She got everything ready and delivered the presentation.

The film *Fish* is about fishmongers at the Fulton Street market in Seattle, Washington. They have a great time selling fish, and their clients enjoying buying from them. One of the points being conveyed in this film is that you have control of your attitude. One of the fishmongers says that he had been out until 4:00 A.M. the night before and had to report to work at 6:00. He points out how easy it would be to be grumpy and just put in the time today. He smiles (a little weakly), snaps his fingers and says No, he chooses what attitude he will have. It's not the situation, not feeling tired and hung over; it's his decision alone.

The facilitative leader creates his or her future and lives in the tension between that future and the present. The circumstances and the good or bad thoughts, emotions and attitudes are all there, like paints on a palette. It is the leader's own decision which ones to use and which ones not to use in painting the reality between the now and the future.

THE PROMISE

This state is when you make the promise to yourself to live your life to its fullest extent. This is not a New Year's resolution to do better, stop smoking, jog more, or drink less. This promise is experienced more as discovering that you have made your promise. You have chosen to *be fully* as the teacher, electrician, or whatever you are. D. H. Lawrence helps us understand this in his poem, "We Are Transmitters." He ends with

> Give, and it shall be given unto you
> is still the truth about life.
> But giving life is not so easy.
> It doesn't mean handing it out to some mean fool, or
>   letting the living dead eat you up.
> It means kindling the life-quality where it was not,
> even if it's only in the whiteness of a washed pocket-
>   handkerchief. (Lawrence, 1972, p. 449)

It is important to create reminders to yourself about this promise, to remind you of your decision.

Don, the marketing vice president of a paper company, was an active volunteer in an international development organization. On a trip to India, he visited Mumbai and Delhi, and went out into the country to the rural villages as well. He became determined to assist in the development work that was taking place there. He was pretty clear that just giving money was not sufficient. His internal promise to himself was to discover the most responsible way for a businessperson like himself to help.

To that end, Don knew that other things would demand his attention when he got back to the office. He thus began creating reminders of his resolve. One of the first things he did was to begin telling his story about rural India. He spoke at his local church, at service clubs, business events, and social groups. Sitting in a place or in a bar, he would start up conversations with strangers about India. He could have sounded like a strident fanatic, but he didn't. He was just someone sharing his thoughts. Don was building a self-story about his caring.

He bought some beads in India that he wore all the time. They were a reminder of his promise to himself. He began putting things in his briefcase that were little symbols to him—a pot of hot spices, a statuette. When airport security wanted to know about these things in the briefcase, about the beads around his neck, Don would explain about India.

The promise level is creating ways to remind yourself how, as Lawrence puts it, you intend to create the spark of a life where it is missing.

THE GREATNESS

Focus is having a living vision of the future for yourself and your world. It is making a promise to yourself about that vision. It is also resolutely honoring the greatness of your life's venture.

In his work on self-mastery, Peter Senge (1990, Chapter Nine) mentions the tendency to reduce your vision down to the current situation. When this happens, you in fact also reduce yourself and your potential. The greatness level of Focus is the experience of expanding the focus of your life to its maximum. This is a very bold and frightening thing to do. Other people may be offended. Who are you to try to claim to achieve something?

There was a film made recently about Cassius Clay/Muhammed Ali, titled *Ali* (Bingham et al., 2001). But even the film did not communicate the massive impact Ali had on the world stage, the sheer scandal of hearing someone say, "I'm the greatest!"—someone who simply meant it. The poet Marianne Williamson understands the power of this. She states in her book *A Return to Love* (1996) that in fact it is not our inadequacy that we are most afraid of. Rather, we fear the power, beauty, talent, and brilliance that we possess. Focus at this level is about accepting the greatness that you are. It's the challenge of looking in the mirror in the morning and letting what you see amaze you.

This third level of Focus is resisting the urge to belittle yourself, maintaining your greatness and that of what you are out to achieve. Being a facilitative leader is guarding the greatness of your role in life with humility and courage. This is not about claiming credit not really due to you. Honesty with yourself recognizes where credit is due. This is about reminding yourself daily that the life you have been given is a glorious gift to the world.

Focus is also about transparency. Lao Tsu puts it this way: "A leader is best when people barely know he exists. When his work is done, his aim fulfilled, they will say: we did it ourselves"(Lao Tsu, n.d.). Of course leadership is necessarily visible. But what do people see when they see the facilitative leader?

In his book *Good to Great,* Jim Collins (2001) talks about five levels of leadership. Companies that have made the transition from good companies to great ones tend to have what Collins calls "Level 5" leaders. When you see Level 5 leaders, you see people with two characteristics. They are humble. They give credit to those around them and take the blame when things fail. At the same time, they are dogged in their pursuit of the values they hold dear. These two characteristics are in contrast with those of bigger-than-life leaders who are more concerned about their public image than with the long-term viability of the organization. Such leaders, says Collins, can bring success in the short term, but they can leave their organizations so damaged that the companies might not survive.

Facilitative leaders are great in themselves, and they need not continually promote their own greatness. They guard the values of the organization first by acting them out. Employees follow what their leaders do, not what they say.

THE ABSURD

The fourth level of Focus is the absurd. At this level, you are an embodiment of what it is to be great, without needing to call attention to your greatness. Miyamoto Musashi, author of *A Book of 5 Rings* (1974), was a swordsman in late sixteenth-century Japan. He realized at the age of thirty that there was no one left that he hadn't beaten. He had defeated all of the best swordsmen from all of the best schools over the entire land. He was, in his world, invincible.

In his introduction, he briefly describes his sixty victories and no defeats from ages thirteen to twenty-eight, and then states:

> When I reached thirty, I looked back on my past. The previous victories were not due to my having mastered strategy. Perhaps it was natural ability, or the order of heaven, or that other schools' strategy was inferior. After that I studied morning and evening searching for the principle, and came to realize the Way of Strategy when I was fifty. (Musashi, 1974, p. 35)

Another dimension of the absurd is your sense of being part of the whole historical process. Loren Eisley, the literary naturalist, describes riding across a plain in East Africa, searching for clues to the archaeological evolution of the area. He notices a crevasse and climbs down into it. He comes face to face with a skull. It was to his expert eyes from a creature whose existence predated *Homo sapiens* by millions of years. The skull was tilted in such a way that it looked up toward the blue sky through the grass overhanging the crevasse. Eisley wondered what unknown creature of the future he would be looking up to millions of years in the future.

The paradox of being great and being humble is indeed absurd. The experience at this level is one of affirmation. The affirmation is not naïve or founded in ignoring life's tragedies. One image that might be helpful is that of walking through a forest in Northern California in springtime. The bright green of new shoots colors the tops of the trees. Tiny wildflowers bloom, ferns are uncurling from their tight coils. Butterflies and insects are about, birds are singing. Every once in a while a Stellar jay swoops down and scolds or a chipmunk rustles through the leaves. Looking down, you can notice the leaves and pine needles from the previous year cushioning the forest floor. You scuff it up a bit and underneath the color is darker and the smell of rot rises up. Toppled trees are covered with fungus, softening into mulch. Death and decay is everywhere, side by side with the new life it is nourishing.

Of course we all like to see the flowers and hear the birds sing. The absurd is the appreciation that the whole cycle is one thing. This is appreciating that your greatness does not belong to you, it belongs to life. To stand in the level of the absurd is to understand, as the pop psychologists say, "It isn't about you." No indeed, this greatness is what life can achieve, and you have turned up inside of it. And of course, just like the forest floor, it comes and goes. No leader is leader forever. For now, you have your day.

The discipline of Focus starts where Senge leaves off, with vision in tension with the truth of the present situation. Then comes the experience of promise. You discover that you are making a promise to be the best you can, not for your own sake but because you care about the world you live in. This promise is an internal resolve coupled with the action and symbols to maintain that resolve. Then comes the greatness of being the very best *you* could possibly be, acknowledging your frailties and having the courage to be great anyway. Finally comes the absurdity of being great and humble at the same time; appreciating the whole cycle of life, of being connected to existence and to its wholeness.

CONCLUSION

It is the discipline of Focus that connects the facilitative leader most to the present, the future, and to the tension between them. Focus is the discipline of tension—tension between Detachment and Engagement, between the now and the yet to be, between the specific place and the universe.

◆ ◆ ◆

Practices for Focus

Whatever practice you choose to deepen your capacity to focus, it should be one that you are comfortable with. Care should be taken when we do these kinds of exercises because we often discover aspects of ourselves that we are unaware of and may be ill equipped to cope with. Until you are experienced with developing your disciplines we recommend that you look for someone who can work with you.

Storytelling

One practice that helps to develop Focus is storytelling.

There are two dimensions to this storytelling for the facilitative leader. The first is maintaining your own self-story. This is telling and retelling the story of what your life is about.

Annual Story. Once a year the facilitative leader can spend a day or two alone or perhaps with your life partner reflecting on the past year and how it has contributed to your life aims. Living in Northern Europe, we find the dark days just before the New Year a good time to do this. It is best done away from the daily grind, perhaps a few days in a quiet, relaxing setting to pull the year to a close without too much interruption.

A day might start off with a special breakfast. Then get started with a long walk, during which you remember the events of the year. This is not a brainstorm; this is the warm-up, gently recalling people, events, high and low points.

Return to a comfortable room to work in. Now begin taking notes, systematically working through the months of the past year. We like to do this backward, starting with December, then November, and moving back to the end of the previous year, like a reverse timeline. Because this is a brainstorm, you can add anything to the list—events in the news, important purchases, movies, and even great football games. Things that happened to children, clients, friends, and pets can all go onto the list. They are all fabric of your year. If you remember something after you have passed that month, just go back and add it onto the list.

Once the whole year is listed, ask yourselves what are some of the themes or threads that run through the year. Write up the themes, illustrating them with points from your timeline lists. Discuss how these themes have contributed to your aims.

All through this talk, take breaks as you need to. Take walks or visit a museum and then come back to the reflection. Times of silence help with this process. Write up your reflections so that over the next year you can go back to it and remember. Next year you can begin your reflections with a reading of the previous year's thoughts.

Team Stories. The second practice in storytelling related to Focus is done with the leader's team. This practice is done once a year, probably related to a planning meeting. Alternately, this can be an ongoing process done on a weekly basis. Essentially the practice is having everyone on the team tell his or her story about the year or the week. If done on a yearly basis, it should be more formal and workshop-like in nature. If you are revisiting the process more frequently, it can be more informal. It is always a good idea to try to capture people's stories in some form. Perhaps after everyone has told their story, the outstanding ones can be typed up for the future. Stories of course need not be only verbal. Some groups thrive on creating sketches, symbols, and even music to tell their stories.

The Vigil

A traditional practice for the discipline of Focus is the vigil. It is used as a way of preparing for a special event and as a way of bringing focus onto an issue or event. Vigils generally take place from sunset to sunrise, although some are longer.

In the Christian Church, the vigil has been used as a way to prepare for some feast days, for battles, and for funerals. Aboriginal peoples use vigils to prepare for rites of maturity and for developing vision. Modern vigils are often used to call attention to a problem, such as vigils conducted in protest of capital punishment.

Prepare yourself for a vigil by deciding what you are holding the vigil about. What situation or hope or fear do you want to stand present to? Set up your space. You might use a candle, a photo, or a symbol as your central point while you are doing your vigil. Once that is chosen, spend a few moments getting comfortable. You do not want to be so comfortable that you fall asleep. Traditionally, people knelt, but sitting in a chair is fine. Over the course of the night, pay attention to your physical and emotional reactions. If you find yourself nodding off, stand up or go get a glass of water. As you wake up, go back to your kneeling or sitting. This will likely be most difficult in the early hours of the morning. Pay attention to your tendency to fall asleep and keep on dealing with it.

When the ending hour comes, spend a few minutes reflecting on the night and on what happened to you. When you have completed your exercise, have a good meal and go for a long walk.

◆ ◆ ◆

Exercise for Focus

The Life Timeline

To consider your own focus, fill out the Life Timeline Chart as follows:

- Write your date of birth on the far left of the chart following, and your intended date of death on the right.
- Mark the decades in between.
- Now recall events from your life and plot them onto your timeline, giving each one enough of a title to keep it in your memory.
- Don't write interpretations yet, like "working hard" or "just floating." Instead, keep listing events. When you have arrived at the present, list

key events for your future—not some idealized notion, but the future you intend for yourself.

- When you have finished with events, move one step up to the "Life Phases" level, and mark the different periods of your life.
- Give each one a title.
- Finally, go up to the top line and give your life a title. You might consider this to be what is written on your tombstone, or you might consider it as the title of the work in progress that is your life.

When your timelines are finished, discuss together as a group:

- What struck you while you were doing this exercise?
- What was difficult?
- What was interesting or fun?
- What would you call this sort of thinking?
- What are other occasions on which you think like this?
- What is the impact of this sort of thinking?

Life Timeline Chart

The Title for My Life
Phases of My Life
Events I Remember from Past and Future
Date of Birth Date of Death

CHAPTER EIGHT

INTERIOR COUNCIL: CHOOSING ADVISORS WISELY

We all have an Interior Council. Our minds are filled with ideas, sayings, advice, and images that guide our thoughts and actions. It is as though a council of advisors sits in our head and makes suggestions. Some of these internal advisors are helpful and sometimes they are not. Some are wondrous and some dreadful. All are important.

Having an interior council is not the discipline. The discipline of Interior Council is learning how to pay attention to and choose the most creative and enabling of the voices that guide your day-to-day life. The discipline is learning to impose your will on your council. The ability to be aware of the voices and to select which ones you will pay attention to and which you will ignore is a key competency of the facilitative leader.

Managing your interior council is the first discipline of the developmental path that focuses on your own self. This is because all of your expression of self depends on how well you can conduct your internal dialogue, your self-talk. You are obviously responsible for what you say and do, but before that you are responsible for what you think, how you choose to interpret what goes on around you. One girl loses her mother as a child and says that it was a cruel injustice from which she can never recover. Another girl may say that her mother was taken away to let her build a stronger relationship with her sisters and brothers. Each girl had the same experience, and yet each of these has chosen a different personal world to live in. As a result, they say and do quite different things.

Managing the voices of the Interior Council is a key discipline in strengthening the capacity to be a self.

This internal council shapes our thoughts, informs our feelings, influences our actions, gives us courage, and motivates us. Facilitative leadership is a profoundly draining activity. Inspiration and sources of new ideas are constantly needed to keep going. There are moments when the only resources you have are the ones you carry in your head. In working with internal mentors, you have the opportunity to work through issues that you have to manage in public. When well managed, your council gives you confidence to go ahead and do what you intend to do, and it gives you deeper appreciation for the issues involved.

WHAT IS INTERIOR COUNCIL?

We all carry the ideas and thoughts of parents, former teachers, friends, enemies, and guides with us. The messages their voices send us come in various forms—memories, stories, and interior dialogue among them.

STORIES AND MEMORIES

In the January 2005 issue of *Harvard Business Review*, Daisy Wademan wrote an article on the advice from mentors that business leaders carry in their heads sometimes decades after the advice was given. In her examination of business guides' advice, she discovered that it was not platitudes that were useful but attitudes, jokes, contexts, or stories that were remembered.

Shelly Lazarus, the chairman and chief executive officer (CEO) of the advertising agency Ogilvy & Mather Worldwide, asked David Ogilvy what advice he would give her as she was in the process of becoming CEO. She reflects every day on the guidance he gave: "'No matter how much time you spend thinking about, worrying about, focusing on, questioning the value of, and evaluating people, it will not be enough,' he said. 'People are the only thing that matters, and the only thing you should think about, because when that part is right, everything else works'" (Wademan, 2005, p. 2).

Ms. Lazarus goes on to tell about a time when a computer crashed just before a major presentation to a client. The financial figures for the media plan presentation would not be available. The media planner responsible walked into the office and in a panic began to walk in circles saying hysterically, "What am I going to do, what am I going to do?" Lazarus's then boss stood in front of the woman, took her shoulders, and shouted, "What are they going to do to you? Take your children away?" They then sat down and planned what to do (Wademan, 2005, pp. 2–3).

While a funny story, it also has an important message. Lazarus reports, "So, when I have a meeting that's really tense, and when everyone in the office thinks the world is falling apart, I disarm the situation, I'll ask, 'Just to be clear, is anyone going to die as a result of our action or inaction? Will Ogilvy go out of business? Will anyone lose a child? Because if that's true, let me know, and I'll get significantly more agitated'" (Wademan, 2005, p. 3). Here the story keeps people focused on what needs to be remembered, and it also becomes a source and style of acting, creating a sense of proportion by using humorous overstatement.

Interior Dialogue

Sometimes the concept of interior dialogue can be captured by a fable or story. A tale called "Two Wolves" talks about managing the interior council.

A grandson told of his anger at a schoolmate who had done him an injustice. Grandfather said, "Let me tell you a story."

"I, too, have felt a great hate for those that have taken so much, with no sorrow for what they do. But, hate wears you down and does not hurt your enemy. It is like taking poison and wishing your enemy would die. I have struggled with these feelings many times. It is as if there are two wolves inside me: one is good and does no harm. He lives in harmony with all around him and does not take offense when no offense was intended. He will only fight when it is right to do so, and in the right way.

"But the other wolf is full of anger. The littlest thing will set him into a fit of temper. He fights with everyone, all the time, for no reason. He cannot think because his anger and hate are so great. It is hard to live with these two wolves inside me, for both of them try to dominate my spirit."

The boy looked intently into his grandfather's eyes and asked, "Which one wins, Grandfather?"

Grandfather solemnly replied, "The one I feed." (Acosta, n.d.)

A leader feeds the ones he or she chooses. They pay attention to all of the voices on the interior council, because to ignore one gives it the opportunity to become more powerful and eventually dominate your spirit.

VOICES OF SEDUCTION

Not all of our inner voices are helpful. We also have advisors who seem to trigger our capacity to be destructive. This is pretty insidious, as we seldom think of ourselves as being destructive. These are the voices that say one more cookie will be okay. You deserve that extra time off. You don't need to call the bank about the overdraft; they know you're good for it. You look good with a few extra pounds. These advisors are seductive; they seem reasonable or fun or whatever you are attracted to.

Being aware of these kinds of advisors is necessary in order to ignore them. You then have some level of control over them.

DIFFICULTIES WITH THE INTERIOR COUNCIL

Developing a rich and meaningful interior life is difficult in today's world. The idea of talking to yourself is seen as a little mad. Living only within ourselves is indeed a danger, and our concern has some validity, even if it is misapplied.

At one time, one or two "heroes" or "heroines" seemed to be sufficient for a lifetime. Not so today. We now find dozens, even hundreds to choose from. Our lives are more complex; and as such we seem to need many more role models. Our heroes don't seem to last as long as they once did. All of our heroes seem to develop clay feet. In our need for perfection, who wants a hero with faults? These heroes and heroines make up a significant part of our interior council.

A third reason for the difficulty in developing a rich interior council today is the loss of the ability to reflect. Few of us really take the time to cultivate our own interior lives. We don't seem to know what to do or how to do it. Perhaps we fear that we will encounter those dark dimensions that reveal our failings. More likely we will come across a capacity to be more than we are. When we do become aware of it, there are no excuses not to be as great as we can be, except our own lack of will.

It is like standing at a door behind which stands the truth about ourselves. We sense that it is there. The door is not locked—all we have to do is turn the knob. And yet we hesitate. Year after year goes by, and we still hesitate.

Our Capacity for Self-Deception

Perhaps the most important reason it is difficult to deal with our interior council is that human beings are illusion-generating creatures. A manager told an employee how much he cared for her and he truly believed what he was saying. Looking at his behavior toward her, it was pretty clear that he did not care for her. He was operating out of an illusion. We deceive ourselves and we are not even aware of it. These illusions we create are self-destructive and destructive of others around us (Arbinger Institute, 2002). Not all of our illusions are positive. A positive mental attitude is well-known to be important in a sports person. Most of us when pushed to our physical or mental limits begin telling ourselves that we can't do it. We continue with this self-story until it comes true. Our illusion in this situation is that we can't do something even though if we disregard this belief we actually can do it. A tragic example of a negative illusion is when a battered child comes to believe that he or she deserves the mistreatment.

In spite of the current belief in individualism, humans are necessarily social animals. We simply cannot function without other humans. We would not survive childhood without an adult to care for us. In day-to-day transactions, a certain degree of cooperation is required. We feel pity for those who suffer. Our concern for others is often acted out. When someone is in danger we try to help. We instinctively care for and help others. We can choose not to, but the instinct is there. We can learn to suppress this instinct. In his book *People of the Lie* (1983), M. Scott Peck suggests a definition of evil as habitually choosing the destructive alternative in a decision.

Refusing to act on this instinct of care for others betrays a foundational aspect of our humanity. From these betrayals we construct illusions about ourselves. We tell ourselves that we are more important or need more or are better than those we know we should care for. We tell ourselves that if they need care it is their fault. We all do it, and we do it often. We could hold the door for someone but we don't. We hear the baby cry in the middle of the night and think we should get up and care for it. Instead we pretend to be asleep so our spouse has to get up and care for the child. When we recognize that what we are doing has negative consequences we justify it as being necessary for some higher good.

A story may help illustrate the process of how simple betrayals lead to the construction of illusions about ourselves and others.

Twenty years ago Hans joined a government agency that was privatized and became the company it is today. At the time it was an exciting place to work. New technology was being developed, new ways of working were being applied, and people respected Hans because he worked for a company with such a good name.

Imagine Hans coming to work when he was twenty-two, fresh out of university. In the first few months of work, he learned his job, made friends, and adjusted to the world of work. One day a colleague, Jan, was sick, and Hans thought perhaps it would be good to cover for some of Jan's work but decided not to. This was the moment when things began to change.

Hans not only did not help Jan, but he had to explain to himself why he *shouldn't* help him. He did this in two ways. He constructed a rationale about why what he did instead of helping was more important than Jan and his work. In doing so, Hans had to create a picture of his work as more important than Jan's. He perhaps thought, "It is critical that I finish the report to my boss that is due in a week. Jan does not have the same kind of deadlines that I have. It is easier for him to adjust his work." He might belittle Jan by thinking, "If Jan had taken better care of himself his work would not need covering. It is pretty inconsiderate of him to leave us with his work. He is not a very effective worker anyway. He is lazy." Whether any of this is true makes no difference; it is the self-story that is important.

At the same time Hans has to build up the importance of himself and his work. He might think that he is a pretty considerate guy who helps people but at this moment he has an important project that has to be completed. "I put in my hours." "I certainly work harder than Jan."

So what has happened to Hans? First, he considered helping Jan—a basic human instinct. He decided not to help Jan, which was a betrayal of that instinct. Hans then began to justify his actions to himself. In order to create a believable justification he has to build up his work and who he is and tear down Jan.

This process begins to change Hans's attitude toward Jan. The change in the attitude means that the things that confirm Hans's image are easier to see. One day Jan leaves twenty minutes early from work, and Hans thinks he is skipping out of work. He is lazy. On the other hand, Hans is a hard worker.

As other betrayals are committed and illusions are constructed about the other colleagues, Hans's whole attitude toward work and the company changes. Hans begins to separate work and life. He learns that he can gain his manager's attention. He began to subtly hint at how things in the department were the fault of laziness and incompetence. Because he was trying to justify his betrayals and wanted to blame others for the various problems, Hans was offering solutions to the manager. They were not real solutions but illusions. The manager agrees with Hans, and in doing so sends messages that strengthen the illusions.

Kenneth Boulding (1961) makes the point that illusions become stable because they are reinforced over and over again. They are also stable because they have an internal logic and consistency.

Hans hears that government workers are not very productive, in fact, that they are lazy. He takes a course on entrepreneurship. By selecting the points carefully he realizes that he is a pretty good businessman, unlike his colleagues. He learns the words of the latest business fads and uses them often.

Becoming aware of his illusions becomes more and more difficult. He becomes proficient at not hearing, avoiding or denying messages that contradict his image. He has selected an interior council that helps keep him in this state. They tell him that he is a hard worker, decent husband, successful businessman, and so on. They also help him blame his colleagues, his wife, his boss, and his company for any difficulties in his situation.

How do we step out of this self-deception? We become aware of our propensities for illusion making. We can learn to face our betrayals and decrease the frequency with which we create illusions. We can learn to identify these illusions and confront the truth of our situation. We act out of our care for others. When it is difficult to do, we don't justify it to ourselves. We find interior advisors who remind us about our capacity to betray our instincts to care.

THE ISSUES OF INTERIOR COUNCIL FOR FACILITATIVE LEADERS

The work of facilitating owes much to the richness of one's Interior Council. You check continually with ideas, sayings, images, heroines and heroes for ways of better understanding and responding to ongoing events. Heroes and heroines may be colleagues (remember how Harry did this), authors (what Peter Senge or Karl Marx wrote), and historic figures (from Martin Luther to Sitting Bull). Further, you may use mantras to focus your awareness, recall images, photos and paintings, raise standard questions on which to reflect, recall poetry or song lyrics or puzzle over Zen koans. . . .

Whether a magpie chaotic collection spree or a soberly structured routine, this dialogue serves as the way the facilitator digests experience to locate its inspiration and nourishment. Understanding your own way of internal dialogue gives you a safe place to return to in the face of whatever experience comes along. (Jenkins & Jenkins, 2002)

When you find yourself having to go beyond your accumulated technique, and have only your intuitions to guide you in a given situation, then your Interior Council comes into play. This means, on the one hand, you need to build and refine your intuitions in a self-conscious way, so that they are ready to serve you when the need arises. On the other hand, there is the struggle to learn to trust that your intuitions will be accurate when you need them.

CHOOSING ONE'S COUNCIL

The process of determining which internal advisors to listen to begins with deciding what kinds of advisors you want. Choosing advisors is only partially possible; we don't have complete control of this.

By the time in your life you have become a facilitative leader, you probably have already been exposed to the majority of advisors you will ever use. Because of this, most of the work of cultivating your internal council is one of selection. You determine which advisors you want to keep; which you may or may not keep; and which you will toss out. Then, you may want to add to the council.

How do you know which to keep and which to toss? Internal advisors you like or enjoy are not necessarily those that are most helpful to you. Equally, those that you dislike or don't enjoy interacting with are not necessarily most helpful either. The important question is, "Is this advisor helping me to grow, to become more effective, to be more responsive to others, to let go, to be more committed, to have greater integrity, to be touched by a sense of wonder more readily?" If one or more of these is true, then the advisor should be kept. If not, then you need to be aware of it but to not pay attention to it.

When you begin to have a profound appreciation of these internal advisors, then you learn to ignore those who dehumanize you or others, and pay attention to the ones who give you courage to be more human. The ones you ignore are not those that you dislike, but those who are not furthering you on your journey. The ones you pay attention to are not necessarily those who you agree with, but those who increase your ability to serve, and offer you the wisdom, skills, and capacity to inspire.

LISTENING TO THE RIGHT VOICES

We have all had the experience of knowing better than to do something and yet watching ourself go right ahead and do it. For example, you might need to fire someone. You might have these kinds of thoughts: "Let's get this over with." "They deserve to be let go." "I hate doing this but it is only this one time." There are others. Here your interior council is advising that you focus on your problem and not on the person being let go. You are desensitizing yourself to the other person's pain and to your own. Instead of serving others you are serving yourself. By repeating this process again and again, you reach the point where you are unaware of the pain of the other person and of your own feelings. When your feelings do emerge, you justify what you are doing by becoming a victim of circumstances. You say, "Someone has to do it." Or, "I'm just doing what I am told." You humanity is diminished. The voices saying these kinds of things need to be silenced and carefully watched for their reemergence in new forms.

Voices that can be and should be kept in these kinds of situation are there, but they are often silent or speak very softly. They ask things like, "What will the person I am firing do now?" "How can I help them through this transition?" "They are likely to experience grief; how can I be with them in that process?" Perhaps the voices say, "This is not fair and I should say something to his boss."

We can return to our story about Hans to help describe the process by which we create a dehumanizing atmosphere in a company by listening to and acting on the wrong voices.

Hans was now a low-level manager in a big European multinational company. He rose as a manager during several downsizing processes over about four years, during which he had to let company employees go several times. The negotiating process in Europe for letting an employee go is long and involves several stages.

Hans had moved ahead partly because of his ability to manage these negotiations well, putting the company at advantage and the departing employee at disadvantage. This saved the company a good bit of money. Some of what he offered the employee was not necessarily legal, but because most employees don't understand the law and do not know their rights very well, it worked.

The employee law was in the process of being changed at a national level and would take effect in January 2005. Many of the benefits enjoyed by employees in 2004 would no longer be available to them in 2005.

In mid-2004, Hans was negotiating with an employee who was being let go. The employee was over fifty and would have a difficult time getting a new job. Hans offered him a six-month training program. Upon completion of the training, in 2005, the specific conditions of termination could be negotiated. Hans said nothing to the employee about the coming change in the law, but he knew that the employee would receive much less compensation if he could be kept on until after January 1. When the employee in question refused the offer of an extra six months and insisted that further negotiations take place through his lawyer, Hans was quite offended. He said that he had tried to keep the relationship on a friendly basis, and this employee had turned their good relationship sour.

It's hard to know in a situation like this what voices Hans may have been listening to. He seems to be quite satisfied with his performance and is making the best of the role he has in the company. His managers find him a fine fellow indeed. All the while, however, his relationship with departing colleagues spreads contempt for him personally and for the company that encourages him to work this way. Departing employees never consider recommending that their children work for the company, nor do they consider looking elsewhere in the company for further work. If those employees can encourage anyone they know to use the services of a competing company, they do so eagerly. Compared to the wave of disgust for the company that Hans is creating, his savings of a few thousand Euros here and there are paltry indeed. Yet he sees himself as successful. It is self-deception, both by Hans and by his immediate superiors, and it is not at all uncommon.

What is important to understand in dealing with someone like Hans is that his behavior is consistent with the voices he has chosen to listen to. Short of some change in his interior council, there is no reason to expect him to change.

The facilitative leader needs to find ways to listen to the right voices on her interior council. To do this we have to overcome the fear of seeming crazy. We have to select many more members for our councils than our ancestors did. We need to take the time and develop the skills to reflect. We need to find ways of reminding ourselves about our illusion-making capacity and find ways of dealing with it.

In dramatic language, Nikos Kazantzakis (1960) describes the discipline of the Interior Council this way:

> It is not enough to hear the tumult of ancestors within you. It is not enough for them to be battling at the threshold of your mind. All rush to clutch your warm brain and to climb once more into the light of day.

> But you yourself must choose with care whom to hurl down again into the chasms of your blood, and whom you shall permit to mount once more into the light and the earth.

> Do not pity them. Keep vigil over the bottomless gulf of your heart, and choose. You shall say, "This shade is humble, dark, like a beast: send him away! This one is silent and flaming, more living than I. Let him drink all my blood!" (Kazantzakis, 1960, p. 71)

Paul McCartney expresses this Internal Council in poems to his deceased wife, Linda. He hears her voice in his head such that she is alive and she is dead (McCartney, 2001, p. 156).

MAKING THE JOURNEY

The process of deepening your relationship to your Interior Council is also a journey. It begins with being startled with the council member. What they say or do seems to have a message specifically for you and your situation. Then the dialogue begins. Questions are asked on both sides. Challenges are given. Ideas are accepted. Finally, a profound sense of belonging together happens.

"Some subconscious thought comes into consciousness that challenges what you are then doing or thinking. You begin to dialogue with that challenging perspective. Should I, for example, be intervening here or not? You develop a profound appreciation for those dialogues" (Jenkins & Jenkins, 2002).

This journey is not linear, but more like wandering around among types of advisors and levels of interaction. It is a bit like those Christmas lights that randomly turn on and off. Some thoughts flash in your mind and seem to never appear again. Others linger, repeating themselves over and over. They may be part of your thinking for years. Still others seem to be out to accomplish a particular purpose. These thoughts come to mind and stay until the problem is solved. The face of someone may appear over and over. You may find yourself singing or humming the same song again and again for months.

THE FOUR LEVELS OF INTERIOR COUNCIL

The four levels of depth in Interior Council are impact, address, dialogue, and union. These are the stages we experience as a member becomes part of the council. Sometimes it is someone you have never met before, or it can be someone you knew many years ago who suddenly appears in your consciousness. Some seem to have an impact for a short while and then sink back into your unconscious.

THE IMPACT

At this level, those internal voices are challenges. These colleagues question the way you do things, the way you act. This level of advisor can also be supporting, a sort of pat on the back, that comes to mind when you are working. The pat is a test of your will to succeed.

Daniel Vasella, chairman and CEO of the pharmaceutical company Novartis, tells a story about meetings at the hospital when he was doing his medical residency.

> The meeting was conducted in a highly disciplined manner; my boss disliked it profoundly when people came in late. In fact, being tardy was unacceptable.
>
> One winter morning, however, the weather was horrible, and the roads were covered with ice and snow. As I drove to work, I realized I hadn't left enough time. Arriving at the meeting 15, maybe 20 minutes late, I was embarrassed and began apologizing as I sat down in the conference room. But my boss interrupted me, "On a day like today," he responded, "only stupid people are on time." (Wademan, 2005, p. 5)

In this example are included both the challenge, a requirement to be strictly on time, and support, "Only stupid people are on time."

The impact is like someone dropping a house on you. You are going along, pretty content and not really concerned about anything, and suddenly you are confronted with a failure or a greatness that you don't want to know about. You go through a whole series of ways of denying the validity of the message. You belittle the messenger. You refuse to believe it. You hide from its truth. If it is threatening enough, you may attack the source of the message verbally or even physically. Most of the time these tactics work. You decide that the message is untrue or unimportant or just someone's opinion.

Sometimes these tactics only partially work, and a small doubt is placed in your self-image. If further messages reinforce your doubt, the doubt grows until a new self-image is required.

Sometimes the message is so powerful or repeated so many times that it causes your illusion to be radically transformed into something more consistent with the messages. Ideally, these messages are also more consistent with reality.

THE ADDRESS

After the impact, the voice becomes more than a simple wake-up experience. The voice begins to speak. It is still more a monologue; it will become a dialogue at the next level. But here you find your interior voices giving you reasons why, why you are great, why you are wrong. They say why you should be going in one direction or in another.

In an interview with *FastCompany,* Michael Useem, Director, Center for Leadership and Change Management, Wharton School, University of Pennsylvania said:

> During the Vietnam War, he's a 22-year old officer in charge of a field reconnaissance run. He stands up with his lance corporal after having been crouched down while studying a map. As the two of them stand, the lance corporal is fatally hit by a sniper in a village about 500 yards away. Pace's first battlefield casualty lies a foot from him.
>
> Pace turns to the radioman to order an artillery barrage on the town. Just then, a 20-year noncommissioned officer, a sergeant, gives him a killer look. Pace got the message. Who knows who is in that village? He calls off the barrage. They cautiously enter the village, populated with only women and children. The sniper was long gone.
>
> That look from his sergeant forced Pace to get in touch with himself so anger didn't overwhelm his thinking, so he could be courageous under trying circumstances. Pace got to that realization through a pretty tough moment in life. But you can do it through meditation, through reading history, and most important, through repeatedly putting yourself to the test and learning from it. ("Everything You Wanted to Know," 2004)

Jon remembers early in his teaching experience being one of the trainers in a course on the west side of Chicago. He was responsible for leading a discussion. Jon tends to be a pretty serious person, and as a new trainer he was very serious about leading the discussion. As the conversation went on, the group became more and more serious. They were nearly morbid by the end. During the evaluation at the end of the day, the leader trainer gave Jon some advice. He said the person leading this kind of discussion has a huge influence on the group's mood. As the group got more serious by following Jon, Jon then got more serious. Jon as the trainer was reinforcing this mood, and it became very uncomfortable for most people. The leader told Jon, "Please pay attention to your feelings as you lead a program." He will always remember that, and most of the time when the group's emotions don't seem to be what he expects, he checks his own to see if it needs to change.

Events in your past become learning points. We have changed because of them. We recall them in important moments. They have become important enough that we cultivate the memories. We tell stories to ourselves and to others; they have become part of who we are.

The Dialogue

Sometimes we argue with these internal mentors. Sometimes we get into discussions with them. This is the level of dialogue. Here you find yourself asking, "What would Fred do here?" "Why would you do that?" You find yourself going back over something that was said and you responded to. You wonder what could have happened if you had responded some other way. You try replaying the scene differently. The key to this level of the discipline is to do this intentionally for critical moments that are likely to come up again, so that you can learn from them.

When we were discussing with colleagues the idea of doing this book, one friend said to Maureen that she simply had to read a certain author; it was just what we needed for reference. The colleague sent a chapter of the book in question. Maureen read the chapter thoroughly and could not imagine what it might have to do with the topic. This, in turn, triggered an internal dialogue. She finds herself asking, "What have I said or done that led my colleague to believe that this chapter relates to the book's content? What assumptions does my colleague have that other readers might have about this material? What message from this article could be construed as relating to the book? How can I address readers who come to the book with the same assumptions and perspectives that my colleague brought?"

This state is the one depicted in cartoons as the protagonist having a devil perched on one shoulder and an angel on the other one, both whispering into opposite ears. In this case, both voices could be both diabolical and divine.

We have a friend who talks to a tree, not trees in general, but one specific tree near his house. The tree is old and damaged. It is rotting in places; branches have been broken off. It is scarred. The dogs mark their territory on it. People have carved their initials in its bark. When our friend is feeling sorry for himself, he walks down the street to talk the tree. He stands in front of the tree and complains about how bad things are. He complains about his wife and kids. He grumbles about his work. He whines about his boss. He says that he is a failure. You know the routine. The tree, according to our friend, talks back. She points out that in spite of all the things she hates about her life she is "sustained in being." Our friend then responds by pointing out how bad off the tree is. The tree is scarred, rotting, and likely dying. She is mistreated and abused. The tree responds that, like it or not, my friend has a life with possibilities just like she, the tree, has a life with possibilities in spite of all the difficulties she has. Both of them can complain about all the problems or reach out for the possibilities and urge them into being.

THE UNION

The fourth level happens after the impact has challenged you with the images and people who populate your thinking, the address provides all of the details of why you are capable of more, and you have entered into the dialogue, in which you discuss what is possible. At this point your councilors give your life meaning. They are so much a part of who you are that it is impossible to know the difference between your own self and your council.

These are the saviors, the guardian angels to whom you go for solace and for permission. They demand greatness from you. After the accidental death of his young son, Eric Clapton wrote "Tears in Heaven," in which he draws strength from thinking about his son in heaven while surely feeling that he does not yet belong in heaven (Clapton and Jennings, n.d.).

Sometimes places seem to be magical. Peter Senge, Joseph Jaworski, C. Otto Scharmer, and Betty Sue Flowers (2004) describe a number of events during which someone has this rather magical experience of place. Senge describes a place in northern Vermont where meetings of the Executive Champion's Workshop are held once a year. The meetings are held in a tent in the middle of a field. The field looks in all directions to the Green Mountains. The first thing that strikes you is a sense of peacefulness about the place. It is more than just a nice setting; it has a history about it. People have brought something to this place. In the case of the field in Vermont, the von Trapp family had purchased it. They had arrived in America quite penniless and traveled through the United States performing until they had saved enough money to buy a piece of land. They chose northern Vermont. At the end of a disappointing search in the area, they decided to pray for twenty-four hours that they might find what they were looking for. The next day the father went to arrange for their departure and ran into a farmer who had decided to sell his farm (Senge et al., 2004).

Such places exist that are special for all of us. Visiting them or just calling them to mind brings a sense of being connected to something bigger and more majestic.

CONCLUSION

The discipline of the Interior Council gives shape and direction to our thinking. It allows us to control to some degree the images and insights that make us who we intend to be. It provides us with courage. We know we are standing on the shoulders of others, and it is right.

Paying attention to and developing those in your memory who inform your thinking and actions is a critical discipline for a facilitative leader. Your Interior Council is the richest resource you have for creativity, logical systems, and reminders of who you are and intend to be. It is our hope that you can bring discipline to this resource.

◆ ◆ ◆

Practices for Interior Council

There are many practices that can be used to develop this discipline for the facilitative leader. In the Interior Council, the discipline creates inner resources that can be called upon in times of pressure or difficulty. They can be elicited in those times of pain or failure. They will not rescue you, but will help you find your way through.

These processes help provide a greater degree of influence over what you think and do. While you can never have total control over your thinking, you can give it direction.

Writing Letters

Writing letters to your inner mentors is one way of developing this discipline. The letters should be done on a regular basis, once a week, once a month. Set aside thirty minutes to an hour in a quiet place where you will not be disturbed. Spend a few minutes reflecting about the concern you would like to have addressed. Select someone or thing or a place that would best help with that concern.

Think about what you would like to say and begin to write. You may want to make more than one draft. Treat the letter as one you would actually send. When complete, read it carefully. Reflect on what the recipient might say in the return letter.

Telling and Writing Stories

One way of strengthening the voices of those you want to advise you is by telling and writing stories about them.

> I used to live in a ghetto in Chicago. It was 98 percent black. It had the highest crime rate in Chicago. People were often killed. Women were raped or beaten. While looking out of the classroom window where I was working, I watched a woman shoot her boyfriend. While sitting at the reception desk a man ran up and asked if I had seen anyone come by. His wife had been attacked. People strung out on drugs, gangs terrorizing, drunks sitting on the curbs, and prostitutes hustling were part of living there.
>
> I lived one block from a little store where they sold whiskey and beer. A woman named Corinne owned the store. The store was divided into two parts. One part was behind a kind of wire screen where the employees worked. You could see the bottles on shelves. You could also see guns

sitting around the place. A shotgun rested against a table. Handguns lay next to bottles of cheap wine and half pints of whiskey. One was always within reach of the staff.

The space on the other side of the screen was for the customers. People would buy a can of beer, sit and talk in her store. It was not a bar but a store. People liked to stay there because it was safe. The guns and Corinne's bravery made it safe.

One evening a group of us were drinking and singing. Steve played the guitar and led us in singing songs together. When the beer got low at around 11:00 P.M. we decided to call Corrine and ask if she would drop some beer off on her way home. Lela called because she knew her the best. Corinne said it was not a problem.

A little while later the doorbell rang and Lela and I went down to open it. We said hi. We asked how she was doing. She said she was fine and smiled. She said the police had stopped her on the way to our place. They wanted to tell her that it was not safe to walk alone at night in that neighborhood. She said with a smile that she could take care of herself and lifted the flap of her purse. Inside was a gun.

I was stunned. I began to see behind Corrine hundreds of women, ancestors going back generation after generation. One, a leader of her ancient people, stood with great dignity giving hope to all who knew her. Some were beaten bloody by boyfriends, husbands, or fathers. More than one was a killer. The oppression of slavery broke and reduced some to little more than animals. A woman cared for the children of others. Another worked sixty hours a week so that her son could go to school. One was chained to dozens of others and laid in blood, vomit, and sewage as the ship they were on rolled in the waves. The montage of good and evil, great and small, loving and spiteful rolled across my consciousness.

Corrine was the latest of a long line of great women. I found myself profoundly honored to know Corrine.

Corrine comes to Jon's mind from time to time. She reminds him that he too has ancestors, good and bad, who go back into the place where humans emerged. They too were worth having.

The process of writing personal stories is a liberating one. The process begins with an event that for some reason was important. Mulling over why it was important and what about it made it important is the next step. This process can take weeks or even months. Recalling the details of the situation and the progress from the beginning to the end is important. Telling the story out loud to someone or to a group is the next step. This seems to provide an understanding of what is important. It reveals the emotional dimensions of the story. The rhythm of the telling seems to help the writing process.

Tell the story again. This time make sure there is time to be relaxed about the length of the story. Normally, we do not use dialogue. We do narrate the story from the perspective of the person experiencing the event.

Now begin thinking about how the story is written. Many narrative structures are available for the storyteller. One begins with setting the scene. Some detail is given at this point. The reader should be able to picture himself or herself in the scene. Next comes the sequence of events that is the story. Making the events full and rich helps to bring the reader along. When the point of the story is made, stop writing.

Now it is time to refine the story. Eliminate everything that is not necessary to create the atmosphere required by the story and the progression of the experience.

Tell the story or share it with others to see their reaction. The story can be further refined if it is to be shared with others. If it is for private use, then further refinement may be unnecessary.

Writing Summaries

Another writing process for working with your interior council is to write summaries of books, articles, chapters, movies, and so on. We have used two ways of doing that. One is to write a one-sentence summary of each paragraph of a book. Then write summaries of each section of a chapter. Then summarize the chapter in a sentence or two. Finally, write a paragraph summarizing the whole book. The second way is to go through the book and take out all of the illustrations, examples, and repetition so that all you have left is the few pages of ideas. Then state those few pages in your own language.

Writing a dialogue with the someone you want to have as an interior mentor is quite useful.

Left-Hand Column/Right-Hand Column

Another technique for developing an Interior Council is called "Left-Hand Column/Right-Hand Column." It is found in Peter Senge et al., *Fifth Discipline Fieldbook* (1994). The following is a version we developed for our clients.

Choosing a Situation. Think of a conversation you have had in the last month or so that you felt did not work well, from which you walked away dissatisfied, and others may have been dissatisfied as well. The conversation can be between you and one other person or you and a group. Here are some examples if you need them:

- You cannot reach an agreement with a close associate.
- You believe you have been assigned an unfair share of the work.
- You believe someone else is not pulling his or her weight.
- You believe you are being accused unjustly.
- The other party misunderstood what you were saying.

Or

Think of a problem or situation in the organization that you would like to do something about. Then think of someone in the organization you wish you could talk to about the issue—either you wish you had the courage to talk to him or her or you wish you had the access.

Writing the Right-Hand Column. Divide a sheet of paper into two columns. Use the right-hand column to write down what you and the other person(s) said (or what you imagine you and they would say). The dialogue might go on for several pages. Leave the left-hand column blank until you have finished.

Writing the Left-Hand Column. Now, in the left-hand column, write out what you were thinking and feeling, but not saying, as the conversation progressed.

Reflection: Using Your Left-Hand Column as a Resource. You can learn a great deal just from the act of writing out a problem, putting it away for a week, and then looking at it again. The writing becomes an artifact, through which you can examine your own thinking.

Use a blank sheet of paper to answer as many of the following questions you can at this time.

- What has really led me to think and feel this way?
- What was my intention? What was I trying to accomplish?
- Did I achieve the results I intended?
- How might my comments have contributed to the difficulty?
- Why didn't I say what was in my left-hand column?
- What assumptions am I making about the other person or people?

- What were the costs of operating this way? What were the payoffs?
- What prevented me from acting differently?
- How can I use my left-hand column as a resource to improve our communications?

◆ ◆ ◆

Exercise for Interior Council

Your Lonely Hearts Club Montage

On the front cover of the 1960s classic *Sgt. Pepper's Lonely Hearts Club Band* by the Beatles, a montage of eighty-seven photos of figures contemporary and historical—from Oscar Wilde to Carl Jung to Sonny Liston to Mae West, along with a stone figure, a hookah, and wax models of the Beatles—serves as the background to the Beatles themselves. You might likewise think of your personal bibliography or the devils and angels that sit on your shoulders or the chorus of voices and influences that surround you. Take the next few minutes to think of the people, places, or objects that form your interior council. Following are some categories to help you brainstorm.

Helped Me to Grow Up	Professional Mentors	Affirmers (they stand up for you, no matter what)	Sacred Forces (they put you in touch with the transcendent)
Supporters (add to your thinking)	Challengers (they push you beyond what you thought was possible)	Destructive Forces (that call forth your dark side)	Critics (they call you and your way into question, helpfully)

When you have made your list (make sure you have considered all of the categories—and add a few more if you wish), choose one name from each of your eight boxes, and think about when you would say Yes and when you would say No to their input.

When done, reflect privately or with some colleagues on your team:

- What is one name (or object) you noted that surprised you?
- Which category was the easiest to fill out? Most difficult?
- How did you decide to add or remove members from your council?
- How can you bring your council to mind when you need them?

CHAPTER NINE

INTENTIONALITY: ALIGNING THE WILL TO SUCCEED

Intentionality is developing the capacity to manage your will, to increase control over your deepest capacities. Standing as the facilitative leader is standing in a position in which every aspect of both your dark side and your greatness are magnified. Intentionality is learning to harness both of these energies.

In the *Star Wars* movie, Yoda the Jedi master says, "Try—there is no try. There is only do and not do." He knows that to say "I'll try" is already gravitating toward failure. Saying "I'll try" indicates that the focus of effort is in doing something, but there is little commitment to succeeding. Your own brain hears not that you will do, but that you will try—quite different things.

Commitment to success is acknowledging all those doubts that are built into the "I'll try" statement that any self-aware person has. It is recognizing personal weaknesses and strengths. As Will Sonnett (played by Walter Brennan) in the 1960s TV western series *Guns of Will Sonnett* used to say, "No brag, just fact." Not only is it true to say "No brag" but it's also true to say, "No victim, just fact." It is unblocking the capacity to care for others. Finally, it is denying the luxury of letting things interfere with accomplishing what you will to do. Intentionality is setting aside all those interior and exterior things that stand in the way of what you intend to have happen.

This does not mean you will always succeed. Life is too random to expect success all the time. Other people have intentions that may conflict with yours. These two things, the specific circumstances we find ourselves in and the actions and responses of others, are only discovered in the acting out of your will. Building intentionality is needed in order to keep on wanting and wanting again what needs to be done.

WHAT IS INTENTIONALITY?

The discipline of Intentionality is the process of developing your capacity to make free choices. It is developing your courage to will something new into existence. It is developing the ability to discern between real boundaries and the barriers invented by your own imagination. Intentionality is the second of the disciplines we discuss related to developing selfhood. Intentionality is the discipline that is in tension with your Interior Council. While the Interior Council is about self-awareness, Intentionality is about self-actualization.

Intentionality is a transformational. It is that act of our being that takes place during the microsecond before we act. It the most radical thing a person can do. It is the act of will that focuses your whole life at turning the everyday mundane into spirit. Intentionality in this sense is not wanting something or having a craving. It is looking at the myriad of possibilities that the future posits as potentialities; choosing the one that best fits you; and willing it into existence. Willing something into being is doing the day-to-day actions required to bring it into existence. Without the action there is no will, just illusion.

FREEDOM

Intentionality is radical freedom. This has nothing to do with wanting to be free. You simply show up free, like it or not. A lot of folks don't like freedom one bit, and spend a good bit of time enumerating all the constraints they have to deal with. But constraints and circumstances make no difference. Freedom is not dependent on externalities. It is not dependent on your internal state either. You hear people say that after they get their act together they will be able to accomplish what they want. This is not freedom.

We normally think of freedom as being without constraints, without boundaries. This is wishful thinking. There are always boundaries. Would you be freer without gravity? The physical world places limitations on what we can do. Our own thinking limits us. Our language, culture, society, and much more create limitations. The paradox in all of this is that we seldom even come near our limits. We create our own limits without being aware of them. We say that something is too expensive. Usually what we really mean is that we have other priorities. We say that when the kids are older, then we can do the things we want to do. What this normally means is that we need an excuse for failing to do what we want to do.

The oil industry has a concept called the "technical limit." The idea is to decide what is the most important factor, called value driver, when drilling a well or installing a pipeline, for example. It could be making it the cheapest, fastest, or most technically advanced. Sometimes there is more than one factor, but normally one overrides all of them—for example, the fastest. The question is then asked, "In a perfect world, in which there were no delays, no mistakes, no late arrivals of materials, in which everyone was optimally trained and did everything they should perfectly—in that perfect world, what is the fastest this well can be drilled?" The answer to this question is the technical limit. Planning a project in light of a technical limit is a very different exercise from planning in light of how well we did this project last time. The assumptions are different.

In one of its foundational courses, the Institute of Cultural Affairs (ICA) talks about four kinds of freedom. The freedom to be lucid is the first. This freedom understands what is really going on in the world, in the groups you are working with and in yourself. Lucidity is freedom from self-deception and to be honest. The second freedom is the freedom to be sensitive. We don't mean weepy. We mean fully present to the situation. This sensitivity hears not only what a person says but also listens to the context in which it is being said. This sensitivity cares for the others in the deep, dark, hidden places where their real weaknesses dwell. The third freedom is the freedom to be exposed. Exposure is acting without having the luxury of the unambiguous knowledge that what was done is the right thing. Exposure in this sense is risk without any justification. The fourth freedom is the freedom to be disciplined. This discipline is not the shallow disciplines such as being on time; anyone with a watch can do that. This is the discipline of being who you are.

MYSTERY

Intentionality is filled with mystery. Joseph Jaworski, who has devoted much of his life to the study and practice of leadership development, points to this with what he calls "Collapse of Boundaries." He describes the Collapse of Boundaries as the process that occurs when walls that separate one of us from the other blur or dissolve. He describes one in an interview with C. O. Scharmer:

> This phenomenon doesn't always occur over something important. I was probably 35 or 38, and in the early stages of the transformational journey I wrote about in *Synchronicity* when I went out in the wilderness in the wintertime. You normally don't go backpacking in the wintertime. One other person went out, a guide photographer. It was very solitary, and I just loved it. At one point I was all alone out there, and this ermine appeared, and she put on an act for me. She started turning flips and jumping in different ways and then would stop and look at me, as if to say, now what did you think about that? And I would nod and smile and then she would do it again. This was out in the middle of nowhere, just a wild ermine. That must have gone on for a long time, it seemed like ten minutes. Finally she gave me one last look and went back down under the snow and I never saw her again. It was very much like these other experiences. I felt a complete oneness with this animal. Jumping ahead, since we're talking about that, I've had that same experience with flowers in the wilderness. (Scharmer, 1999, p. 4)

CREATIVITY

When you actually intend something to happen, good things seem to just happen. It is not that they are guaranteed to happen, but in the normal course of events they do. Help arrives from all over. We think that two things happen. When you intend something with all your will, the first thing that happens is you find solutions more readily and what would in normal situations be problems become either nothing or an annoyance. The second is when you are intensely prepared to accomplish things, others often step in to help. Things seem to go your way for some unexplainable reason.

Intentionality is preparing your spirit, which is the source of creativity. It is aligning who you are both consciously and unconsciously with what you want to achieve. Humility is needed here, as well as gratitude. Care for others and attention to your deepest desires is part of this.

Everyone has had the experience of finding him- or herself in the moment just before doing something realizing that it is the wrong thing to do and nevertheless going ahead anyway. Intentionality is the ability to minimize these moments.

To do this, purpose needs to be brought to our thinking. We create the framework, the perspective, through which the world is seen. Our intentions create our world, and that world determines what we experience and how we respond to those experiences. In an interview by Brad Spurgeon, Colin Wilson, the British intellectual, describes this process:

> The key to it is through effort, concentration or focus and refusing to lose one's vital energies through pessimism.
>
> What it means basically is that you're able to focus until you suddenly experience that sense that everything is good. . . . We go around leaking energy in the same way that someone who has slashed their wrists would go around leaking blood.
>
> Once you can actually get over that and recognize that this is not necessary, suddenly you begin to see the possibility of achieving a state of mind, a kind of steady focus, which means that you see that things are extremely good. . . .
>
> The problem with human beings so far is that they are met with so many setbacks that they are quite easily defeatable, particularly in the modern age when they've gotten separated from their roots. (Spurgeon, 2005, p. 4)

Intentionality is about preparation for action. It is the necessary alignment of will needed to act out who you are. The ICA describes this as "the action before the action." What is meant is that an activity is preceded by an act of will, an intention. This intention need not be conscious, but it is often so. At times our conscious intention is not aligned with our unconscious one.

CREATING AN IDENTITY

Intentionality is also about creating your identity. Japanese folklore speaks of three selves—the self you present to the world, the self you present to those closest to you, and the self only you know. This way of thinking assumes that we live on many levels and expose those levels differently to different people. We make adjustments to our identity all the time, especially the one we present to the world. We play different roles for our bosses, our families, our parents, and so on. Too often we are told to "be yourself," but there are many selves to choose from. Self-consciously deciding to play the appropriate role is an important dimension of being intentional.

Amy Tan, the best-selling novelist, is also on occasion a rock and roll singer, playing the role of a dominatrix. She dresses in thigh-length black leather boots, a skin-tight black leather tank top, a biker's cap, dark sunglasses, and a whip. Imagine the shift in identities between that role and the role of Ms. Tan, the daughter in a traditionally oriented Chinese family, as she describes in her novels.

An identity is more than imagination or something you are acting out. It is "who you are" in reality. Great actors are capable of acting out different roles on demand. Roles have to do with language, tone of voice, posture, mannerisms, thinking, commitment, and more.

The great director, actor, and coach Constantin Stanislavski, who invented what is now know as "The Method," had actors bring themselves, their own emotions, to the stage, rather than a character. Method actors are said to bring greater integrity and depth to the stage. Before Stanislavski, actors were trained to bring an external representation of the role.

DIFFICULTIES OF INTENTIONALITY

Modern society presents many stumbling blocks to intentionality. We are overwhelmed with possible demands on our time and attention. The belief that we can act and avoid obligations is also blocking our capacity to bring intention to our life. We are afraid of being responsible for our actions.

Claims on Our Time

We've noted before that we all struggle with continual demands on our time and attention. Yet we often—unconsciously or not—allow and succumb to those demands. We can spend our whole lives flitting from one demand to another. We are under the illusion that we can prevent lost opportunities for money or friends or whatever is important to us. What opportunity do we miss if we are not accessible? The humor in this is that we lose opportunities unconsciously all the time, but because we are not aware of them we don't miss them at all.

We also value the flow of communications and distractions because they offer escape. It is nice to look at a text message and excuse yourself from an excruciatingly boring presentation. We look busy and therefore important. After all, it is the modern world, the only constant is change, and it is good to be busy.

In the Greek epic poem *The Odyssey,* Odysseus desires to hear the voice of the sirens. They are creatures with female heads and the bodies of birds. They sing their songs to sailors traveling near their islands. The songs are so beautiful that listeners are lured to their deaths on rocks. Odysseus ties himself to the mast of his ship so that he can hear but not respond to their seductive song. He has his men block their ears with wax so they cannot hear the song.

Unfortunately, we have no such simple escape from the sirens that make demands on our time. The propensity is to give partial attention to many things at once. One of today's most precious gifts—our undivided attention—is rarely given, even to ourselves. Intentionality is the process of setting aside all of those distractions—pleasures, desires, and competing demands on our time.

Avoidance of Obligations

Another aspect of contemporary life that makes intentionality difficult is what might be called a desire to avoid obligations—to respond to the whim of the moment without negative consequences. We do things that we know have consequences in the short or long term as if those consequences did not exist. We use petroleum-based products and know that by the end of the century there may well be none left. Unless alternatives are found in many aspects of life today, we will have less electricity, less automobile and airline travel, fewer plastics, higher rates of cancer, increased flooding, more damaging weather patterns, and much more. We tell ourselves that these things are not our responsibility or ask, "What can one person do?" Rather than choosing to act in the context of our whole situation, we limit it to something we think is manageable. It is easy to bring great purpose of will to a small decision.

Sometimes this avoidance of consequences is done in subtle ways. This can often be seen in organizational decision-making processes.

Jon is on the board of a nongovernmental organization (NGO). Some of the board members are able to describe the risks inherent in any course of action. Someone will suggest a direction to take, and these people point out the negative consequences of going that way. Someone else will make a suggestion, and they will point out the dangers of that direction. Dangers are pointed out again and again until the entire group becomes paralyzed. The risks are often reasonable and even likely. Any given risk has many shades of grey, as does any benefit. Each shade should be examined in detail. A suggestion that we look at the risks and benefits of each action as a way of moving beyond the circle of dangers that has been created results in the response that this method has dangers inherent in it, too. This NGO chooses to be trapped by avoidance.

We can be trapped by our patterns, and they can also liberate us. Consider writing poetry or playing music. Once you have decided to write a poem in a particular form or a composition in a particular style, say haiku or jazz, then you follow the rules of that form. Your choice of form was part of your creative invention. Even if you create your own form, you set in place the rules that you follow in order to showcase your creative message.

Fear of Accountability

Another impediment to intentionality is our fear of accountability. If we avoid intentions, then in principle we would have no accountability. This fear seems to come from wanting to be able to say, "It wasn't my fault."

Transferring blame is common practice in the organizational world. It is so common that it can be readily predicted in business simulations. We use "The Beer Game," a logistics simulation, to teach how small events can have big effects on a system. The game is a simulated beer distribution network in which the objective is to minimize costs across the entire network. Groups of sixteen to eighteen people play the roles of Factory, Distributor, Supplier, Wholesaler, and Retailer. It costs $1 a barrel to store the beer and $2 a barrel in lost revenue if an order comes in that cannot be filled. Over the course of twenty-six rounds, someone invariably places an order for more beer than is needed, which creates a re-action across the rest of the chain so that every station increases their order "just in case" until there are hundreds of barrels in back order or in stock.

In debriefing the game, the question arises as to what caused the problem, and someone always responds that it was the customer's fault. If the customer hadn't bought any beer there would have been no problem. It is immediately obvious to all of the players that this certainly can't be the problem, and yet the ease and obviousness of transferring the blame is irresistible.

In real life, the head of one of the training departments we worked with succumbed to such thinking. When the department was having a difficult time delivering on courses, he announced to the account managers to stop selling courses. If this had been a temporary part of an overall strategy for improving capacity it would have been okay. It was not; it was the solution to the lack of capacity problem. His lack of capacity was reframed into a "too many customers" problem.

Being truly intentional is difficult for many reasons. We have very many things and people wanting our attention. We for some reason think we can avoid the consequences of our acts. We fear being responsible for our actions by transferring blame and claiming successes that often we are only a part of.

THE ISSUES OF INTENTIONALITY FOR FACILITATIVE LEADERS

ROLE AND IDENTITY

Managers have for too long focused on the externalities of the roles they play. They learn the "techniques" of communicating, and yet they fail to communicate. They learn the methods of inspiring leadership and don't bother to inspire. They fail to bring their real selves to the roles they play.

As a facilitative leader, you can create a particular identity by imagining when you played that role in a similar situation before. Imagine what it felt like and how you behaved. What were your emotions? Now imagine the circumstances that triggered your emotion and reactions. To recreate your self, don't focus on the externalities of the role, but on the circumstances, the things you brought to that moment, the feeling you had that changed the way you behaved. Once you recall them accurately, they will re-trigger the role. The real you will be brought to the role you are playing.

Bringing your real self to the roles you need to play is not easy. It is about aligning who you are with the role necessary for the place you are in. It is aligning the energies of your self and your role.

ALIGNING ENERGY

Aligning energy first requires acknowledging your own weaknesses. It is being humble. Your own blocks and failings are taken into account and set aside or used to deliver the needed event. "Usually as soon as I focus on my intentions, I know if I'm trying to be 'learningful' or be a loudmouth" (Ruete, 1999). Ned Ruete under-stands that we can choose to focus on understanding, hearing, and learning from others or we can focus on our need to say things. What we like about this statement of Ned's is that he knows that it takes an effort to realize which one we are focusing on. It is not au-tomatic. It is also possible to move from being a loudmouth to being "learningful."

This doesn't mean self-depreciation or being a victim, but rather acknowledging your own limitations. Jon, for example, is a white American male living in the Netherlands. His linguistic abil-ity is low and he understands little and speaks less Dutch. He is at that age between middle-aged and elderly. Friends and colleagues are dying, injuries take longer to heal, and his memory seems to take longer to access than a few years back. All of these things have consequences for what Jon can do. Some are positive, some are negative, and some are both.

Acknowledging your frailties is not the same as being victim-ized by them. Because of his age, Jon is expected to have rather stuffy, conservative attitudes, and little interest in new technolo-gies. We were at a cocktail party once, and in the course of intro-ducing us to someone, our host mentioned that Jon was working on his friend's Web site. The guest struggled his way through the image of this "old man" designing a Web site.

Experiencing Gratitude

Aligning the energies of your self and your role also involves being grateful. This is difficult, because in some circles gratitude seems to have become a moral obligation. We don't mean you have to *do* anything to be grateful. It is something that happens. You discover that you are grateful for being in a difficult situation or for a tragedy happening.

Gratitude is not the first response you have in these situations. But at some moment in the experience, you have a chance to choose how you are going to relate to what has happened. You can be grateful or hateful; accepting or denying; blaming or absolving. You have a choice. It may come days or months or even years later. Being open to the possibility of being grateful is a key to becoming aware of it yourself. Being grateful does not mean that you are not suffering. After this awareness deepens, you become capable of choosing to journey to gratitude for the tragedies that we all experience.

Being grateful for the nice things, the things you already like, is easy and requires little or no discipline. It is much more difficult to be grateful when things are not going well. And yet, as the following story shows, perspectives on what is the good can change:

> A long time ago a very powerful chieftain had a friend that he grew up with. They were close and did many things together. The chieftain's friend had one particular habit. Whatever happened to him, whether good or bad, he would pause for a minute and then remark, "This is good!"

> One day the chieftain and his friend went hunting. The friend acted as gun bearer, preparing and loading the guns the chieftain would shoot. One time either the gun was faulty or the friend had done something wrong—when the chieftain fired the gun it misfired and blew his thumb off. His friend looked at what had happened and stated, as was his habit, "This is good!" The chieftain was furious at hearing the remark; said it was not good and had his friend arrested and put in jail.

> Some time later the chieftain was hunting in an area known to be populated by cannibals. Soon the cannibals captured him, bound him, and began to prepare him for their meal. As the preparation

went on they noticed that the chieftain was missing his thumb. Because this defect was considered an ill omen, they immediately released the chieftain and sent him home.

On returning to his home he recalled his friend and the occasion on which he had lost his thumb. He immediately went to the jail and released his friend. The chieftain told his friend that he had been right that it was good that he had lost his thumb. He told how he had escaped the cannibals because of his missing thumb. He said that he was sorry for sending him to jail and that it was bad of him to have done it.

His friend said, "No, This is good!"

The chieftain said, "What do you mean? You spent a year in jail for my anger. What good can that be?"

"If I had not been in jail, I would have been with you when you met the cannibals."

This gratitude is neither abstract nor a mere ritual. It is found in the moment, in a specific situation. The discipline is to find the courage to see and live the goodness in whatever situation in which you find yourself.

Seek to align the event—everything said, done, and embodied—with the best possible outcome. Strip off the distractions and superfluous diversions; add the finesse elements that can turn a good experience into a terrific one. You may visualize the day unfolding before your eyes, to attune yourself to its rhythm.

EMPATHY FOR OTHERS

Intentionality is developing a state of empathy for all of the people who are in the group. It is acknowledging the built-in drive to care, and it is intending to care. The discipline is developing your capacity to care for others. Care for others is easier when the person you are caring for is someone you like. It is more difficult when the person is less likeable. Care is not just feeling empathy, pity, or concern. Care begins with concern, but is meaningless without action.

The intention to care has embedded in it the intention to act. The process of feeling care without the will to act has a different quality; risks are viewed differently. Having to ask how this concern will be practically acted out changes the way the object of care is viewed. The circumstances become more important. The way the situation will change becomes part of the concern. Rabindrath Tagore wrote of this: "I awoke and saw that life was service. I acted and behold, service was joy" (Walsh, 1999, p. 254).

With Intentionality, your conscious and unconscious wills align. You are fully aware of the weaknesses and strengths of yourself and others. You recognize where skills, knowledge, or courage are lacking and so you find yourself seeking help. The foundation of Intentionality is care for others. Intentionality has you care for yourself but it is in order to care for others.

THE FOUR LEVELS OF INTENTIONALITY

The reason Intentionality is a discipline is that we all face obstacles that have to be overcome. The four experiential levels of Intentionality are burden, passion, intervention, and expenditure.

THE BURDEN

The first level of Intentionality is the recognition that you are responsible for your own thinking, deeds, and stance. You are responsible for the things you create, the things you destroy, and for many things on which you have no observable influence. You are responsible for your happiness, sadness, anger, and indifference. You are responsible for your thoughts and ideas. You are responsible for what you read and understand. Often this realization comes in an unexpected moment, a chance encounter or comment.

When Maureen gave birth to our first son, Jean-Paul, she felt that a world of responsibility seemed to descend on her in a single day. There had been time to adjust to being married, and while she was pregnant, Jean-Paul was obviously there, but he was part of Maureen. On the day he was born, however, there was instantly someone else, another person, with continual, pressing needs. She loved stepping into this new world, but it was clear that there was now a lifelong new responsibility that had not been there the day before.

When we lived in Mumbai, a leper used to sit on the sidewalk begging outside the building we lived in. Every day, Jon passed him, and he smiled and nodded as Jon walked to work. He seemed always in a good mood. One day Jon went out very early in the morning and the leper wasn't there. Not many people were about yet. As Jon walked down the street, he had to step around brown bundles—men, women, and children wrapped in cotton blankets sleeping on the street. Jon wondered as he walked where they all went during the monsoon, the rainy season. As Jon got to the corner, he saw the leper just waking up, unwrapping his blanket, and sitting on a concrete slab, the porch of a small shop. With him were a woman and two small children. Jon realized that this was his family. He couldn't believe that the mundane life of wife and children would also be granted to a begging leper. He started inventing reasons why it couldn't be true. He suddenly realized that all of the brown bundles in their tens of thousands, and all of the thousands of lepers all over the city had those who cared for them and whom they cared for. He felt helpless realizing that, no matter what he did, most of those people would live and die caring for their families there on the street. Suddenly he was completely humbled by the mass of suffering on every side as he walked along the street.

In this moment of being overwhelmed by the burden, a kind of paralysis sets in. Absolutely nothing you can do will be sufficient. The forces that keep problematic situations in place are too powerful. The numbers are too great, life is too short, I am not up to what is demanded of me. I am too weak, not clever enough, and lack the determination to do what needs to be done.

At that moment it is easy to give up, to try to block out the awareness of the world around you, yet it won't go away. You have more than enough reasons not to try or to try and fail. You know that all of your reasons are in fact excuses. This burden is yours to bear. The burden gives Intentionality its realism. It is neither sad nor happy; it just is. The burden gives eyes to see honestly. You see hope and possibility and you also see disconnects and the potential for failure.

THE PASSION

The second level of Intentionality is the passion, when the awareness is transformed into an overwhelming desire to do something. Jon's leper beggar becomes a kind of symbol, a representative of all of the suffering in the world, and you personally are responsible to act on this. All of the programs and agencies and the relief efforts are irrelevant; only you are responsible. The passion is the state of care becoming manifest. While foolish in the eyes of others, you find yourself determined to make a difference.

Juanita Brown, international consultant and co-originator of "World Café" tells the story of an event in 1966 that points to this state. The United Farm Workers in California were trying to organize farm laborers working for the DiGiorgio Corporation, the largest grower of table grapes in the United States. The workers were hired in Mexico, transported to California, and lived there in DiGiorgio housing while they worked. All were supporting families.

Cesar Chavez and his United Farm Workers could not enter the private property where the laborers worked and lived. There were guards at the gates who prevented unauthorized people from entering. Fear prevented the farm workers from leaving the camp to attend union organizing meetings.

The workers had the right to vote to be unionized and yet the organizers had no way of having the face-to-face conversation necessary to convince them that they could vote for a union. The organizers were becoming discouraged and even Chavez was beginning to lose hope.

He called a meeting of everyone who would come, including the surrounding community—men, women, and children. He explained the situation realistically and honestly. He said he really didn't know what to do and would like their help. Many people contributed to the discussion. As the meeting wound down, an old woman stood up and spoke softly in Spanish:

> Well, I know I'm not qualified, but there was something. . . . I had an idea, maybe just a small idea, but maybe it can help. If we cannot go in to visit the workers, maybe there is a way they could come to us. I believe only God can help us now. Why don't we build an altar, a small Church on the public road across the street from the camps. We can hold Mass and a prayer vigil every night. I know there are priests who will help us. The workers can come across the street to Mass and the prayer vigil. The growers can't stop them from coming to a prayer vigil, can they? And they can't stop us from holding one, can they? And as we pray together with the workers from the camps, they will come to know who we are and

what we stand for and then they can vote in a better way for their future. (Briskin et al., 2001, p. 10)

At this moment things began to happen, a flame began to burn. Chavez's old station wagon was parked across the road from the camps. An altar was built in the back. Workers began coming to Mass. A few attended the vigil at first, and then many. Elections were eventually held and the United Farm Workers gained the right to represent the farm laborers.

Sometimes it is a single person in particular circumstances that seems to ignite passion in people. A story such as Juanita Brown's does this. Being intentional is being open to these moments that awaken passions, and it is more. Intentionality is creating the conditions within yourself where your passion is brought forth.

What are the triggers, your personal triggers, that call forth passion? How do you overcome your reticence and fear of this passion?

THE INTERVENTION

The next level of Intentionality is called the intervention, and it comes after the burden of recognizing your own participation in the world and knowing you are capable of doing something about it, and the passion, in which you accept the burden of care you carry and act on it.

It is at this point that concrete action is envisioned. Something clicks, and you can see how what you intend can be done. Up to this moment it was more theoretical. It could be done in principle. Now you can see how to start, where it will be difficult to do, and how you will approach these difficulties. You understand the technique of the action you intend. Later you may have to do it differently, but now you are clear.

The directions after that first step are many and depend in part on what happens during and immediately after that first step. Your step may produce any of a number of different results. Other people may react in a diversity of different ways. New options may open up that didn't exist before you began, and old options may no longer be viable.

It is a bit like billiards. You know that after sinking the present ball, if you place the cue ball in a certain area of the table, you will have many options for sinking the next ball. Which option is best will depend on the specific spot in that area of the table the ball lands. Naturally many shots require placing the ball in a very precise location. Working with organizations is similar. The key is to know when an approximate goal is best, which leaves several opportunities, or a precise goal, which leaves very few options available.

Sometimes in strategic planning you are interested in what might be called "practical proposals" or "strategic directions." These are plans that can be implemented in a diversity of different ways, some direct, some indirect, and some even counterintuitive. Here you are looking for direction, while avoiding locking yourself into a fixed approach. You are trying to choose a general direction, like choosing an area of the table, not a specific point.

In connecting a directional proposal to possible implementation routes, you are standing in the intervention level of Intentionality. You can see any number of possibilities, including the obvious and the not so obvious. This is more than a list of nice ideas. The list and the process of creating it are inspiring. You try on many different images of yourself and of your organization.

We know a hairdresser who generates possibilities for satisfied customers in a wonderful way. He asks himself the question, "How can I create an atmosphere in which people have such a great time that they come back just to be in the atmosphere?" Having asked himself that question, he keeps on generating more and more new answers. On Friday afternoon, an hour or two before closing, he sets out wine and snacks in the entrance of the shop, for anyone who drops by, customer or not. "Did you know," he says on the first day after the test, "I got twenty-one new appointments during that wine and cheese hour last Friday!" He has installed a music video system that shows the videos simultaneously inside and outside the shop, so there are always a few observers standing outside enjoying Oasis or just chatting. From time to time one of the staff turns on the bubble machine, filling the shop with bubbles. In warm weather, he moves some of the chairs outside so that customers can enjoy the sunshine along with their haircuts. During the first week of classes this year in our university town, our friend rented a double-decker bus, filled both levels with chairs, and offered haircuts at reduced prices in different locations across the city. There was a drawing for a student to win a free apartment for a whole school year. Who knows what will happen next?

THE EXPENDITURE

The fourth level of Intentionality is the expenditure. This is the deepest level of Intentionality. At this level everything is in place for flow to happen. In a conversation between Tom Callanen and John Ott, Callanen is reported to have said:

> During college I was a member of Middlebury College's lacrosse team. During my senior year, we were playing Williams College for the New England championship. I'd read about sports teams entering "the Zone," but I'd never really experienced it until that game. From the opening whistle we entered this space that seemed like everything was happening in slow motion. Roy would win the face-off, and I knew where he was going to run and when he would pass it to me. And I'd move in that direction, and he'd make the pass just as I'd seen it. I would turn, and I knew exactly where A. J. would be for my pass, and then for his shot on goal. In that first five minutes we scored five unanswered goals. Not only did it seem like the moves of my teammates were scripted, but it also felt like that other team was somehow participating in the dance as well. (Briskin et al., 2001, p. 26)

We've been in meetings where we've had similar experiences. Sometimes a meeting starts off perfectly from the very beginning, and sometimes something is said that clicks the event into place. It can happen in any sort of gathering. The experience can be very short in duration, or the length of an entire project.

Maureen and Jon spent a year on a team of five people doing planning consultations with local communities. They ranged from a jungle community in Venezuela to inner-city neighborhoods in Washington, D.C. We worked with local people, supportive volunteers, content experts, and our own organization's permanent staff in each location. The planning consultation lasted a total of four weeks, including setup beforehand and documentation afterward.

Hours were very long, and the team of five was not really very well suited for one another. Once we began doing our work, however, we grew into a remarkably effective unit.

One of the times that the "magic" happened was in a village in the central mountains of Italy called "Termine" (The End). Termine was geographically just that. Perched on a saddle in the mountains, there was a sheer drop on the north side and three small valleys on the south. Once the road reached Termine, there was nowhere else to go.

We had a sense as we drove around the village that something would be special here. We had done a number of consults together by that time. We knew our roles, and each others' strengths and weaknesses. We trusted each other to cover for our failings and to use our strengths.

Since the village had no public place large enough to meet in, the team built a tent on the football pitch, anticipating sunny weather that never came. Planning workshops in the tent called for managing a leaky tent roof that occasionally sent streams of water down the homemade blackboard. None of this was a problem. As a team we either worked out a way to solve the problem or found an alternative approach. Some of it should have been hardship, such as ducking the residue of bedpans hurled out of upper story windows on the way to the morning team meetings and having only one heated workroom, the air grey with the smoke of a leaky woodstove. As we were aware that this was exactly the way the community lived, it was cause for humor rather than complaint.

The spirit of Intentionality can capture you anyplace, even in a hairdressing salon, a sports competition, or a village development project. When this happens, things seem to work for you, and even when they do not work, it simply is not a problem—you can find another way.

This sense of the imminence of success in everything is the consequence of the expenditure level of Intentionality. Once you are committed, many kinds of possibilities open up to you. This level of commitment is not easy or taken lightly. It is total commitment. Partial commitment or commitment with reservations, while sensible, does not work at this level. It is all or nothing.

CONCLUSION

Intentionality can also be described as the capacity to develop mental toughness. Disappointments become opportunities to evaluate how to improve. This is the capacity to set disappointment aside once the learning it delivers has been discerned. For those who have developed mental toughness, failures become triggers by which they can raise their game.

While the following practices and exercises will help deepen your capacity to be intentional, the basic issue is one of mental attitude.

◆ ◆ ◆

Practices for Intentionality

Many practices exist in the arena of Intentionality. At the simplest level, most time management systems are a practice of intentionality.

Personal Risks

We have a friend who has a set of practices that he works every month. At the beginning of the month he identifies three personal risks. One is a new physical risk. One month he might do a bungee jump or learn to swim (he is afraid of water). One of the risks is an intellectual risk. For this risk he might attend a challenging lecture series or read a book that he knows will contradict his own thinking about something. He might read something that is far above his head such as computer programming. The third area of risk is emotional. He will select something that he has avoided dealing with. One time he visited his father, whom he hadn't seen in several years.

The first key to this practice is to pick things that are risky, but not so overwhelming that you can't do them. The second key is to do them regularly. Once a month is the schedule that our friend has set for himself, and it seems to work.

Time

The simple process of identifying how you spend your time can be a place to begin. Draw or type on your computer a 24/7 chart, seven columns wide for the seven days of the week and twenty-four rows deep for every hour of the day. Set aside a few minutes every day for one week during which you write down what you were doing the day before. Record what you really did, whether it was sleeping, sitting at the computer, driving, talking to a customer, eating lunch, bathing a child, whatever. If your schedule varies a great deal from week to week, you might try doing it for a month just to get an overview of how you spend your time. You might then color code the different kinds of time you spend. Choose a code that tells you something useful, whether it is how much of your time is your own and how much in service to your boss; how much is work and how much is family, or how much time you actually spend in sports and fitness.

Now look at how you are spending your time. Ask yourself, "What is enjoyable? What is difficult? What is important and what is really important? What time is spent refreshing myself? How could I change the way I spend my time?" If you do this practice two or three times a year, you will begin to manage your time. You can do the same thing with finances, carbohydrates, or any other resources you are concerned about managing.

Risk Management

Another practice has to do with risk management. There are many different ways to do this. Often this is done in conjunction with looking at a new opportunity, for example, a job offer or the possibility of opening a new line of business.

First make a list of opportunities you face. If you are considering one single opportunity, list all the various aspects of that opportunity. At the same time, make a separate list of the risks involved were you to move on the opportunity.

You will put each list onto a separate 3x3 matrix. Across the top of the matrix, write "High Influence," "Medium Influence," and "Low Influence," for the degree of influence you have on that risk or opportunity. Low influence, for example, would include things like weather, the housing market, and government regulations. High influence could be the selection of whom you choose to work with or your timing. Down the side of the matrix, write "High Impact," "Medium Impact," and "Low Impact," for the degree of impact that item would have on the direction you wish to take.

Fill in the matrixes with the opportunities and risks you put on your lists. Use the two charts to think through how to minimize your risks and maximize your opportunities.

Practical Care. It is easy for people to forget that others are affected by their decisions. It is easy to think that senior management positions are filled with people in touch with what is happening in their organizations. It is easy to believe that abstract decisions of strategy by executives are more important than the day-to-day operational decision of the workforce. Some leaders use rather simple, symbolic acts to keep connected to the realities of the whole organization.

The management board of an NGO decided that they needed a ritual that symbolized the practical aspect of their responsibility for the people in the organization. They decided to clean the sidewalk outside the NGO's office building. They did this every day at 8:30 in the morning. When it snowed they shoveled snow. When it rained they used brushes. When it was sunny they used brooms.

One of the big airlines required that all senior managers spend one week a year doing the work of a frontline worker. A vice president may spend a week working as a baggage handler.

The owner of a one-hundred-person cleaning company has lunch once a week with a group of five of the cleaners. Each week it is a different group, so that over the year everyone has a chance to have lunch with him. At the lunch, any topic is discussable. Whatever people say is not to go outside the room. Whatever anyone says will have no effect on their performance evaluation or work life.

◆ ◆ ◆

Exercises for Intentionality

Profiling Yourself in the Group

To work with your intentionality, think about how you act when you first stand in front of a group.

Look at the 5 × 5 × 5 form following. The form consists of one row across the top, a second row with five columns, a third row with twenty-five columns, and then five rows of twenty-five columns.

Think of the first five minutes of your last group session. In the first row write down what those five minutes accomplish. In the second row of the form, write down the five actions you take when you first start a session. These actions should have about the same weight (length of time or importance). In the third row, for each action listed in the second row write down five sub-actions that make up each of the five actions listed. You now have five actions in the second row and twenty-five actions in the third row. In the last five rows, you can begin to fill in five actions for each of the twenty-five actions in the third row. You do not have to fill all of them in, but fill in at least three.

Row 1   Row 2   Row 3

When you have completed your form, reflect privately or together with a team:

- What is one activity that you wrote down that was surprising for you?
- What was the most difficult part of doing this?
- Select one of the categories from the bottom five rows and say what it is, why you do it, and how it contributes to the group process. (As a group you might discuss several of these. You might ask, "Is there something that could be done in a different way?")
- How could you improve the first five minutes of your facilitation?

CHAPTER TEN

SENSE OF WONDER: MAINTAINING THE CAPACITY TO BE SURPRISED

Having a Sense of Wonder is being open and responding to the miraculous. It results when you are carrying out your best and most authentic understanding in the service of your most powerful resolve toward what is needed. Wonder is present when you experience that instant of awe, a simultaneous combination of dread and excitement after which you seem to have a new appreciation of life.

The facilitative leader evokes drive, commitment, and creativity, being open to and eliciting wonder. Having a Sense of Wonder is a choice. It is looking at reality, with all its warts, and deciding it is worth the excitement. It is being open and responding to the miraculous. It is cultivating awe in day-to-day experience.

In *Nausea* (1969), Jean-Paul Sartre describes his protagonist, Antoine Roquentin's, disgust in watching a glass of beer on a café table. Roquentin's disgust is not with the beer, it is with himself, which leads him to realize there is no meaning to existence save that he exists. With the coming of this insight, he can choose how to act out that existence.

Keeping the capacity to be delighted by groups, events, and even ourselves is difficult in a time of skepticism and cynicism. Having a Sense of Wonder is being able to see possibility without succumbing to naïveté.

A Sense of Wonder is the nexus between Interior Council and Intentionality. Your Interior Council is about the past. It is tradition, your advisors, what you have read. It is those things from your own experience that you want to keep aware of, to keep alive. Wonder brings that past to bear on the present. The discipline of maintaining a Sense of Wonder informs you of who should belong to your council of internal advisors.

Intentionality is about the future. It is one's desires about the future put into willing a difference. It is conceiving how to bring the new into practical form. A Sense of Wonder brings that potential future into the present moment. Wonder is the source of that future.

WHAT IS A SENSE OF WONDER?

Rudolf Otto in "The Idea of the Holy" (1958) talks about a sense of wonder or sense of awe as a precognitive awareness that produces the simultaneous emotions of fear and fascination. The two interesting aspects of this definition are "precognitive" and "fear and fascination." Precognitive is awareness that comes before you can think, before the category comes to mind that puts the experience into a box. It is that moment between the experience and the thought about the experience. The discipline is to pay attention to those instants and savor them. (Jenkins & Jenkins, 2002, p. 8).

They are unbelievably common when you pay attention to them.

The simultaneous experience of fear and fascination is also part of the discipline. If fear overwhelms us, we flee or fight. If fascination overwhelms us, we indulge in the delight of the experience. The discipline is to broaden our capacity to experience both at the same time. While you cannot create this feeling of wonder, you can certainly be open to it. The one thing you can always expect is to be surprised.

Situations, buildings, mundane things like water and wind, even ourselves, all have the capacity to be wonder filled. The potential is always there. We have to train ourselves to participate in it. A paradox exists here. The miraculous seems to be present all the time, but its appearance is out of our control. We have to be open to it, and yet we can't determine when it happens. If we are not open, then it surely will not happen. If we try to force it in to being, it will not happen.

Wonder is touching the not me, the unknown. Perhaps, it is being touched by the unknown. From childhood we carefully construct a world within which we live. We add to it as new experiences come along. Boulding points out that sometimes anomalies appear and we adjust our world or deny the reality of these extraordinary disruptions to our world (Boulding, 1961). Thomas Kuhn makes the same point in his book *The Structure of Scientific Revolutions* (1970). Scientific revolutions are the results of information that does not fit current theories and that over time erodes the viability of those theories until a breakthrough happens and a new theory emerges. Like the resistance to change in an operating image that Boulding talks about there is also resistance within the scientific community to changes in theory. In both cases there is a sense of awe that frequently accompanies these moments.

Maintaining a Sense of Wonder also enables you to test for real life. If as contemporary physics and psychology say, we invent our own universe of meaning, then how can we distinguish what is real from what is simply our own creation? How do we avoid illusions? Perhaps we don't.

Two tests seem available, however. One is to test our experience against that of others. This may introduce the problem of groupthink, in which we created shared illusions in a small group, as in the investigation of the *Challenger* disaster. We can create illusions as a whole society, such as M. Scott Peck described about the United States and Vietnam in *People of the Lie* (1983). Collective illusions are arguably better than individual ones. There is at least the possibility of interaction with others.

Another test for reality is the sense of awe. In the split second between an experience and our thoughts about it, reality intrudes. This is Rudolf Otto's "precognitive" awareness. Whenever that gap appears, we know that something real has happened. The struggle here is making sense out of what the "real" was. In that moment we are freed from the old and from the world we ourselves have created.

If you keep your senses sharp, you yourself are simply amazing. Your good points, strengths, vices are not amazing in themselves and neither are your bad points, weaknesses, and virtues. The amazing part is that these things lie together, side by side.

Difficulties of Maintaining a Sense of Wonder

Maintaining a Sense of Wonder is difficult today for a number of reasons. We don't perceive or understand much of what is available to our senses. We try to put everything immediately into a box so that we don't have to deal with it. We need to tap reserves of courage to do this work.

The Problem of Perception

Much of what is available for us to experience we miss completely. It is filtered out before it even registers. We would be simply overwhelmed with data if this were not so. We get used to things to the point that sensations do not register. The odor of the dog or cat, after a while, can't be smelled unless we choose to. We walk down the street and our partner says, "Did you see that sign? (that haircut? that display?)" You hadn't seen it. Trivial? Not really. What is unimportant to our operating image is often not even seen, heard, or registered. Sometimes what we disagree with we don't see either.

We create understanding about what we are experiencing out of what we already know. Drawing on experience is important, even critical, to learning. This same ability can block coming to new conclusions. We draw conclusions with little data and often quickly, before we even are exposed to the whole experience. It is difficult to delay coming to conclusions as soon as possible.

When U.S. car manufacturers first visited Japanese factories, they reported that they had been shown fake factories, because there was no inventory. The only way to make sense of the lack of inventory they saw was to have an explanation consistent with what they knew (Senge, Scharmer, Jaworski, & Flowers, 2004). We do this because it helps us to understand and to deal with the world we live in.

It is one thing to delay closure and another to reopen our thinking after we have decided what something means. There are clues about when we need to rethink our understanding of something. When the same problem keeps coming back, we might want to look deeper into the situation. When we need to keep adding exceptions to the rules of how things work, we might look at the assumptions we are making. When we are uncomfortable with something, when we have "it just doesn't feel right" responses over time, we might look at the processes by which things are done. When we experience fear and fascination, we can know that the new is trying to break into our consciousness. There are lots of other clues, but none of them guarantee that something is wrong or needs to change.

The Control Box

A second reason for this incapacity to maintain a Sense of Wonder is that when we do experience awe, we tend to categorize the experience, to label it in an understandable way. We all have a need to control the world around us. Moments of wonder are out of our control; we did not create or schedule or influence them; they happen when and how they will, out of range of one's agenda, strategic plan, budget, or even ability to manage. "Expect something wonderful to happen to you today!" could be a blessing or a curse. In either situation, you do not control it. Those of us who insist on living in a world that we control simply have to avoid the breakthrough of wonder into our lives—a heavy price to pay indeed!

We lose a great many insights by imposing an order that is not necessary. Harrison Owen (1990, p. 87) describes two approaches to creating walkways on a new university campus. The first way is that architects can plan them ahead of time as part of the overall campus design. What frequently happens once students begin to claim the campus is that pathways are worn into the grass on the routes that are especially convenient. These emerge from the way the campus is used—the route between popular classes and the café, for instance. Sometimes it is possible to forbid students to walk on the grass, to hold to the architect's intended design.

Another way to approach the problem is to install no pathways when the campus is opened, and as pathways emerge to pave them over. This is more organic and in some ways more practical, but it means that the architect has to give up control of student traffic management. More accurately, it puts traffic management in the hands of the students.

Information and communication technologies have enabled us to control our work and lives much more than was the case even ten years ago, making our lack of control of nature more troublesome than ever. There is controversy today in areas like flood control and forestry and wildlife management. Forcing rivers into a single path can result in disastrous flooding. Allowing occasional brush fires to clear out underbrush may help prevent destructive forest fires. Allowing some predators to survive may cost the occasional sheep, but permit a healthier overall balance of ecology. In all of these matters, the value is control. We have grown to expect our lives to be very much in our control, and when they are not, it seems as if something is terribly wrong.

What if it weren't a problem? What if that was just the truth of existence trying to tell you something more important than your current goal?

Courage Required

A third reason for the difficulty with maintaining a Sense of Wonder is that it requires courage. It is work, because in order to maintain an open stance we have to pay attention to details, dynamics, and patterns that we would not otherwise have been aware of. This is the discipline of setting aside one's judgment in order to listen to what the universe has to say to us in a given moment. There is no guarantee of results.

Being open to new ideas and new experiences requires courage of several different kinds. We have to be ready to admit that our understanding of a situation may simply be wrong. This is the courage to be wrong. John F. Kennedy's book *Profiles in Courage* (1956) documents this dimension of courage. Of course, Kennedy demonstrated his own courage following the Bay of Pigs fiasco when the U.S. government sponsored the failed invasion of Cuba by anti-Castro Cubans and mercenaries. Kennedy took responsibility for authorizing it, when he could simply have transferred blame to the previous administration or the CIA.

There is also the courage to act. It is one thing to be aware of a mistake and to admit your part in it. It is another to point to someone else who was right. Finally, it is another sort of courage to turn around and move in a new direction.

One has to put himself or herself into a "corrected" frame of mind in order to move between acknowledging a mistake and acting to correct it. Often you hear people only go halfway; "Yes, I was wrong; that's just the way I see things." Then someone else steps in to address the problem in a new way. To go all the way means taking charge of a new approach to the same problem. This means going back to your assumptions and forcing yourself to change them to fit the reality that has intruded. This is a unique sort of courage.

THE ISSUES OF A SENSE OF WONDER FOR FACILITATIVE LEADERS

"Facilitation is maintaining a sense of wonder about those we work with; it is dread and delight about the group that is currently in front of us. This discipline is appreciating the group and the individuals that make it up. It is also being conscious of their dis-relationships and being in a state of wonder about them" (Jenkins & Jenkins, 2002).

Being present to wonder requires that we be willing to set aside our known world and pay attention to the unknown and allow it to speak to us. Being facilitative, which is to say enabling groups, is greatly enhanced by this ability to keep in touch with wonder. Facilitators who are open to the experience of wonder and who can enable others to experience it are able to tap huge reserves of energy. They seem to be more aware and more effective. Creativity is released. People are motivated. Relationships are deepened. Trust is enhanced.

D. H. Lawrence (1972) in his poem, "New Heaven and New Earth," points to how renewal of the spirit takes place. He begins with a sense of weariness. He is tired to the point of sickness because everywhere he looked he saw that he had corrupted it. He saw that he had corrupted everything, nature, machines, people, friends and foes. He was sick to the point of despair. He knew everything because he had polluted everything. All that was left was despair.

He then describes death and how that begins to relieve the weariness. At the end he dies. Nothing has meaning or purpose. All is gone. It is good to be put to death, to find yourself in the black, dead earth. It is good to be nothing, absolutely nothing.

He then points to the experience of wonder. At the moment of being trampled to death by constantly seeing yourself, you reach out. You touch something that is not you. A shock runs through you and a spark ignites and flame bursts into existence. So you put your hand out a little further, and it is true you are touching the unknown, the truly unknown.

This is a moment of awe (Lawrence, 1972).

CREATIVITY

In workshops that deal with and solve difficult problems, occasionally something takes place that is outside the experience of those present. There seems to be a period during which the problem is unsolvable; it is overwhelmingly complex or difficult. It seems impossible. We might keep up a brave face, but deep down we feel it is impossible.

In the process of looking for a solution, sometimes a comment is made or an idea expressed, and it is like a flicker of light in the darkness. Many people in the group may not see it or understand the potential of the idea, yet a few people do. These few may make comments or suggestions supporting the insight. This is a moment of wonder. The facilitator's job is to enable the idea's exploration and growth. There may be outright hostility toward the idea, which needs to be controlled until the idea is explored further. Naturally, these moments of insight do not automatically result in a good idea. The first idea may be unrealistic, but others often emerge because of the first moment.

A good facilitator pays attention to these moments and enables the group to see the idea's potential and to give it space to prove its worth.

MOTIVATION

These experiences of wonder can be profoundly moving. You can sense excitement in a group that has had this kind of experience. Groups are inspired by them and are driven to creativity.

We once led a strategic planning workshop for the human resources staff of a large Dutch company. There were about fifty people working over three days. During the last session, the group created a 120-day timeline with people signing up for the twelve action arenas that had been identified. Everyone agreed to a role in the execution. By the end of the 120 days, every goal had been reached except one.

RELATIONSHIPS AND TRUST

People who share certain kinds of experiences of wonder have a special sort of relationship. They have shared a moment of marvel. When they continue to work on the new reality that has emerged, their relationship deepens.

Trust is critical to organizational health. A person can be trustworthy but not trusted. Clearly trust is built on integrity, doing what you promise to do; consistency, applying standards to everyone equally; communicating clearly and regularly; not tolerating incompetence, bad behavior, and dishonesty in feedback; and confronting and dealing with painful situations. It is also built on creating those moments in which meaning and purpose are obvious to everyone.

Jon worked with the corporate processes manager of a big multinational who had these traits of evoking trust. He was understated but decisive. He did not preach that people had meaningful work. He enabled them to see it for themselves. At staff meetings he asked, "What was the high point in the past week?" "What was the low point?" "What was it that made it high or low?" He would compliment people for their contribution to the mission of the company in specific terms. Everyone that Jon talked to about this manager said they would work for him at any time and anywhere.

For the facilitator, wonder may first be experienced as an intrusion. You had an image of the group or its task or yourself, and that understanding is challenged. You find yourself caught up in the excitement and fearsomeness of the challenge presented to you. Then you find yourself with a profound sense of respect of the source of the challenge. Finally, there is the sense that this is as good as it gets.

THE FOUR LEVELS OF WONDER

Like the other eight disciplines, this one has four levels. In this case they are encounter, entrapment, collegiality, and adoration. Having a Sense of Wonder comes from several directions. Sometimes it is experienced as wholly clear. Sometimes the past provides a source of wonder. Jon remembers one of his first walks in Rotterdam. There was a statue of a man with his arms raised in the air. He looked like something Picasso might have done—angular, distorted. There was a jagged hole chiseled out of his center. Jon's friend explained that the statue was called *The Hole* and commemorated the bombing of Rotterdam by the Americans near the end of World War II. Thousands of Dutch civilians had been killed. Jon was hearing of this for the first time, and was in shock. It would have been easy to put distance between himself and what had happened; he was only three when the bombing occurred; mistakes are made in war; it was critical that the harbor be crippled in preparation for the invasion. Yet something is set free in being present to all that being an American is.

Sometimes it is the future that surprises us. We have all had the experience of hearing someone describe a future reality, perhaps a park, a building, and a new organization. It is hard to believe, and yet the energy of the speaker can bring us into the dream. All the more amazing is the experience of finding exactly that reality some while later, standing before us.

Sometimes we surprise ourselves. We do things we've never done before or thought we couldn't or wouldn't ever do. Our success can surprise us, and sometimes our own cruelty can be shocking.

The Encounter

The first level of a Sense of Wonder is the encounter with the mysterious. Jon was teaching a Training of Trainers course in Poland a few years ago. The participants were teachers in Polish business schools. Most of them had a great deal of experience with teaching, but that had meant lecturing. Very few interactive methods had been used. Even the lectures lacked much passion or effective communication with learners. One of the methods in Jon's course was preparing and giving dramatic lectures. One of the participants was a woman in her mid-twenties, sophisticated, businesslike, and attractive. When it was her turn to lecture, Jon was looking forward to a masterful presentation. She stood up and seemed instantly to turn into a little girl flirting with Daddy. Her voice pitched higher, she giggled. Her posture turned into the hunch of a preteen caught doing something naughty. She was a completely different person, utterly unsuited to the workplace. Jon was stunned; he struggled to give feedback. How in the world could this happen to someone? Where in this woman's experience did this bizarre self come from? This is the kind of thing that happens with the encounter. Suddenly you are facing something that is beyond your control or understanding. It can be a positive or a negative encounter, but it is inexplicable.

One day you wake up late and a bit distracted, dress hastily, and as you walk into the office, a colleague says, "Nice tie!" That's a surprise; usually no one says anything about your clothes. You look down, and surprise again, it is a very nice tie! You chose it yourself! It seems like your whole existence has been approved.

At this level of the discipline, the issue is to be open to what is going on. The Polish woman seemed to represent a whole system of relationships between men and women in Eastern Europe. Jon felt challenged to do something. As he watched the presentation, Jon considered a myriad of options of how to respond. But the starting place was simply standing present to the amazing transformation he was witnessing.

The response to the encounter is paying attention and standing present to what is happening both externally and internally. Being present to the immediate moment and the historical context that created this moment is also part of standing present. Knowing that your own biases are also creating your understanding of the situation is important part of standing present.

THE ENTRAPMENT

The second level of Wonder is called the entrapment. This is the experience of no escape, nowhere to run to, and nowhere to hide.

There are always moments of encounter that we slip away from. It is unexpected but not really interesting. Sometimes, however, an encounter comes that really seems to have your name on it. You find yourself, for whatever reason, intrigued and bound. This mysterious moment is yours, and you are going to take it on, whatever it takes. This is the awareness that drives radical change, from improving one's golf game to rebuilding an organization—an individual feels called upon to respond to what is happening. . . . This is really about *me*!

A few years ago our biggest customer was reorganizing, and our company's role had been cut back by more than half. Our employees at the time were very upset. The cut in income meant that some employees who had never done acquisition before would have to begin to do so. No one's position was as secure as it had been. We were holding meetings with the whole team to plan new directions for the company, but the mood was very negative. Two individuals had found jobs elsewhere, and those remaining were very angry. One day the office manager turned to Maureen and said, "You claim to be able to improve the quality of life in teams—how come your own team is such a mess?" Suddenly the difficult situation was more than just a quirk of fate to work through—it was about Maureen's integrity. It began as an encounter with an unexpected business event but suddenly grabbed hold of Maureen. This is the level of the entrapment.

In the early 1970s we were part of a team developing a course called "New Individual and New Society." As apprentice trainers, Jon and Maureen were accustomed to working with the youth subgroup, totaling about twenty people (the adults in the course numbered over a hundred). It was a weekend event running Friday evening through Sunday noon. On Saturday night, the head teacher asked that Jon do the morning lecture to the whole group.

Jon said he had never done that presentation before. Perhaps one of the more experienced trainers should do it. Jon suggested a number of alternatives, but the head teacher was having none of it. Jon said he thought he would be terrible, but the teacher kept insisting. Finally, out of excuses, Jon agreed. He got a pot of coffee, found his notes, and spent the rest of the night preparing a lecture.

The morning session was opened by one of the other trainers. Jon was next. He walked to the front of the room and looked over the largest group he had ever stood before. To his right was the exit door to the building. His mind was blank. He rattled his papers, looked at all the people, and again looked at the exit door thinking, "If I walk out that door I will never have to do this again!" Another thought came to him: the first sentence of his lecture. He looked at the participants and began to speak.

In that moment, between the two thoughts—one of leaving and one of starting—Jon moved from the level of entrapment to the level of collegiality.

The Collegiality

This is the third level of the Sense of Wonder. Jon's example of the eight or ten hours that transpired between being asked to do a lecture and completing it the next morning became for him a source of strength that has lasted a lifetime. It was a dreadful experience that has become a friend and companion.

What had been an experience of being trapped suddenly may turn into an experience of being honored by that which intruded and trapped you. You realize that if you had not had that intrusion, you never would have made the discovery that it brought you. You actually look forward to the next intrusion, albeit with a sense of some dread.

We did a strategic planning session with a training department of about a hundred people. When we got to identifying blocks, we omitted our customary emphasis on the distinction between a problem and a root cause. Though we ordinarily go into some detail on what comprises a root cause, we assumed these learning professionals would automatically look beneath appearances to search for root causes, and we just put the group directly to work, without much context. But what a shock when we got our evaluations! We got responses like "Lack of trained professionals" and "Lack of e-learning training."

It was easy to blame the lazy participants, to blame the short workshop program, to blame ourselves for being incompetent facilitators. What we realized with reflection, however, was that we had been given a gift—a clear demonstration that our original approach had been right all along—no matter who the participants are, you have to seriously stress the difference between a problem and a root cause. Being inside of a problem can make even the most professional of us incompetent analysts. The realization didn't help much with that workshop, but it indeed proved to be a blessing.

A few years ago, Jon was asked to do some training of facilitators in Serbia. The program was funded by USAID and was run by a private American development company. Jon arrived in Belgrade late the night before the program and stayed in one of the big hotels. He noted that the building, about twenty stories high, was burned. The next morning a driver arrived to pick him up, along with one of the community development officers. She had a degree in psychology and was quite articulate in English. The driver was funny and clever, and his English was understandable.

Along the drive, the officer and the driver pointed out various points of interest. Like much of Central Europe, there was a mixture of poverty and wealth, with the emphasis on poverty. One spot in particular was a bombed-out hospital. NATO had hit it during the war. This was at the end of ten years of sanctions that had reduced one of the better-off countries of Central Europe to a skeleton of its former self. Jon commented that they must despise NATO and the United States. They said they did, but that acting on that hatred would neither help them or their country.

During the three-hour drive to the course location, Jon's understanding of the people of Serbia and their past dramatically changed. As in many situations, when you got beneath the public images to the actual people, a more complex and more hopeful reality emerged. There are both truly awful, self-serving individuals who have sway over much of public opinion, and at the same time there are wonderfully generous and great souls, looking for ways to restore Serbia to the world community in a responsible way.

Here was Jon who as an American was responsible for the destruction, hurt, and anger he was witnessing. He found himself caught between guilt and blame. One part of him suggested succumbing to a sense of collective and historical guilt. His government had waged war on this small country; it had used ten years of economic sanctions it knew would not work; and it had failed these people at the end of World War II when Tito took over. At the same time Jon wanted to blame the Serbs for their destruction. Their national pride, their looking the other way when Croats, Bosnians, Kosovars, and others were being butchered and their permitting malevolent leaders to act without checks, all made it inevitable that they would bring this suffering on themselves. Neither response was adequate. Between these two and the experiences he was having was something amazing.

Cultivating a Sense of Wonder is disciplining yourself to become open to these moments of challenge as friends, blessings in disguise that help you to deal with the world you live in.

THE ADORATION

At some point you realize that these moments of awe-filled transformation are more than colleagues. You realize you are not forced into these moments of awareness; it is a co-creation. Whatever it is that puts you into these moments is you yourself, your attitudes, your selfhood, your own responses, and who you are. It is this realization that is the level of the adoration; it is something you find yourself grateful for.

We use the term *co-creation* because what you do with these moments of awareness is your own choice. It is a continuing series of choices. An opportunity is offered by a situation in your life, you respond, the opportunity changes, you respond again, and so on. It is like an ongoing dialogue between friends. The ideas evolve as the dialogue continues.

There is no reason to be thankful for these challenges and affirmations that come as defining moments; you are just thankful. Other responses are possible, such as anger or resignation. The discipline increases the frequency of the times you are thankful. It increases the number of moments you are aware of. You find yourself more sensitive to the different kinds of awe.

In the adoration, the experience is that of connection. Suddenly you are connected to yourself, all of yourself, the things you hate the most and the things you are the most proud of. They make a single whole. You experience being connected to the past, all of it. The future and all of its all unrealized possibilities are all part of you. You and the other are united in a dance of co-creation.

The duality found at this level is reverence and humility in tension with confidence and courage. Joseph Campbell, in his classic work, *The Hero with a Thousand Faces* (1949), described the moment of adoration with an Irish fable of the five sons of the Irish king Eochaid.

Fergus, Olioll, Brian, Fiachra, and Niall went hunting one day. After some hours in the forest they found themselves lost and thirsty. They stopped to rest, and the eldest Fergus went in search of water. After some time he found a well that was guarded by an old woman. She was an ugly hag. She was more than an ugly hag. She was covered with dirt from head to toe. Her teeth were rotten and green; her hair was matted with dirt, twigs and leaves. Her eyes were dim and runny. Her nose was off to one side and flattened against her face. Her skin was wrinkled, her arms bent, and her hands knobby and clawlike. Her bandy legs ended in huge fat ankles. Her feet were flat and shovel-like. Her toenails were broken and jagged. A few were blackened. She reeked of rot, sweat, and decay. She could be smelled from some distance away. In short, she was disgusting. Fergus greeted her and asked, "Are you guarding the well?" and she said, "It is." He asked, "Would you give me permission to take some?" She replied, "I do. It will cost you a kiss on my cheek." He said, "I will not! I would rather die of thirst than kiss you." He then left, returned to his brothers, and told them that he had not gotten water.

Olioll, Brian, and Fiachra went in search of water. They too found the well and the hag. They asked her for water but refused the kiss and so returned to their brothers without water.

Finally, Niall, the youngest brother went and came to the well. He yelled out, "Give me some water, woman!" "I will give it and you will give me a kiss," she replied. He answered, "Before I give you a kiss, I will give you a hug." He went to her, bent over, and gave her an affectionate hug and a kiss on the cheek. When he stepped back there stood the most beautiful woman he had ever seen. She walked with womanly poise. Her skin was smooth and without a flaw. Her eyes a pale blue that seemed hypnotic. Her teeth were like a string of matching pearls. Her mouth was red as rowanberry juice. Her arms were elegant; her hands smooth with long, tapering fingers. Her legs were long and graceful. On her feet were sandals. She wore over her shoulders a crimson cape of the finest fleece closed with a silver brooch.

Niall asked who she was, and she said she was "Royal Rule." She granted him water, blessed him, and explained that both as a hag and as a beauty she is Royal Rule, which requires a gentle heart to release the beauty in the hag.

In mythic form, this is the discipline of maintaining a Sense of Wonder. At this level, the humble and reverent heart can embrace even the most disgusting of situations, people, and problems.

Conclusion

We fail to have a Sense of Wonder unless we discipline ourselves to maintain it. We need to set aside our cynicism, our belief that the world is out to do us harm. We need to learn to see, to experience the awe that is available in every moment. We need to learn how to set aside our capacity to judge, to put things into boxes and learn how to appreciate the unknown. We need to learn to have courage, the courage to be open to the new, the courage to be wrong, and the courage to act to correct the wrongs we have made.

◆ ◆ ◆

Practices for a Sense of Wonder

In the day-to-day living of a leader it is easy to forget the best reasons for choosing to be a leader of a specific group. It is easy to succumb to the various temptations we have talked about. Exercises and practices are not only ways of strengthening your capacity to act out of the discipline; they also become rituals that remind you of the need for the discipline

Expanding the context of the situation can enable you to see the relationship between what is happening and the world and times in which we live. It can be useful to ask yourself how the mystery, the depth, and the greatness of the group with whom you work is manifested (Jenkins & Jenkins, 2002).

When one of these procedures is done once as a way of bringing awareness to a group, it is an exercise. When these are done regularly with a group they are then a practice. We are putting it in the practices part of the chapter but it could have gone to the exercise part also, depending on how it is used. Each practice following would be done in a regular routine.

Contemplation

The most obvious practice related to the discipline of the Sense of Wonder is contemplation. One might focus attention on an object, such as a flame or a stone. One might focus on an idea, a saying or a Zen koan. Sit in a comfortable position. Focus your mind on the idea or object. View your focus from several perspectives in your mind. Think of its history or formation. Just look at it. Think of nothing else.

One other approach to this is called a Spirit or Consciousness Conversation. These are done in groups wherein there is already a reasonably high level of trust. The conversation is about something thoroughly mundane and everyday such as cats, stairs, fire, or water. The conversation is an exchange of experiences about the topic, exploring its impact on our lives from several perspectives. The following is an example of how a conversation about water might go. Notice that the leader is not aimed at analyzing the topic, but rather inviting participants to tell about their own experiences of wonder.

> *Leader:* Sometimes water can be so beautiful. When have you
> ever experienced water as beautiful? I remember when I
> was a teenager; my family was camping near Mount

Lassen in California. We were walking along a stream, toward its source. As we went around a bend, there was a waterfall sparking in the afternoon sunshine that filtered through the evergreens. It was only nine or ten feet high, three meters or so, but fairly wide. It fell through rocks and small plants that clung to the side of the cliff. It sparkled and danced. Water at that moment was simply beautiful. When have you experienced the beauty of water?

Participant 1: I remember sitting on a beach watching the waves come in and slowly retreating as another wave broke. There were so many colors in the water. It was breathtaking.

Participant 2: When I was a kid we used to go to a lake every summer. We stayed in a cabin. Late at night we would walk along the shore to look at the moon's reflection, as it seemed like a pathway to heaven.

Leader: Sometimes water can taste so good. Not necessarily what comes out of the tap, but water can taste so good at the end of a hot day. I was traveling with my family when I was ten or twelve, driving from Los Angeles to Taos, New Mexico. We had a 1954 Pontiac, no air conditioning. My father hung a canvas sack filled with water on the bumper to keep it cool as we drove through the desert heat of 110 degrees Fahrenheit (43 degrees centigrade). After a couple of hours we stopped and had a drink. It was so cool and delicious. When has water tasted great to you?

Participant 1: When you drink from a clear mountain stream. It tastes like the forest, but it is great.

Participant 4: There is nothing like a huge glass of water in the morning after a night of drinking. It makes a huge difference.

Participant 3: I grew up on a farm. Sometimes we would be in the fields and in the middle of a summer afternoon my mother would bring a cooler filled with jars of water.

Leader: Sometimes water can be frightening. I'm sure you have all seen the horrific pictures of the tsunami last year. When I was in the Navy I made a couple of trips to the Mediterranean. I was in what is called an LST—a Landing Ship Tank. It was about six hundred feet long and carried trucks and Jeeps on the main deck and tanks below. While crossing the Atlantic on the way back we were caught by the edge of a hurricane. I remember standing in the wheelhouse watching waves cover the front half of the ship as we crashed up and down. The water that covered the deck was blue-green and several feet deep. I was terrified. Have you ever had an experience of water that was frightening?

Participant 2: In a water safety program I took one time I had to jump from a platform about twenty feet above the water. We were to jump feet first, cross our legs and cross our arms holding onto the life jacket. The thought of hitting the water scared me to death.

Participant 4: I also did safety training. In our case we had to practice escaping from a helicopter. We got into the cabin of a simulated helicopter. It would drop into the water, float for a few seconds, roll over and sink. We had to get out of the cabin. The disorientation of the crash and rolling over combined with panic. Because of the pressure of water rushing in, you were supposed to wait to get out until the cabin was completely full of water, but your panic was so strong that it was very difficult to learn.

Participant 2: I was once caught in a riptide when I was swimming. It sort of grabbed me. I was pulled under and rolled over and over. I knew I should relax and then I would float to the surface, but I kept starting to panic as I ran out of breath and thought I was going to die. Then I floated suddenly to the top, broke the surface and was safe.

Leader: When have you seen water being destructive? When I was twelve or thirteen we lived on a hillside in South San Francisco. Our row of houses was the topmost row. Behind our house you could walk up to the top of the mountain. One spring we had a mudslide. A sort of thick stew poured off the mountain, rocks, trees, dirt, and water. It missed our house, but the next four below us were all hit. The gardens disappeared; the fences were tossed aside, the mud pushed open doors and filled rooms. Everything was pushed downhill. When have you experienced water as destructive?

Participant 3: One time I watched a flash flood run through a village. It carried buildings, cars, and everything. People scrambled to escape.

Participant 4: My old house and its rotting roof is a testament to the horrendous damage a little leak here or there can do if you let it go. It's amazing!

Leader: Water is such an everyday thing. They say our bodies are 95 percent water. We can't live without it. It is both life giving and so destructive.

Naturally a dialogue like this feels artificial, but the exercise is clear. The aim is to build together an appreciation for some mundane aspect of existence.

Group Context

Another exercise related to the Sense of Wonder has to do with the content you give to groups with whom you are working. You might begin with the vision/mission statement of the group. You might begin a discussion about what the group does to contribute to their company. Ask them to view this beyond the work process relationships, to include social, cultural, and other aspects of their relationship with the company. Shift the focus then to the company. What does the company contribute to society? Products and services surely, but what else does it contribute? Things may come up like taxes, training, stability of the community, and so on. A final question could be, "If an historian of the future were describing the company's most important contribution to the world, what might they say?"

The aim here is to look with a Sense of Wonder even at the everyday relationships in which we work, to recast our relationships in a new light.

◆ ◆ ◆

Exercise for a Sense of Wonder

Mindful Music

We pay heavily for our busy, harried lives. One cost of our distracted lives is that we rarely take time to appreciate what is around us: the wonders of nature, events that happen to us, even everyday pleasures like eating and listening to music. We rarely give these things the opportunity to offer their full benefits. Likewise, we miss the stunning mystery, depth, and greatness of our colleagues, participants, and of ourselves.

In this exercise we focus on a piece of music, to try to appreciate what is there. You want to develop not only concentration but also greater sensitivity and clarity of awareness. Listen as carefully as you can. Try to catch the subtleties you may have missed before: the delicate notes, the background rhythms, and the emotions that arise in you. Try to hear with all of your senses; feel the vibration, taste, and see the sound in all of its glory.

This is an individual exercise. Any music can be used, but you might try beginning with something classical. Sit or lie comfortably and take a moment to relax. Then listen and enjoy as fully as you can. Periodically you will find your mind is adrift in fantasies and that you were largely oblivious during the last few minutes. When that happens, simply return your attention gently, just as in meditation, but this time focus on the music instead of the breath.

A way to help yourself to focus on this exercise is to take a large sheet of paper and a box of colors. As you hear the music, choose the main color the piece brings to mind. As you hear the music, draw what the music brings to mind.

Think back over what you have just done.

- What do you remember from this exercise?
- What did you notice about the music?
- What were some of the emotions you felt during this exercise?
- What was different in this music from most music you listen to?
- What was different in your listening?
- What or whom in your life could use your appreciation?
- How might you practice that?

CHAPTER ELEVEN

AWARENESS: KNOWING WHAT IS REALLY GOING ON

We have chosen to call this discipline Awareness. It could equally be called Knowing or Wisdom or Consciousness or even Conscientiousness. Awareness is consciousness of yourself, of others, of the universe in which you live, and of the mystery of existence. We have all had moments (perhaps mini-moments) of illumination, those "Ah-ha!" flashes of insight. Who has not woken up in the middle of the night with a great idea about a problem they have been working on? We sometimes find ourselves in the midst of a difficult situation, and we become aware that it is clear we don't know enough about it to create an effective solution. From time to time we discover depths in ourselves and in others that we never dreamt possible.

Awareness as a discipline is part of the final developmental path: life. This path is the most profound and most difficult. The interaction between Awareness and Action is played out in Presence. It is where you invent your life as it is and will be.

Awareness is intimately connected to the discipline of Action. A way of putting it is the old traditional saying, "Action removes the doubt that theory cannot solve." Others have put it, "The only way you know something is by changing it." Anything that has never been done before can only be proven to work by doing it. The other side of the coin is that good action is based on good theory.

Jose Ortega y Gasset (1962), the Spanish philosopher, put the problem in a way we find helpful. To live in the environment we find ourselves in, we need to do something. We have to eat, breathe, and so on. That something we have to do is not imposed on us by the environment. We have to decide what to do moment by moment. We have to decide what we are going to be. These choices have to be made by us. We can transfer the mechanisms of choice to others, but the choice is ours.

Joseph W. Mathews (1996), one of the founders of the Ecumenical Institute, spoke about Awareness as follows:

> Doing compels you back to knowing. And if you ever find that you know anything, that's dangerous because that compels you right back to doing. The minute you see something in life, brand new imperatives are given and grounded in the new thing that you see. It's almost as if you can't ever separate the knowing from the doing. They also are intimately related to one another. (Mathews, 1996, n.p.)

What Is Awareness?

Some attributes of awareness involve managing one's own image and the messages one receives, using different ways of knowing, and developing perspective.

Messages

Kenneth Boulding (1961) developed one useful understanding of how we become aware. He talked about an "operating image," a picture of the world, of ourselves, of others, and of how things work. This image is created by "messages" we receive throughout our lives. They are any input from our senses. The flow begins even before we are born. Out of the tens of thousands of possible inputs, only a relative few are selected by a complex system of values and constructs built into our personal architectural design of the world.

Messages have one of four effects. First, they can have no effect; they can pass right through, sort of in one ear and out the other. When someone says, "Did you see that?" and you have no idea what *that* was, is an example of this "no effect" meaning of the message. Second, messages can add to our image. When we hear that Sacramento is ninety-six miles from San Francisco and we did not know that, nothing earth-shattering happens, but we have a little clearer understanding of Northern California.

Third, messages can revolutionize our image. One of the effects of privatization has been to dramatically change the images of former government employees. They have to create a new image of their employer, who they are, what their work is, and who their clients are.

The fourth effect of messages is that they can increase your certainty or uncertainty. You might consider yourself a pretty good project manager. Then, a series of projects that you run fail, and you may begin to doubt yourself.

Boulding helps us understand why we are not more aware with his concept of resistance. He says we resist the doubt and the change by tending to select those messages that are not hostile to our image. The causes of this resistance seem to be the amount of reinforcement the image has received. If we hear hundreds of times that quality costs, and every time we try to buy something of quality, we find that it costs more than something with less quality, our belief that quality costs is strongly supported by experience. Another thing that contributes to resistance is how internally consistent the image is. This ability to resist change is both useful and a problem.

Some messages do get through despite our defenses against them. Messages that are very strong or repeated very often can get through. Even then we explain them away or strike back at them by attacking the messenger.

Our image has places where it is clear and without doubt. We "know" that our friend is trustworthy. In other places it is not clear and rather in doubt (Boulding, 1961). The key to Awareness is managing our own image of the world, how it works, and who we are in it.

DIFFERENT WAYS OF KNOWING

Many researchers have described different ways of knowing. Howard Gardner (n.d.) identifies eight intelligences or ways we know:

1. Verbal/Linguistic intelligence
2. Logical/Mathematical intelligence
3. Visual/Spatial intelligence

4. Bodily/Kinesthetic intelligence
5. Musical intelligence
6. Interpersonal intelligence
7. Intrapersonal intelligence
8. Naturalist intelligence

By being able to use more of these intelligences, our awareness increases.

PERSPECTIVE

Perspective is another dimension of awareness. The saying about being able to stand in another person's shoes is what this is about. Perspective enables deeper, better, and more complete understanding, creates the potential for creativity, and increases the possibility of more effective action.

A way of taking different perspectives was developed by Edward de Bono. In several of his books, he talks about using perspective to generate creative ideas. One of his more famous ideas is the "Six Thinking Hats" (1985). The idea here is for a person to look at a problem from six different perspectives. The perspectives are associated with six colors. The Red Hat is about emotions, your immediate, instinctive feelings about the situation. The Black Hat is about the dangers, difficulties, and problems in the situation. The Yellow Hat is about the benefits of the situation, what can be gained or gotten from the situation. The Green Hat points to the creative aspects of the situation, the changes or modifications that are present. The White Hat is about knowing the situation. What do you know, would like to know or must know about the situation? The Blue Hat is about the processes of thinking about the situation. What is the best way of organizing thinking or the sequence of processes applied to the situation? (de Bono, 1985). He is asking people to use their own internal perspectives to view a situation.

DIFFICULTIES OF AWARENESS

In our time with its increased complexity and rapid change, gaining and maintaining awareness is difficult. Many things contribute to this problem.

Schooling

Schooling systems discourage curiosity in primary grades, and by the time secondary classes are started our children have learned to not ask. Children before they go to school ask their parents questions when they occur to them not when the curriculum calls for them. The parents answer at the moment of asking. If the ideas are too difficult, they will help the child understand. In the classroom the curriculum dictates what is learned and when it is learned. A great deal of work is being done to rectify this problem, but the solutions are not yet clear.

We are taught fragmented and seemingly unrelated ideas. Our system of academic specialization often increases the lack of relationship between disciplines. The history of color woodprints in seventeenth-century Japan has nothing to do with quantum physics at the University of Chicago. It is increasingly clear that models that unify knowledge are helpful. They give us hooks on which to put new knowledge. They give us ways of seeing relationships between things. Creativity is often the product of seeing relationships between diverse fields of thought. A scientist looks at moles digging and conceives a new way of digging tunnels under the English Channel. An oil engineer buys a bottle of wine in a duty-free shop and the sleeve inspires a new system of pipes. The simple elegance and placement of elements in a print of Mount Fuji could spark an insight in a physics problem. Creating these unifying models is difficult and not really possible for a single person.

Sense of Responsibility

We think we should respond to the problems we see in the world. At one time it was normal to see someone that is in difficulty and immediately help them. Today the number of people in difficulty often overwhelms us. One response to this is to stop learning about the difficulties in the world. Another response is to harden our feelings for people in trouble. We see a car accident but drive on by. We sometimes fear being taken to court or sued. If you gave first aid to someone and did the wrong thing, you could lose everything. There is a sort of collective, "I don't want to know." Jon remembers teaching in a course in Seattle some years ago. At the end of the second half-day session a course participant came up and said that she realized that what the teachers were saying was true but that she did not want to live in that kind of world, and she left.

THE ISSUES OF AWARENESS FOR FACILITATIVE LEADERS

Maintaining a high state of awareness is a great deal of work. First, it is learning how to be still, to be silent. It is being aware of the present, of this moment as it unfolds. It is looking under the surface of the now and seeing the dynamics of the present. Second, it is paying attention to the space we occupy. The mistake we make is paying attention to the things in the space. The awareness we are talking about is being conscious of the relationships in the space. It is a quiet acknowledgment of the human effort that has constructed the spirit of the space. Third, it is paying attention to the future as it emerges. Most of the time we extrapolate from the past; we construct the future based on what has happened up to this moment. In this kind of awareness, the unknown future tingles at the edges of our senses and seems to beckon us in a direction. The touch is so light that if we are not paying attention we can't experience it.

Awareness is also consciousness of the larger context in which we work. We expand our attention to the larger world; in this we learn to know the world. When the authors were doing community development work, one of the first things we did before the planning consultation was to walk the community. We would walk around the boundaries. We visit as many significant sites we could. We would ask questions about the community. We would ask how things were done. Most of all, we listened to the villagers talk about their village. All of this was done in translation for most of the projects, and that meant that we needed to pay much more attention to the way things were being said. The history of the place was also a source of important insights into the dynamics of the community. In all of this, what was important was to maintain a sense of appreciation about the way things ran *in this place*. The community sensed that belief in the appropriateness of the way the community had constructed its life and they then shared in and contributed to the energy that was being created.

LISTENING

In an interview by William Taylor (1999), Harvard's Ronald Heifetz points to one problem of today's leadership.

> Most leaders die with their mouths open. Leaders must know how to listen—and the art of listening is more subtle than most people think it is. But first, and just as important, leaders must want to listen. Good listening is fueled by curiosity and empathy: What's really happening here? Can I put myself in someone else's shoes? It's hard to be a great listener if you're not interested in other people.
>
> Think about some of the best-known leaders in the airline business: Jan Carlzon at SAS (Scandinavian Airlines System) in the early 1980s, Colin Marshall at British Airways in the early 1990s, Herb Kelleher at Southwest Airlines today. These executives are always flying on their own airlines' planes. They're always talking with customers. They're always encouraging ticket agents and baggage handlers to be creative about helping customers to solve problems. They're in "dynamic listening" mode, asking questions all the time—and not getting seduced into trying to provide all of the answers. (Taylor, 1999, n.p.)

Listening begins with the attitude of curiosity and care. It is inquisitive. It asks questions and genuinely wants to know the answers. This creates a crucial internal state open to maintaining awareness.

MANAGING INFORMATION

To expose ourselves to the information that we need to keep aware of is a lot of work. It is work to make sense out of that information. It is work to be constantly going through the process of learning and changing.

It is also difficult to seek the truth. The truth needs to be tested through action in order to know if it is true. Because the source of a piece of information is an authority, in the old paradigm we tended to automatically believe it to be true. In the new paradigm, an authority making a statement has no relevance to the truth of the statement, no matter how powerful the authority is. The idea still needs to be demonstrated in reality. How do you know an organization? Try changing it. How do you know if a prophet is false? Wait and see what happens with his prophecies. As Margaret Wheatley (1992) points out, information in the new paradigm is not the facts but the relationship between the facts.

What could be more factual than accounting? In his interview in *FastCompany* with Baruch Lev, the Philip Bardes Professor of Accounting and Finance at New York University's Leonard N. Stern School of Business, Alan M. Webber (2000) says this belief is not necessarily true. He first describes the common wisdom about the field. "Accounting is all about accuracy. Accounting is all about hard numbers. Accounting is all about accountability. Accounting is a time-honored tool for making hard decisions about dollars and cents, about profits and losses" (Webber, 2000). He then goes on to explain that Baruch points out how irrelevant the old approach to accounting is in the postmodern world.

The value of a retail outlet may be more in the way the staff interacts with each other and with clients. We go to a small snack shop near our house about once a week. There are a great many other restaurants nearby, and yet the one we go to is nearly always full. The seating is okay and the food is good but a little quirky. The experience is great. The owner and all of the waitresses greet people when they come in. They smile and are friendly. The photos on the walls are of people we know: other merchants on the same street or staff at leisure. The music is nice. We go not because of the food but for the atmosphere. A change in any of these things would diminish its value, and yet none of this is reported to the tax authorities. The truth of value is not found in the inventory or the cost of rent but in the responses of clients and suppliers in the relationships with neighboring shops and the niceness of the staff.

The difference between knowing in the old paradigm and in the new paradigm is clear. In the old paradigm what was important were the tangibles. They could be measured. Their value could be determined. Their life expectancies could be estimated readily. In the new paradigm, intangibles like knowledge and capacity to innovate are important.

We all have the experience of information overload. In the new paradigm, part of the discipline of Awareness is that the leader takes responsibility for the way he or she acquires and handles information.

ACQUIRING INFORMATION

There are three issues in acquiring information: perception, different perspectives, and scale.

Perception

Perception has to do with attentionality, the process of knowing what is important and becoming aware of those things that are critical to know. Using all of one's senses improves attentionality. Different people use their senses in different ways. Some senses are more acute for some of us than others. A colleague of ours can walk into a room and know by smell who was there before he arrived. Apparently, he can distinguish different body odors for different people.

A story might illustrate what we are describing.

A young orphan boy of nine or ten years greatly desired to be the greatest swordsman in all of Japan. He went to the best teacher and begged to be his student. The master was old and had no student. He told the boy to leave. The boy persisted and persisted and finally the old man agreed. The boy began by carrying water from a stream up the hill to the master's hut. He carried water all day and, exhausted, fell into his bed after a meager meal. This went on until the boy became convinced that he had made a mistake in his choice of teachers. On the day he decided to leave, he was carrying water up the hill when without warning he was struck from behind. He did not even see who had done it. A few hours later he was struck again and later struck again. This last time he realized that it was the old man. He was so startled that he forgot to leave. Day after day the boy tried to avoid the pain of the bamboo stick. Slowly over time he became aware of things around him. He avoided obvious ambush places. He learned to dodge the stick a few times out of a hundred. One day he carried his water up to the door of the hut. He stood at the door for some time. He then walked through to be struck over and over as the old man said, "You knew, you knew and you used this door! At least try to make this interesting." (Jennings, 2001)

The boy knew unconsciously that the old man was there and yet he ignored his own intuitions, an important learning for the boy.

Different Perspectives

The ability to view a situation, problem or potential solution from different perspectives is critical for a leader. Perspective enables deeper, better and more complete understanding, creates the potential for creativity and increases the possibility of more effective action.

Often these perspectives are those of different roles, functions, or personalities. The leader might ask him- or herself what finance would say about this, or manufacturing or sales. By seeing a situation from many different viewpoints the leader comes to appreciate both the situation better and the importance of the view.

We had a boss who would come into the office between 5:00 and 6:00 A.M. He would be working on a project of one kind or another, but the real reason was to be available to people. Anyone could come into his office during this hour and talk about anything. He would listen and ask questions. He would engage in the thinking of the other person and help them clarify whatever they were concerned about and guide them to think through solutions. Sometimes he would give advice, but often not. He had a profound understanding of many different perspectives, but not all. Over time and with some struggle, he would add a perspective that he did not have available to him. What made him a leader in this area was this capacity to add perspectives.

Scale

Scale is another of aspect of attentionality. Scale has to do with the distance from, breadth and depth of, or time frame applied to the problem or situation.

When looking at a financial report, it is possible to look at different levels in the report. You can look at a specific transaction, a summary of all similar transactions, a summary of all transactions, the bottom line of the whole report, or this report in a larger framework such as the past ten years. Each of these levels of information gives the viewer a different perception of what is happening to the company.

In John Whitmore's *Coaching for Performance* (1996), like all batting coaches he suggests to baseball batters to concentrate on the ball, but in addition he asks the batter to notice the direction in which the ball is spinning. This reduces the scale of the problem and changes what they are aware of and what is important. At the same time the batter's ability to hit the ball increases. Many organizational change experts suggest that one of the healthy aspects of an organization is a clear understanding of its larger purpose. This is to take a step back from the organization and look at it from a distance.

Understanding the breadth of a situation is also important to be able to change it. To be able to see all of the things that influence an organization helps create a better understanding of the context in which it operates. One of the places the issue of breadth shows up is in problem diagnosis. We all know that we see symptoms of a problem and not the real problem. Getting to the real problem is to understand the dynamics of an organization.

A great deal has been written about the destructive effects of managers and executives operating on a quarterly time frame. Choices are made so that quarterly numbers are maintained. Change programs are evaluated within weeks or a few months of initiation and criticized for not being effective. A new program replaces the old one. The long-term problems are often not even seen, let alone taken on. Short memories and the need for quick results combine to undermine any chance for real change. By taking a longer view, leaders learn the patience needed for real change to happen.

Developing the ability to shift scales, perspectives, and ways of perceiving the situation are important for leadership. These form the ability to become more aware.

Handling Information

Handling information means building the capacity to organize information and to use that organization effectively. This discipline understands how creating, discerning, and using meaning brings structure to information. There are different ways of structuring information. One is to use an existing structure. The second is to understand how to build models based on existing information.

Existing Structure

A model or structure of information for us has a number of characteristics. A model is relevant, internally consistent, simple, elegant, and beautiful. It must be connected to experience, to reality, in order for it to be useful. Models also need to be simple, simple enough to be used and complex enough to be useful. It is a bit like a map for a trip on a freeway over several hundred miles. The map does not need to be very detailed. To find a specific house the map needs to be much more detailed. A model that is elegant is refined, precise, and has a certain grace in form. A beautiful model is pleasing to see and use. Models, for example, with fractal-like characteristics—repeating patterns throughout their structure—have extra resilience.

A model is also inclusive. It takes into account all of the information available. It is tested against a number of circumstances. It should work in a number of situations.

Social Processes

One such model is the Social Processes model (Figure 11.1), which is used in a number of ways. One is to compare the compatibility of a company's culture with that of a country. A careful description of how the company works is placed in each of the categories in the triangle. The same is done for the country. Possible points of difference and similarity are noted. Decisions are made about how to deal with the differences and support the similarities. The advantage of this kind of model is that it tends to be more inclusive than standard business models that focus on economic and legal issues.

Another way this model is used is to look at trends. The focus of the analysis is defined. For each of the categories in the social processes, changes are noted over a period of time. Often this is fifty-plus years, but it can be shorter or longer depending on what is needed. One or more major trends are noted, as are minor trends. Emerging trends are noted. Counter trends are described. Plans can be developed to respond to these trends.

Awareness is knowing about the many models that are available, which ones are useful, and when they are useful. Sometimes the models you need are not available and you have to create your own.

FIGURE 11.1. THE SOCIAL PROCESSES

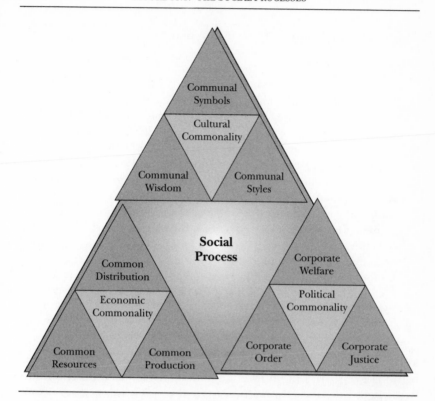

Model Building

Often models to help structure information need to be built. This can be a time-consuming process.

In its simplest form, the process goes like this: Ideas are generated. They are then organized into categories. These categories are tested against criteria and then modified if necessary. Inconsistencies are corrected. Missing data is searched for and added to the ideas. The process is repeated at the next level of the model.

In a sense, everything can be changed, from the original design to the criteria the model is tested against. It is important to maintain one's values throughout the process.

STORIES

The ability to tell and listen to stories may be the key to leadership.

> Stories, including narratives, myths, and fables, constitute a
> uniquely powerful currency in human relationships. Stories speak
> to both parts of the human mind—its reason and its emotion.
> Stories provide a tool for articulating and focusing vision. Stories
> provide a medium of communication, both internally within an
> organization and externally to customers, potential customers,
> business partners, business rivals, investors, and others. Increas-
> ingly, various companies are becoming aware of how stories can
> serve as a market research tool, a public relations and marketing
> tool, and a tool for learning and communicating important insti-
> tutional knowledge about effective business practices, adapting
> to innovation, etc. Stories provide a tool for conceptualizing and
> identifying challenges and opportunities. Stories provide a power-
> ful tool for capturing and leveraging knowledge, one that is com-
> plementary to logical thinking, what we think of as "just the facts."
> (McLellan, 2002)

A great deal of work has been done over the past decade on
knowledge management, and one of the interesting developments
is the use of stories in knowledge management. Organizations are
becoming aware of the value of stories and story telling. "The
World Bank and *IBM* have run storytelling programs, *Hewlett-
Packard* has created a corporate mythology—key stories that illustrate company values—while *Nike* executives tell new employees
tales from Nike's history. In Britain, the *Countryside Agency, Royal
Mail* and *Met Office* have all looked at this too" (Murdoch, 2004).

Terry Bergdall (2005) uses both hard data and stakeholders'
stories in evaluating community development projects. These stories become part of the history of the communities and help bind
them together.

Steve Denning (2002) suggests that there are seven types of organizational stories:

1. Springboard storytelling that ignites transformational change
2. Storytelling that gets people working together
3. Storytelling that transfers knowledge ("Uh-oh!" stories)

4. Storytelling that communicates who you are ("Who's There" stories)
5. Storytelling that transfers values ("What We Stand For" stories)
6. Virus stories: Storytelling that transforms the narrative dynamic
7. Storytelling that leads the way to the future (the "Amen!" stories)

We see stories as having four functions for leaders: transmitting values, creating and supporting community, solving problems, and enabling personal identity.

Transmitting Values and Knowledge

Stories and storytelling transmits the core values of a company. This function is critical to making sense out of situations that otherwise would be disasters. The poisoning scare concerning Tylenol is a good example.

Some twenty years ago, bottles of Tylenol were laced with cyanide and seven people died in Chicago. Johnson & Johnson's chief executive officer, James Burke, ordered all of the millions of bottles removed from the stores and spent a huge amount of money informing the public of what had happened. According to Alicia Korten, an expert on stories:

> Through that investment he gained two things that were precious—he may have saved some lives, and two, he gained a story—a story that is embedded in the public consciousness as to what Johnson and Johnson stands for. The story is now famous. . . .
>
> What Johnson and Johnson has is something I call a Core Values Story. A story that communicates to others what their values are, and also a story that makes them clearer as a company about what they stand for. In addition to being a good ethical decision, it also turned out to be a tremendous business decision. Here they have a story about their values embedded in the public consciousness. (Korten, 2003)

The story is both an internal story and a public story. It communicates to employees and to the public what the values are at Johnson & Johnson. Core value stories to a large degree embody the values of the community. They are often stories about origins, struggles, and destiny. They can be about corporate heroes.

Some stories are used in induction programs to prepare people to work for a company. Such a company is Nike. "The best way for a company to create a prosperous future is to make sure all of its employees understand the company's past. That's why many veteran execs at Nike spend time telling corporate campfire stories" (Ransdell, 2000, p. 44). In Nike's case, these stories are for the most part for internal consumption.

> Most people have heard of Nike CEO Phil Knight, a middle-distance runner who turned selling shoes out of his car into a footwear-and-apparel colossus. But few know of Nike cofounder Bill Bowerman, Knight's coach, or of Steve Prefontaine, the now-deceased runner who was also coached by Bowerman and whose crusade for better equipment inspired Bowerman and Knight to build the Nike empire. Yet, inside Nike, those three figures are more relevant to the company's sense of identity than any of its superstar spokespeople. (Ransdell, 2000, p. 44)

Every new hire hears these stories from senior managers and executives. For Nike this is not a passive process. Technical representatives go to Eugene, Oregon, and run on the track where Bowerman coached and visit the site of the car crash where Prefontaine died.

Stories can also transmit knowledge. A salesperson might tell a story to junior salespeople about how she closed a deal. The story communicates more than facts. It shares the way decisions are made and thus the ethics at play. It communicates emotions, conflicts, and successes and the human side of the organization. By creating drama in the story, the storyteller involves the audience so that they are part of the process.

Creating and Supporting Community

Stories and storytelling help create and support communities: communities of practice, teams as communities, business as communities, and social groups as communities. Traditionally these are stories told of beginnings, endings, and the struggles in between. When we worked in a village in Peru, we heard many stories of the beginning of the community. They all revolved around what was called the "founding families." The village is located in the coastal desert, inland a few miles from the Pacific Ocean and the coastal highway. It is on a plateau overlooking the Mala River. In this desert almost nothing grows, so it was simply a flat plain of sand and rock a few miles square. These founding families contructed homes and dug an irrigation canal five miles long along the side of a mountain cliff. They created fields and irrigation ditches and planted fruit trees, cotton, beans, and potatoes. Over the two-plus years it took to do this, they had to carry water up the side of the cliff. They camped out for the whole time while the work was being done. It is hard to believe what it took to make a living and build a village at the same time. The people of today are still proud of these founding families. A five-day-long fiesta is held each year to celebrate this beginning. The stories we heard contained all of these elements but more. They were stories of struggle, sacrifice, and creation.

The stories make connections between people. They enable people to see the connections among themselves, other members, and the community as a whole. The stories enable people to identify with the community. Even though we were outsiders and not really part of the village community, we felt proud of the founding families. Somehow we were included in the story.

The stories connect people to the land. Every house, street, and irrigation ditch had a story connected to it. While we were there, each section of the village constructed a "mini-park" in their part of the village. When the mayor complained about young people sitting late at night playing the guitar and engaging in some flirting there, the mini-parks became part of the story of the village.

Solving Problems

Stories and storytelling have at least three functions in problem solving. They can be used to remind people of the values of the organization and as such create a framework within which to make a decision. Stories are used to communicate knowledge that is important in understanding the situation and how the problem might be solved. Stories also are used as problem-solving tools.

John Seely Brown's (2001) analysis of photocopy repairmen, which we mentioned briefly in Chapter Four is a case in point. The company in question has a complete series of repair manuals and training processes for company representatives and technicians. The reps go to the customer's site and make any repairs necessary. The technicians act as support for the reps when they could not find a solution to a problem with a machine. The policy is that if the process suggested in the repair manual and taught in courses didn't succeed, then the equipment was to be replaced. For a variety of reasons, the repairmen and the technicians were reluctant to replace machines.

> Solving the problem *in situ* required constructing a coherent account of the malfunction out of the incoherence of the data and documentation. To do this, the rep and the specialist embarked on a long story-telling procedure. The machine, with its erratic behavior, mixed with information from the user and memories from the technicians, provided essential ingredients that the two aimed to account for in a composite story. The process of forming a story was, centrally, one of diagnosis. This process, it should be noted, begins as well as ends in a communal understanding of the machine that is wholly unavailable from the canonical documents. (Brown, 2001)

When the repairmen don't have a solution, they begin by telling stories about what has happened so far, what tests have been run, what the results are, and why these results are of little help. They begin remembering some similar photocopiers or symptoms and recall how they were dealt with. Users are asked to share their experiences with the machine. In this flow of gathering information, recalling similar situations, possible problems are diagnosed and the machines are tested. Slowly a solution is arrived at, far more frequently than the manuals and training suggest is possible. The company saves money, the customer is satisfied, and the repairmen's self-esteem and reputations are intact.

At the other end of the problem-solving spectrum is the use of storytelling and stories in strategic planning. Three obvious ones come to mind: scenarios, appreciative inquiry, and Lego Serious Play. All of these are about using and telling stories. In scenario writing, the stories are about the future of the organization. Scenarios offer real alternatives to each other and to the present moment. Appreciative inquiry begins by asking people to tell stories about when they experienced the organization functioning at its best. Naturally, the questions evoking these stories are much more specific to the issue being addressed. Lego Serious Play combines the use of storytelling and the tactile and visual experience of constructing a future using Lego blocks.

Enabling Personal Identity

Stories also create an identity. They form our "self-story." Our self-story is both public and private. Or rather, parts of our self-story are public and parts are private.

A story is more than a chronology of events. It is also an interpretation of those events. It includes the emotions surrounding those events. It tells about what is important and suggests why that is so. Like corporate stories, personal stories are indicators of values and purposes.

Stories can be about how you came to be who you are. Stories can be about overcoming problems—mental health, obesity, addiction, disease, accidents, disasters, and more. Every professional group seems to have stories of "the worst I ever"—the worst class, the worst customer, the worst software catastrophe, the worst patient, and on and on. Stories are also about the future, what I am going to do, what I will become, why I am making this particular move. One interesting change from the old to the new paradigm is in CVs. Time was when a CV was a documented list of what you did—facts and dates, period. That was what an employer needed to know. Increasingly, employers look for your story about what you did. It has to fit the facts, of course, but your interpretation of the facts gives relevant information about you that the facts alone never reveal.

Constructing a personal story consciously is an adventure, sometimes painful, but often enlivening. Not easily done, it requires both a close look at the facts of our lives and keen decisions about what we intend to say those facts mean. This is important because in today's paradigm, what we say the stories mean becomes what they mean.

THE LEVELS OF AWARENESS

Awareness has four levels, being sensitive toward the self, sensitive toward the world, sensitive to possibility, and sensitive to awe. Leadership depends on being brutally honest about the current situation. Leadership is about seeing the truth, both the positive and the negative aspects.

SENSITIVITY TOWARD THE SELF

Self-awareness is about paying attention to your internal and external life. You know both the things you do well and those things you don't do well. Unfortunately, neither your own reflections are very trustworthy nor are those external to you. By continually asking, "Why are people responding the way they are, and why am I responding the way I am?" some patterns will emerge. When they do, changes can be tried to see if different responses occur.

We all have dark sides to our personalities. The dark side emerges when we face situations in which we are destructive to others or are self-destructive. Normally we are not aware of them, so we need to have them pointed out. Feedback from trusted friends or colleagues is critical here.

Sometimes becoming self-aware can take place in an instant, such as in this traditional Zen story:

There was a young monk in China who was a very serious practitioner of the Dharma. Once, this monk came across something he did not understand, so he went to ask the master. When the master heard the question, he kept laughing. The master then stood up and walked away, still laughing.

The young monk was very disturbed by the master's reaction. For the next three days, he could not eat, sleep nor think properly. At the end of three days, he went back to the master and told the master how disturbed he had felt. When the master heard this, he said, "Monk, do you know what your problem is? Your problem is that *you are worse than a clown!*"

The monk was shocked to hear that, "Venerable Sir, how can you say such a thing?! How can I be worse than a clown?"

The master explained, "A clown enjoys seeing people laugh. You? You feel disturbed because another person laughed. Tell me, are you not worse than a clown?"

When the monk heard this, he began to laugh. He was enlightened.

SENSITIVITY TO THE WORLD

Awareness of the world has to do with the ability to expand the use of your senses and being aware in new kinds of ways.

Drew Brees, the American football quarterback from San Diego, practices passing the ball. "The receiver is watching the quarterback walk another five yards down field, waiting as Brees pivots and fires. The football smacks the receiver's hands square in the palms. 'The first time it happened, I couldn't believe it.' Said Malcom Floyd, a rookie receiver" (Jenkins, 2005, p. 5). The difference between this quarterback and others is that he does this with his eyes closed.

While talking with the coach at our gym, he described similar things in gymnastics. He described how no matter what direction you are looking in, you are always aware of exactly where you are in relation to the floor or the bars or rings. It is not a matter of seeing, but of sensing the space.

Similarly, you can walk into a business and immediately feel the state of health of the organization. A healthy, creative company feels different when you experience it, although it is difficult to pin down in specifics. It certainly has to do with the way the space is kept, what employees do and say with each other as well as with clients. In a sense, every part of the company is represented in the reception area, or the manufacturing plant, or the customer service outlet. Every part reflects the whole, like a hologram.

SENSITIVITY TO POSSIBILITY

Recently, studies by Professor Richard Wiseman as reported in RedWorld.biz (2004) have been conducted into why people are lucky. There is a difference between chance and luck. A person has no control over chance. Chance is the random acts that happen to us. Interestingly, luck doesn't have much to do with chance but with what a person does with the circumstances they find themselves in. Lucky people create their own luck. Lucky people see opportunities that unlucky people do not see.

> Some of the research looked at, for example, how we see opportunities in life. So in one experiment we asked people to flick through a newspaper and to just count the number of pictures or photographs in there. About halfway through we would place a huge half-page advert saying spot this and win £100. Well it was the lucky people that saw it—the unlucky ones didn't. It's a very good

example of how you create your own luck. The unlucky people are often so focused they don't step back, see the bigger picture and see the opportunities. (RedWorld.biz, 2004)

Wiseman has four principles of lucky people:

1. *Maximize Chance Opportunities.* Lucky people use chance to their benefit. They are aware of opportunities, create them, and act on them. They can do this by building strong networks, are laid back in their lives, and are open to new ideas and experience.

2. *Listen to Your Lucky Hunches.* Lucky people pay attention to their intuitions and act on them. They develop their ability to sharpen their intuitions by using practices such as meditation and other techniques to clear their minds.

3. *Expect Good Fortune.* Lucky people expect things to get better over the long term. This allows them to keep going when things have gone wrong. This also develops positive relationships with others.

4. *Turn Bad Luck into Good.* Lucky people use self-talk and self-created attitudes to deal with bad things that happen. They recognize that things could be worse, they move on from ill fortune, they assume responsibility for the situation. (Pink, 2003)

Ann Watson, another researcher on luck, suggests several factors that people use to improve their luck. They have extensive social support networks and use them. Lucky people take more and greater risks than unlucky people. They see opportunities where others do not. They have positive intent and a high level of self-awareness. They persevere, staying with something long enough for the results to come to fruition. They are flexible in finding solutions to problems. They take responsibility for what they do and who they are (RedWorld.biz, 2004).

Sensitivity to Awe

Leaders appreciate those moments that seem to appear out of nowhere and add delight and significance to their lives.

One aspect of this is to see beyond the appearances of mundane things. We fail to see through reality to the complexity of relationships that constitutes it. Take a typical dinner. On the plate is a boiled potato covered with parsley and butter. The potato is much more. It was prepared by a cook, served by someone, and will be cleaned up by someone. The cook bought it at a store paid for by money earned at a job. A stock person put it on the shelf. A truck delivered it to the store. Someone unloaded the truck. It had been stored in a distribution center. Another truck brought it to a distribution center from the farm. The farmer who grew it is also present in that potato. Worms, bacteria, fungus, and the weather created the dirt it grew in. A magnificently complex network of relationships brought that potato to you; it's a miracle arriving on your plate. Our capacity to be present to these relationships can be developed, and leaders are continually improving their capacity to see beyond appearances.

Leadership also has the capacity to be surprised. Being open to the unknown allows surprises to happen. Being able to *not* put experiences into a box is important here. The sort of "It's only a potato" response prevents us from being surprised. This response is so quick we are unaware of it. To de-box the potato, we have to go back to the precognitive moment in the experience, when we experience the potato and hadn't put it into the potato category. Paying attention to the uniqueness of the experience is important if we are going to be surprised.

Conclusion

Developing the discipline of Awareness is more than knowing a lot or being able to espouse theories. It is being sensitive to what is happening around you and what is happening inside you. It is developing the capacity to understand the world, who you are, and how these two interact. It is appreciating being surprised by what you don't know and don't understand. It is putting this understanding and knowledge in a context so that you can act if you choose to. It is the ability to move from one framework or perspective to another to better comprehend.

Time needs to be taken to develop the capacity of Awareness. Becoming aware, you would think, is just a matter of opening your eyes and paying attention, but it is that and more. It is having models of reality that help you understand what is going on and enable you to act effectively. We believe that this time and effort is the path to Awareness.

◆ ◆ ◆

Practices for Awareness

Here we offer two good starting points for Awareness: Journal Writing and Personal Feedback.

Journal Writing

A journal is a Web blog, book, notebook, or any collection of written thoughts in which one writes about events in detail, especially including descriptions of the situation, feelings, opinions, beliefs, hopes, fears, reflections, and the like.

People use journals for a variety of reasons, including self-understanding, focusing awareness, getting organized, solving problems, keeping a record of creative ideas that would otherwise be lost, stepping back and reflecting, as therapy, celebrating or expressing gratitude, and/or keeping a record of events in your life.

Different techniques are used to keep a journal, including the following:

- *Stream of Conscious* or *Free Writing* is writing whatever comes to mind. The stream of conscious writer records everything. When they reach a block in writing they can write, "I can't think of anything to write." Or "I am bored out of my mind." Or whatever comes to mind. It may seem chaotic or disorganized and unreflective, but the discipline is to keep writing. The idea is that as you continue to write you will begin to uncover deeper aspects of yourself. An alternative to this method is called *Focused Free Writing*, which begins with a topic and you try to write as much about that topic as you can in the same way as free writing.
- *Descriptive Writing* is putting down in great detail what is happening in the world around you. It is important to not only what has happened but your and others' reactions to these happenings.
- *Mind Mapping* begins with a circle or square in the middle of a sheet of paper that contains the central idea being focused on. As ideas about the topic come to mind, a line is drawn from the circle or square with the topic in it to another shape in which the new idea is put. A number of subtopics are connected to the topic. As ideas are generated about the subtopics, lines are drawn from them to shapes with these sub-subtopics. This continues until the page is full or all ideas are exhausted.

- *Prompts* can be use to stimulate thinking and writing. A list of questions or important issues is created and each one is placed on a slip of paper and put in a bowl. Select one slip of paper from the bowl and begin writing about it. As thinking runs down about the first idea, pull another slip and continue writing. A list of words can also be placed in a bowl and used as prompts. An interesting creativity exercise is to select several slips of paper and write about the relationship among them.
- *List Writing* is a technique in which you don't create narratives but simply list of things. You can start with something like "What are the events of the day?" or "What have I learned today?" If these lists are going to be used later, it is a good idea to put them in complete sentences; if they are simply a list of words it is easy to forget what they meant.
- *People sketches* are verbal descriptions of other people. Several may be done of the same person over time. They need to be in great detail, appearance, expressions, moods, comments, gestures, and so on. Your responses to these things are good to record.

There are a number of other techniques, but these should give you an idea of the kinds you can do. The discipline of course is to do it regularly and frequently. Spending ten to thirty minutes a day is a good target for journal writing.

Personal Feedback

As second useful technique is to put yourself into situations where you can receive personal feedback. We suppose that this is the role that the popular image of a court jester played for royalty. An effective leader finds ways of getting an understanding of what they are doing well and what they are doing badly.

A practice used by the Institute of Cultural Affairs and continued by our company, Imaginal Training, is to do a debrief at the end of every day during a program, whether a two-day course or a month-long research project. We ask three basic questions:

1. What went well today?
2. If we were to do this again what could we do to improve the program? and
3. What might each of us do personally to improve our performance?

The key is not only to create a system of providing feedback but also to utilize the insights to improve performance.

◆ ◆ ◆

Exercise for Awareness

Meeting the Rock

To consider awareness, select a rock from the ground. Look at the rock closely. Look at the various sides to the rock. Now fill in the following boxes:

Look at the whole rock:	
What are some shapes that you see on the rock?	Describe in as much detail as possible the shape, its edges, interior, color, texture, and so on.
Select one of the shapes you see. (Draw or describe one of them.)	
What are some of the shapes within that shape? (Draw or describe one of them.)	Describe in as much detail as possible the shape, its edges, interior, color, texture, and so on.
Select one of the shapes you see. (Draw or describe one of them.)	
What are some of the shapes within that shape? (Draw or describe one of them.)	Describe in as much detail as possible the shape, its edges, interior, color, texture, and so on.
Continue the process until you have to imagine what you are seeing. (Use the back of the sheet to continue.)	

When you have finished your charts, discuss together:

- What are some of the shapes you described?
- What was the most difficult part of the exercise?
- If you were to observe a group in the same amount of detail what would you have to do?
- How could you become more aware of the groups you work with?
- What would be a symbol or ritual you could use while leading a group to remind yourself to be more aware?

CHAPTER TWELVE

ACTION: EFFECTIVE DOING

Dee Hock (1999) quotes from W. N. Murray's *The Scottish Himalayan Expedition* to point to what action is.

> Until one is committed there is always hesitancy, the chance to draw back, always ineffectiveness. Concerning all acts of initiative and creation there is one elementary truth the ignorance of which kills countless ideas and splendid plans. The moment one commits oneself, then providence moves too. Multitudes of things occur to help that which otherwise could never occur. A stream of events issues from the decision, raising to one's favor all manner of unforeseen accidents, meetings and materials assistance which no one could have dreamed would come their way. (Hock, 1999, p. 308)

Action is an important step toward the development of selfhood. It is critically understanding the world, accomplishing what you want, and being a presence. In applying your understanding to the situation you live in, you learn whether that understanding is valid and how it could be improved. Action tests your thinking while thinking gives you a direction to your action.

We have unfortunately separated thinking and doing in our society, although the bias toward thinking is changing to some degree. Managers are thinkers and employees are doers. Creativity is thought of as inventing an idea, not of making it work. From our perspective they are both required and of equal value.

The way you behave determines what kind of presence you have in a group.

Action is in tension with Awareness. Our action is based on an understanding of the world and what it is about. As Ortega y Gasset

(1962) says, in order to survive we are compelled to do something, no matter the situation or our disposition.

Not only are we driven to act, but we also have a desire to be effective in what we do. We act in order to accomplish something. Sometimes we are not sure why we are doing things. Not infrequently, we realize in the midst of acting that we are doing the wrong thing. It is not unheard of for us to do things that are clearly self-destructive or destructive of others; even we are aware how wrong they are. We smoke (or used to). We eat too much. We select partners who are unmistakably bad for us. Whether we act for our own interests, the interests of others, or even in destructive ways, the action has some purpose, even if the purpose is wholly unconscious.

WHAT IS ACTION?

We are not using the word *action* here in the popular sense of, "Don't just stand there; do something! Anything! Now!" It is not action for the sake of acting. It is not acting for the sake of doing something that seems useful even if it is not effective. It is not doing something to deal with personal or collective guilt. It is not about *you saving the world*. All of those reasons are focused on *you* and not on the purpose of the action. Effective action is about accomplishing something; it is detached from the self.

Effective action is also something more than mastering technique. In Daisetz T. Suzuki's introduction to *Zen in the Art of Archery* (Herrigel, 1989), he says, "If one really wishes to be master of an art, technical knowledge is not enough. One has to transcend technique so the art becomes an 'artless art' growing out of the Unconscious" (p. vii). In this kind of action, a profound mastery of skills is required. Constant practice is needed. At some point skills and self get in the way of mastery and must be given up to be effective. This is not only a matter of Zen. Learning theorists speak of "unconscious competence," which is to say the individual has a skill so well developed that he or she exercises it without thinking about it. If you habitually drive a car, you may find yourself pulling into your driveway at the end of the day without having thought through in much detail how you got there—you have indeed transcended technique!

Effective action is being able to do the seemingly impossible. This chapter is about developing the competence to succeed at what we intend. The effective actor also turns the failure to reach goals into opportunities while never denying the failure. Action is always about managing change. In a changing world we are always either initiating, going along with, redirecting, or blocking change of some kind or another.

Effective action transcends the tension between immediate action and paralysis by analysis. At one end of this tension is spontaneous, unreflected action. From this perspective, thoughtful preparation is seen as a self-imposed trap, hindering creativity and freedom.

From the other end of the tension, spontaneity is seen as simply irresponsible, giving permission to do whatever comes to mind without regard for consequences. Here is the meticulous planner who thinks through every detail and accounts for every contingency. This is responsible, claim its advocates. It takes into consideration as many of the known factors as possible. To its detractors, this is death by planning. It is a way of avoiding action and risk in a futile search for certitude.

Another approach altogether is avoidance. Simply waiting until the problem goes away or is corrected by the system is an effective approach requiring the least effort and cost. Organizational systems do act on problems and often solve them or at least move them around in such a way that they are not immediately discernable.

All of these approaches sometimes get things done, personally and for the organization. Action as we are talking about it here, however, is not just getting something done. It is bringing your full self to bear on the world. This is not just acting, but moving in union with life in such a way that change happens. People confuse activity or nonactivity with action, and it is not the same thing. A Zen artist may spend hours sitting on a beach before a canvas and then in a few seconds produce a masterpiece. The hours spent sitting are not to plan the painting, quite the opposite. The mind is settled; calm is achieved. The paint is mixed and brushes are prepared. In a moment the painting appears. What emerges is unknown until it is completed.

Difficulties of Action

Why is action difficult today? One issue is time pressure. We all act in increasingly shorter time frames. When a change process is introduced and the results are not immediate, the process may be dropped. A great deal of literature has been written about managing change. Companies shift from one change process to another in the hope of getting better results faster.

Katzenbach and Smith (1992) describe the development process of a work group into a real team. During the initial transition period, productivity often declines while issues like creating shared purpose and approaches are worked through. The team who expects to become a team instantly can only do so by creating a superficial bond, and this is something that the first winds of real crisis can blow apart.

A similar thing happens physically when you enter a fitness program. When we first began to go to the gym every morning, the instructor tested us and developed a program for both of us. What was most helpful was his statement that for the first month our fitness would actually deteriorate. We would then become more and more fit until we reached the level we wanted to sustain. Had he not said that and worked with us on a daily basis at the beginning, we would have limped home never to return in that first painful week. Would that board, executive teams, and managers were given the time it actually takes for change to genuinely take hold, or had the courage to demand it!

The Issues of Action for Facilitative Leaders

Effective action is intent, the capacity to will successful activities. Action is found in the execution and not in the plan, no matter how comprehensive or elegant that may be. What happens is what determines the future, nothing else. Action is effective to the degree that behavior changes in the organization.

Three issues face a leader when considering action. They all have to do with effective action: intent, implementation, and impact.

INTENT

In this book we spend an entire chapter on intent (see Chapter Nine: Intentionality), but here we would like to spend a few paragraphs looking specifically at its influence on action.

We continually run into situations in which change plans are sitting on a shelf, never looked at again after the end of the planning process. Enough planning was done to create a plan, but not enough was done to create change. The intent is different, and it may take some work with you as leader and with the group to clarify the intent. To be effective, action begins in these cases before the planning process ever begins. Different practical questions come to mind when the end product is change rather than a plan about changing.

Another issue in the area of intent has to do with revising plans. Plans sometime crumble under the onslaught of the arrival of new information. A plan is a few weeks old: new data appears that suggests that the plan may need revision, and teams can get stuck trying to figure out what to do. When do you revise plans and when do you stick with them? We find that by setting revision dates for plans, such as at the end of a quarter or every half-year, it is easier to put new information into a file to be looked at when the revision is done. The decision to look later must be made self-consciously. Sometimes new data does mean that the plans need revision, but it must not be allowed to freeze the process.

If plans are continually being revised whenever new information arrives, perhaps the planning process needs to be looked at. This pattern of behavior needs to be looked at. Is enough data gathering being done? Are projections overly optimistic or pessimistic? Are the issues being looked at in enough depth or breadth? Are the root causes being discerned?

A third issue regarding intent has to do with execution. Here again, the intent is change, not planning, but how can that intent be realized? A plan is created. It needs to be checked, published, and rolled out. This can take weeks or even months. When a really great plan is created, especially when those affected by the plan build it, a great deal of motivation exists. Unfortunately, this motivation is easily dissipated. The very best time to begin executing a plan is the moment it is completed. Anything that can start immediately, even as documentation and approvals are progressing, can use the rich flood of motivation that exists, and keep it flowing and building until the rest of the documentation is in place.

IMPLEMENTATION

A second action issue for the facilitative leader has to do with the way a plan is implemented. There is a bias toward serial implementation of plans: first complete this part and then start that other part, and when it is done move on to the third part. Naturally, some things depend on others, and in these cases serial implementation is necessary. However, this is not often the case. Not everything has to wait.

In large-scale change, the more things that can take place at once, the more integrated the change experience becomes. While it is easy to isolate change processes that are aimed at only one thing at a time, it is harder to ignore a process that is taking place in many different points at once. It avoids the tendency to identify a change process with the first group for whom it is rolled out. ("This seems to be really just a process for the secretaries, not us.") In this approach, every aspect of change process that can begin at the same time is begun.

Different people are interested in and have passion for different things. This approach taps into that motivation from the very beginning. Some people will begin to work on one area and get frustrated or bored and move to another area. The parallel approach provides them with a way of contributing when this happens. We find that if this part of the project is self-organizing, it can have a greater chance of success. In a workshop done by Shell's Wells Global Network, representatives from around the world used the self-organizing process called "Open Space" to select and work in parallel on projects that affected them locally. Projects were linked to work spaces and volunteers went to work on the project or projects they had enthusiasm about. The time to work was limited, as many people wanted to work on more than one project. In this process people were required to select areas in which they have the most interest. Working this way wherever possible allows people of divergent interests to get involved, a process that is much more difficult when people are only involved when their part of the change process comes along and then withdraw when it is done.

In this scale and type of change project, a kind of synergy is created. People see more going on. Things are happening. Morale increases. As things are accomplished, new ideas develop and are implemented. This same process happens in business organizations.

We did a workshop with the personnel staff department of a company of thirty thousand people. The workshop took three days, and at the end there were a number of projects that needed to be started within the next ninety days. Most would be completed in that time frame. First, we asked for people who would be responsible for implementing each of the project areas. Then we asked people to volunteer for one of the projects that they were most committed to getting done. Everyone signed up, and was ready to report their successes at the end of the ninety days.

The company was downsizing, and this department was getting new tasks all the time to carry out the staff reductions. Even though some of the reductions would include themselves, morale remained high as teams put their tactics into place.

IMPACT

Much of the impact of any action a leader takes is not in the new stuff or office or factory that have been acquired but in the perception and behavior of employees, suppliers, and clients. For change to happen, people need to see and believe change has happened. They then act in a new way that is consistent with their perceptions. The stuff can be used to reinforce the perception of change, but the real change is in the people themselves. Care needs to be taken in changing the way people think and do. This section will talk about the balance in large-scale efforts between quick and easy actions and actions that require more effort, time, and money. It will discuss what we call symbolic acts. It also will talk about the issue of impatience.

Obviously, some actions take longer than others. Commissioning, creating, and installing a new computer system will certainly take longer than hiring a new assistant. In most change processes, the small, quickly implemented activities are much more numerous than the big steps that take significant time and effort. These myriad short-term, easily done things need to be balanced with those that take longer and need more work.

Think of the image of the two swords of a Samurai warrior. "A *katana* is the long sword that is most associated with Samurai." The blade is approximately twenty-four to twenty-nine inches long. The *ko-gatna* is the short sword and is really a knife that was also used as a weapon. Some Samurai were proficient at throwing it (Locke, 2003). While most warriors used the swords one at a time, some used both at once.

A project may include many, even hundreds, of easily done, low-cost projects that contribute to the overall plan or increase the visibility of the change process. Consider these the change process "short swords." Although no one of them makes a big difference in itself, the sum total of activities can be impressive. Above all, short sword activities offer engagement and motivation. These activities are a bit like a pointillism painting in which the artist uses little dots of primary colors placed close together with the effect that if you step back the eye rather than the brush mixing them reproduces any color that the artist wants. These little dots of action when seen from a larger perspective are experienced as a high degree of change. When a project comprises short sword things alone, however, fundamental structures never improve, even though lots of people are actively involved and very motivated.

The fundamental, long-term projects, physical or social infrastructure, may take months or even years. Much of this work needs professional expertise and is not especially stimulating. Think of things such as installing electricity in a community, changing financial systems over to a new software program, or rolling out new personnel management policies. Funds need to be raised, contracts awarded, paperwork sorted out, and programming done. This sort of project is virtually invisible until construction starts, and no one benefits until it is operational. In fact, the day-to-day experience of people may be worse while systems are in transition than it was before. When the focus of a project is on these things alone, no matter how substantial and eventually rewarding, people can easily become disenchanted and demotivated. By the time new services start, they may have forgotten that they were the ones who proposed the changes in the first place. Nevertheless, it is these changes of fundamental systems that may have the greatest impact in the long term. These substantive projects can be seen as the "long sword."

The trick is to use both of these swords together, in a creative and coordinated way, with each one reinforcing the other. Sustaining motivation means creating a balance of activities such that work is going on in several different spheres at the same time. When a lull appears, short, quick activities should be initiated.

Another dimension of maintaining momentum in a project is creating ongoing indicators of change, so that people are continually reminded that something new is happening. Wherever possible, change needs to be made visible. We are all familiar with billboards that announce the future location of a highway, office building, or apartment block long before construction begins. It shows there is change afoot. The same principle can apply in any change process. The manager of a wide area network for a telecom company understood this. The department had performance measures that came out every week, but few people took the trouble to look them up. Our colleague coded each team with a color, and posted on the bulletin board at the end of every week colored circles that corresponded in size to the productivity of that team. Everyone in the office knew at a glance how they were doing.

SYMBOLIC ACTS

Some acts have greater impact on the spirit and motivation of a group than others. Some of these actions make a positive, exciting statement about the organization. Some say how important what they are doing is. Some acts honor the past or the present. Some anticipate the future. Understanding and enabling symbolic action is a key task of any facilitative leader.

Often these acts are quite small but highly significant. In the first of what could be contentious and difficult negotiations between labor union officials and a major Dutch company, just as everyone was sitting down opposite each other, one of the leaders of the company's negotiating team stood up and walked around the table pouring coffee and tea, beginning with the head of the union team. This gesture reduced the tension, demonstrating what the style of dialogue could be like.

Some acts make a huge difference. They change the way things are perceived. The people in a small Peruvian village where we once worked believed that the difference between a dusty nowhere and a proper village was that a village had a well-maintained plaza in front of the church. In this dry, desert area, flowers are especially important in a plaza—they demonstrate quite visibly that someone cares enough to water the plaza every day. One of the early acts of the development project was the construction of a plaza. An old millstone had been found when the village was first built some hundred years previously. It was a relic of the pre-Spanish civilization that had once thrived in the valley. It was the community's physical link with their own heritage. The stone was about three feet across and weighed hundreds of pounds. The youth of the village built a base on which the stone could rest and mounted it in the center of the plaza space. Irrigation canals were dug and trees and flowers planted. A sidewalk was constructed and benches installed. Over a period of a few months, the voluntary labor of a few young people tuned an empty space into a real village.

Sometimes symbolic acts simply say that change is happening. They give people courage to keep going. Our personnel department colleagues knew their change was real the day that they moved into new quarters. Only on that day did most of them come to believe that something real was happening. Skepticism turned to cautious belief.

IMPATIENCE

Impatience can be an issue for facilitative leaders. Results in projects and change processes need to be quick, sometimes unreasonably quick. The impact of quarterly financial reports and the need to respond immediately to competition is well known. Yet many change processes take years of quiet effort before results can be seen. In this sort of situation, actions do not result in noticeable change for a number of years of effort.

Pressure to do something immediately—this ingrained impatience—also results in desiring simple solutions to complex problems. Of course, problems can be made more complex than they need to be. The more common failing, however, is to overly simplify them. A common example from event facilitation is the dominant participant in a meeting. The simple issue is that one person is grabbing too much airtime and needs to be stopped. The facilitator should stop it, now!

It is not at all a simple situation, in fact. People may dominate discussions for any number of reasons. The facilitator must have patience enough to understand the dynamics in the group before responding.

Running a meeting is a very simple task compared to some of the matters that we face in leading projects—increasing market share, cutting costs, attracting skilled new employees. We live in a world of growing complexity. The amount of time it takes to analyze any situation is growing because of the number of perspectives that need to be considered. Yet we block our ability to act effectively when we oversimplify.

A related way in which impatience impedes effective action is the tendency to jump to solutions. A problem or opportunity is placed on the table, and there are one or more obvious courses of action. This creates two difficulties. Normally when a problem or opportunity is presented, only the symptoms are described. The whole situation may not yet be well understood. The complexities may not yet have been explored. Underlying causes may not yet be understood. The relationship between the problem or opportunity and the various parts of the organization may not yet be clear. And yet, solutions are at hand. The temptation is to apply the obvious solution, get moving, and avoid the risk and irritation of having to invent and sell a new approach.

One company, needing to cut costs, had an annual pattern of freezing all of its outsourced projects in November because of budget overruns. A favored strategy to deal with this was to keep a project running, but submit its November and December bills in January, which simply carried the problem over to the following year, when the freeze had to come earlier. An alternate solution was for suppliers to stop work with the understanding that they would resume in January under the new budget. To recoup their losses at the end of the year, suppliers added personnel or raised prices when they resumed in January. The freeze was an obvious solution for dealing with a budget overrun, but it only managed to increase costs year on year.

Finally, impatience impedes action by leading to unintended consequences. In a downsizing process, the assistant editor of an internal journal was let go on short notice. Some months later, the department began receiving complaints about subscriptions not being changed or cancelled. The assistant editor had for years handled subscription issues, even though it was not part of her job description. During the reorganization, she had never been required to report what work she actually did, and that function had simply fallen through the cracks. This was not the last straw, but within a year the department was sold off completely and the journal abandoned.

Beyond impatience is avoidance. Sometimes we put things off because we simply do not know what to do, or we hope they will go away or that things will perhaps get better of themselves. The great difficulty with avoidance is that is does indeed work occasionally, like curing a cold. You can treat your cold and it will go away in ten days or so, or you can just endure it and it will go away in ten days or so. Unfortunately, this happens just often enough to make avoidance seem to be a viable option, even though it is not.

THE FOUR LEVELS OF ACTION

The discipline of Action has four levels. The first level is mission, followed by the venture, the election, and finally ecstasy. It is the experience of deepening your capacity to act effectively and meaningfully. If Awareness is about understanding, then Action is about accomplishing. Action is doing the vision found in Focus and experiencing the delight found with a Sense of Wonder.

THE MISSION

This first level is experienced as though what you are doing is exactly right for you and the world in which you live. You hear people say, "I suddenly knew this is what my life is all about." Mission is both an "Ah-ha!" experience and a choice. You hear people say, "Live for the weekend!" as if five days a week are not living, and two days are real life. This seems an excessively high price to pay for anything. There is work/life balance, which at its extreme becomes a drive to reduce the price in meaningless work time that has to be paid for the more meaningful family and personal time. We are exaggerating here, of course, but the trade-off of the organization's time versus your time is no exaggeration. Our society suggests this dichotomy, but it is we who choose to split our lives in half this way. In the discipline of Action we make another choice, a choice for connection.

Leaders in the discipline of Action have connected home and work, family and colleagues into a single whole—one life. The mission level of Action is throwing yourself into getting your hopes and dreams, your vision for society and your organization into reality. This is not doing for the sake of doing but doing for the sake of the world. It is interior activity and stillness.

We have often had the opportunity to participate in very intense research assemblies, consultation workshops, and training courses. These programs tend to start the day at 6:00 A.M. and run right through the evening with preparation for the next day. Especially in pilot programs, these are very exciting times, punctuated with real breakthroughs. The time is simultaneously exhausting and exhilarating. There are fantastic breakthroughs and total defeats, and a profound sense of cooperation among the team. When you see people from such a team even years later, you may still feel connected by the bond of that single month's or week's great work together.

The same thing may happen in family events. Some years ago, our family bought a new house and moved into it on very short notice. We painted together, laid carpets, put up shelves, installed the kitchen, and left the old house spotless and empty with about two hours to spare. When we are together now, ten years later, we still laugh together at some of the events of those busy days. This being connected to mission is the first level of Action.

THE VENTURE

Contrary to what our society says, doing is not just putting in time. It is bringing our life energy to bear on something that needs to be done, no matter how trivial or underrated that may be. Following mission is venture, wherein you come to see your every action contributing to your mission. If it isn't, then there is no reason for doing it. It feels wrong, inappropriate, a waste of time. In this situation it is activities that are meaningful, not your thoughts or what you have to say about your activities. There is a Ukrainian folk song that goes something like,

> On Monday morning you told me you loved me,
> but Monday night you were with someone else.
> On Tuesday morning you told me you loved me,
> but Tuesday night you were with someone else . . .
>   and so on.

Clearly what happened at night spoke more clearly and effectively that what was said in the morning.

At the level of the venture, you are focused onto having your say by doing it. This means working through everything it takes to do your mission to its ultimate. If you listen to interviews with coaches of Olympic athletes, you hear a level of concern with sport that few of the rest of us aspire to. There is attention to every element of movement, to proper warm-ups and cool downs, to every item the athlete eats, how long he or she sleeps. It is total training. It is absolutely clear on the intended outcome. Sometimes you see this as well in facilitative leaders—here is someone who honestly is concerning herself or himself with every tiny aspect of the work. This is the venture.

The venture is creating the future. It is pushing the boundaries. The slogan, "don't work harder, work smarter" has become commonplace, but in fact few of us ever consider what it would look like to push our own limits. In his book *Dark Star Safari* (2003), travel writer Paul Theroux decides to travel alone from Cairo to Cape Town by public transport only because everywhere he goes, people say that no one could ever do that—he would surely be murdered, contract a deadly disease, encounter a terrible accident, or some such. Theroux describes his strategy of traveling not as an influential tourist, but in nondescript clothes as patched and shabby as his co-travellers, carrying not much more than his notebook.

What would it be like to live at the limits of what we can do? What strategy would it take to do what seems impossible? In the venture this is the question we are asking. In his book *The Tipping Point: How Little Things Can Make a Big Difference* (2002), Malcolm Gladwell looks at the process used by New York City to attack a level of subway crime that seemed completely out of control. The first phase of the crime reduction plan was dealing with graffiti. Most "professionals" thought this was the wrong focus. They believed that more police in the cars, surveillance cameras, and tougher sentences were the answer. What worked were a few counterintuitive measures like keeping the subway cars free from graffiti. Systematically, subway line after line was converted into a "clean" line, that is, in which no cars were allowed to run with graffiti on them. When a car came into its end station, graffiti was either removed or painted over before the car was permitted to leave the yard again.

Next came a crackdown on fare beaters. The system was losing $150 million per year because an estimated 175,000 people were not paying fares. Each crime was for $1.25 and considered by the transit police not worth dealing with, as other more serious crimes were taking place in cars and on platforms. Up to ten plainclothed police officers were assigned to the fare turnstiles. Each person going through without paying was arrested, handcuffed, and put in a line until there was a "full catch." A bus was fitted out as a mobile police station, and the processing time reduced from taking most of a day to less than an hour. The added benefit was that of those arrested, one in seven had outstanding warrants for their arrest for other offenses, and one in twenty were carrying illegal weapons. "Minor, seemingly, insignificant quality-of-life crimes . . . were tipping points for violent crime" (Gladwell, 2002).

For each of us there is a critical limit connected with our mission. There are indeed things we cannot accomplish. Most often, however, that critical limit is far beyond what we think it is. Whatever we aim to accomplish, the Venture is the experience of seeking ways to push the limit. It involves unearthing those steps that can make our action effective.

This means understanding what you really intend. The leading U.S. manufacturer of beer can openers went bankrupt when pop-top cans grew popular. The owner reflected that he had thought he was in the business of making kitchen utensils, when really his business was opening cans. These distinctions are commonly made in business. Consultants ask, "What business are you in?" However, this detailed consideration of objectives could well be useful to ask oneself personally, to ask in the family and in the nonprofit association. Once you are clear what you intend, you can choose strategies that apply and stop worrying about the rest. Life becomes not more difficult, but simpler.

THE ELECTION

The election is the third level of the discipline of Action. Election is the experience that existence is helping you along in your doing.

At the election level, you are going along pushing the boundaries, and something unexpectedly helpful happens, moving you forward without your own effort. Just as you were considering giving up, a sponsor is found, a new project appears, funding becomes available.

One of the necessary tasks in our former work of community development was fund-raising. After every community consultation, visits were made to potential donors in the area to provide support for the new programs. Two of us were visiting donors in Memphis regarding a project in Pace, Mississippi. On one visit, the businessman listened to our story and immediately wrote a sizeable check. As he walked us to the elevator, he confessed that he never ordinarily made such donations, but when he saw us and heard our story, he just knew it was something special. We had given just the same story any number of times to any number of donors without this response, but inexplicably something happened there.

Not everything is positive at this level. There are choices between right and right and between wrong and wrong. While still committed to the direction you have chosen, all steps into the future can be problematic, dangerous, or painful. The downside of every possible action is clear. Not acting is as much a problem as acting. With courage you go ahead, even as your commitment is assaulted by doubts and the knowledge of destructive consequences. You do what is required because it is required, not because of external pressure or internal need, but because it seems existence needs it. Here is the paradox of serving. You experience yourself as both nothing, a servant, and as connected to all, the king.

THE ECSTASY

The fourth level is ecstasy. Here time seems to stop and the moment becomes eternal. It is as if you suddenly become aware that you are standing in an amphitheater. As you look out at the huge crowd, you realize this is all of existence awaiting your next act. The universe is holding its breath in anticipation of what you do next. You experience yourself as part of a league of giants whose work you are completing. Future giants await you so that they too can contribute to the process of co-creation.

Miyamoto Musashi (1974) calls this level the void:

> People in this world look at things mistakenly, and think that what they don't understand must be the void. This is not the true void. It is bewilderment. (p. 95)

He goes on to say:

> Until you realize the true way, whether in Buddhism or in common sense, you may think that things are correct and in order. However, if we look at things objectively, from the viewpoint of laws of the world, we see various doctrines departing from the true way. Know well this spirit, and with forthrightness as the foundation and the true spirit as the way. Enact strategy broadly, correctly and openly. (Musashi, 1974, p. 95)

Action is being at one with what history is calling into existence, what Musashi calls the "true way." The Institute of Cultural Affairs describes this kind of action as taking place in the empty space between the "no longer" and the "not yet." Most people choose to spend most of their lives outside of that region if they can. It is surely safer and more satisfying to live and work where the rules are clear and expectations can be met. We live in times in which that can be very difficult to arrange.

The future only comes into place because of those who are willing to step out beyond what currently works and try out the new directions. In his inauguration speech in 1994, Nelson Mandela placed himself between the no-longer apartheid and the not-yet reunited South Africa:

Out of the experience of an extraordinary human disaster that lasted too long, must be born a society of which all humanity will be proud. Our daily deeds as ordinary South Africans must produce an actual South African reality that will reinforce humanity's belief in justice, strengthen its confidence in the nobility of the human soul and sustain all our hopes for a glorious life for all. (Mandela, 1994)

This is Action at its ultimate stage.

CONCLUSION

The discipline of Action is selecting what one intends to achieve and then thinking it through in such a way that it can be done. Those who have defined their objective and focused their life to achieve it find that the world cooperates with them in a way they could never have anticipated.

◆ ◆ ◆

Practices for Action

A wide variety of practices can help in the discipline of Action from regular workouts, preparing for a marathon, to Ikebana or Tai Chi.

Martial Arts

Tai Chi or *Tai Chi Chuan* can be translated from the Chinese as "supreme ultimate force." It is based in the idea of the dynamic duality of the yin/yang, male/female, active/passive, dark/light found in all things. "Force" means, according to Christopher Maijka, "the means or way of achieving this yin/yang or 'supreme-ultimate' discipline."

> Tai Chi, as practiced in the West today, can perhaps be best thought of as a moving form of yoga and meditation combined. There are a number of so-called forms (also sometimes called "sets"), which consist of a sequence of movements. Many of these movements are originally derived from the martial arts (and perhaps even more ancestrally than that, from the natural movements of animals and birds) although the way they are performed in Tai Chi is slowly, and gracefully, with smooth and easy transitions between them. (Maijka, n.d.)

While different users have different aims in practicing it, our aim in suggesting Tai Chi for helping with the discipline of Action is to develop a tranquil mind. It is a practical road to learning focused on the precise execution of the movements. Some of the movements contribute to our understanding of others: a two-person exercise called "push hands" develops sensitivity to and responsiveness to another person's *chi* or vital energy.

Japanese Art

A number of Japanese arts may contribute to developing the capacity to act effectively, including *kendo* (swordsmanship), archery, the tea ceremony, and *ikebana* (flower arranging). All of these have a long tradition of finding spontaneity in very rigid sets of activities. All require careful preparation of your mind before you act.

Developing the discipline of Action does mean practicing acting and not thinking about acting. It is not theory or planning, it is doing. It is developing and mastering a set of skills by repeating the same actions over and over until they become automatic, disconnected from thought. When this is achieved, then spontaneity is possible. In the world of organization, these same kinds of disciplines can be applied in the way meetings are run, plans are made, and reports are prepared.

◆ ◆ ◆

Exercise for Action

Risk Planning

To work with your action, think about risks you've taken in the past year. The question here is not whether they worked out "successfully," or whether you kicked yourself later for trying them. The question is in what ways you've been willing to stretch yourself, to go farther than the limits of your certainty.

First, consider a few of the risks you've taken. They may be intellectual, like tackling material that's thoroughly new for you or moving into a new culture or language. Or you may risk yourself physically, with a longer jogging circuit than you're sure you can achieve, or a longer fast than you thought possible. Risk can be emotional as well—confronting thorny relationships, taking several days of silent retreat to consider your life, or making peace with painful areas of your past.

Perhaps equally interesting is to consider where you have passed up risks, where you've stuck to what you are sure of. The point here is not to look at risk for the sake of foolish frivolity, but risks you need to take to keep your own spirit and ethical fabric in peak form.

Risks I've Taken Lately	Risks I've Avoided Lately

First write out risks you have taken lately in the left-hand column and risks that you avoided lately in the right-hand column. Looking at these lists, consider where you haven't been stretching much lately. How might you take a step in the needed direction? Brainstorm a bit using the boxes following, and then circle two or three risks you might undertake in the coming month. A stretch risk should be something rather frightening to consider.

Intellectual Risks I Could Undertake	Physical Risks I Could Undertake	Emotional Risks I Could Undertake	Vocational Risks I Could Undertake

You can reflect on this exercise individually or with a team:

- What sorts of risks do you find important for yourself?
- What is difficult about this line of thinking? Fun?
- What would taking these risks contribute to your presence as a leader?
- What might you do to ensure you went through with such a plan?

CHAPTER THIRTEEN

PRESENCE: INSPIRING AND EVOKING SPIRIT IN OTHERS

Presence is the final discipline. It is the focal point of the other eight. It is where the tension is found between Awareness and Action. It is the intersection of knowing and doing. Presence is based on care, and it acts out that care in sacrifice. Presence is charisma, inspiring and evoking spirit in others. Presence is the unique manifestation of spirit at a particular point of history. At this moment in society's journey, facilitation—enabling collective direct decision making—is part of the spirit of the times. Facilitation creates new freedoms and new responsibilities for individuals while enabling more diverse and creative interaction among groups, communities, and networks. Presence is the facilitator's capacity, the discipline of enabling new forms of individual innovation and collective interaction.

WHAT IS PRESENCE?

Presence is the magical quality of someone who combines care for others as individuals, in groups, and as societies. Such people are sensitive and insightful about barely discernable emerging futures. They act at the boundary between the possible and the impossible. When they are present life seems more meaningful, more possible, more exciting. Yet they are not a domineering force, but one that enables others to be greater than they are. Presence is not something that is reproduced in a cookie cutter process. Because in each period of history a new presence is required, and because each person who answers the call to be a presence brings his or her unique gifts to their time, no two are ever alike. You as a presence will be the only one. Yes, there are some characteristics of people of presence.

Presence as we describe it here is the point at which the past and future meet, where society is being invented to meet new needs and to remedy new issues. Perhaps "inventing" the future is not really the right term. Presence is more like co-creating the future. It is as though many potential realities are vying to come into being. At the same time, each of us is in the process of becoming his or her highest self. This highest self is aligned to some potential future. Michelangelo is reported to have said that he saw the statue of David in the stone. His job was simply to remove the unnecessary rock. David was there already just waiting to be released. Had Michelangelo not had his sight and skill, the work of art *David* would never have come into being. Could another sculptor of great vision and skill have seen David in the stone as well? Another David would have been sculpted. In this example, Michelangelo was becoming his higher self while he and the stone were co-creating the future.

THE DARK SIDE OF PRESENCE

Presence also has its dark side. Charisma can lead to demagoguery and misuse. Jon was present when a presentation was given by Claus Otto Scharmer to members of the board of directors and senior executives of a large Dutch company. The contrast between Scharmer's presence and that of the company director at the time was notable.

The director arrived a few minutes before the session was to begin. Barely acknowledging anyone from his company, he was introduced to Dr. Scharmer and said, "Okay, let's start." He went to his seat, and when everyone else was seated, he observed that two of the twenty-four seats were empty. He yelled, "Who's missing here?" A couple of names were mentioned, and again he yelled, "Get them on the phone and get them here or else get replacements!" The rest of the management were clearly accustomed to this way of operating, perhaps a bit relieved that they were not the missing ones.

Scharmer began his presentation. The director interrupted with frequent challenges, asserting his knowledge and power.

Scharmer, unruffled, answered every point clearly and respectfully. His knowledge of the issues of leadership and organizational change was remarkable, yet at no point was his tone anything other than respectful and patient.

Halfway through the program there was a break. As the session began again, the director challenged less and contributed more. By the end of the session, the director had become part of the group, engaged in shared discovery.

This director is a well-known charismatic figure in the Netherlands. His charisma is a dark presence, however, based on the force of his personality and his ability to have his way. He demonstrated both within a few minutes of arriving in the room. This power is one of control. On the other hand, Dr. Scharmer has charisma, but it is based on his care for the group and genuine interest in how they can recognize and embody a new kind of leadership.

The major differences were not about power or personality, but in their relationship to the future of society. The director's charisma is based on the traditional command-and-control paradigm. At the time of this anecdote, he was actually retarding development of anything new in the organization. Scharmer, on the other hand, was a living example of a new kind of leadership, a new social model.

This director is not at all unusual. Many leaders act in the same way, afraid to risk a new style to suit the new challenges in their businesses. The command-and-control mode of leadership can achieve what it seeks, namely control. However, this dark charisma does not generate commitment or creativity; it generates obedience. Scharmer's positive approach stimulates attitudes and behaviors in an organization that the power approach cannot reach.

DIFFICULTIES OF PRESENCE

It is difficult to act with Presence today because we lie to others and ourselves so often and so routinely that we lose the feeling of honesty. We learn a set of responses to our own failures and mistakes to choose from, depending on the seriousness of the mistake and how directly related we are to its consequences. These are options such as:

- Ignore it and it may go away or others may not notice.
- Downplay its significance.
- Deny that it was a mistake: "That's just what we intended all along."
- Transfer the blame somewhere else: to others, the situation, the equipment, and so on.
- Flee: If one gets away fast enough, no one may notice your involvement.

These responses are so common and familiar that they form the basis for any number of jokes, cartoons, and humorous slogans. We learn them so early in life that we are largely unaware of them until someone calls attention to a particularly obvious or outrageous one. These little maneuvers work well enough, often enough, that they are hardly noticed. This is deceit, however. It is precisely in these deeply ingrained habits of avoiding the truth of ourselves and our situation that we lose our ability to be truly present to a situation and to others.

Second, it is difficult to deal with the discipline of Presence because we have a fear of standing out. The head that sticks up too far above the crowd tends to be knocked down. Presence moves one to stand out, but it does so without calling attention to itself. It is quiet power. Presence is transparent. What you see when the facilitative leader who practices this discipline is present to the situation is the spirit of the organization. This presence is wise. They see through the illusions they and others create. This presence acts in the knowledge that something is always possible, even when all seems impossible. This presence offers all who see and have the courage to act the opportunity to create the truly new.

A third reason why presence is a difficult discipline in today's world is the struggle of being all you can be. We tend to either belittle ourselves or blow ourselves up all out of proportion. The choice of becoming your particular presence at first seems exciting, interesting, and fun. What if I really could make a difference in this situation? As we move closer toward it, however, the prospect becomes frightening. We begin to touch our own greatness and recoil from it. When we have the courage to stick with it, others may well insist that this is the wrong path. They point out that it's not your job; you're no saint; you probably don't have the ability to influence anyone anyway. Our friends may be offended by our transformation and become more distant.

Presence is an individual discipline that necessarily has a collective side. An individual on his or her own has no presence any more than a leader can lead without followers. This collective dimension is more than the obvious. We have said earlier that Presence happens when an individual manifests the spirit that is emerging in his or her times. It is also true that the people who respond to that spirit, those who recognize a leader, also define it. They bring their own understanding of who that individual is and what his or her leadership means. The followers add and suppress aspects of the leader's presence to suit their concerns and needs. It is an interactive system of mutual creation, sustenance, and limitation, in which both group and leader are shaped by their interactions. The development of charisma is also influenced in similar ways with the larger world.

THE ISSUES OF PRESENCE FOR FACILITATIVE LEADERS

Presence is important for the facilitative leader. Presence as charisma does not overwhelm or intrude unnecessarily or excessively. It is accepting of the group as it is, and it challenges the group to be all that it can be. Presence steps inside the spirit of the group and calls forth its greatness.

EVOKING SPIRIT

Facilitative leaders are important at three moments in the life of an organization: at the beginning, during those moments when the spirit lags, and at the ending.

A facilitative leader has his or her own unique charisma. At the beginning of an organization, the facilitative leader attempts to put form onto the grasp he or she has of the spirit of the times. Initially, that form involves talking about the issues. As the leader finds people who respond to what they say, a story begins to emerge. It is told in many settings, and it changes as it is told. If all goes well, the story becomes increasingly powerful and compelling. At the same time, the group is making the story tangible, whether it is a computer in every household or a new approach to Montessori education. Prototypes are built, methods tried. More and more people are attracted to the idea because it is so inspiring. One way of defining leadership at this point is "empowering spirit." The key for the facilitative leader is to find the best form for that particular dimension of spirit that they encountered. If they pay attention and act with care and integrity, what they build will last.

When spirit lags in an organization, it is the job of the facilitative leader to revitalize it by returning to the source where it came from. Sometimes this is quite literal. Nike takes its employees to the sites where the company founders worked to see and experience firsthand the place where their organization began. Sometimes it means recreating the environment in which the spirit started. Nike European Headquarters has photos of early pioneers in the company hanging throughout the entrance hall. In a nearby shipping center, a pair of shoes worn by John McEnroe in one of his biggest victories is displayed at the entry in a glass case. These things represent more than just décor. Everyone participates in at least an hour of sport a day. Facilities are available; managers make the time available to employees and join in themselves.

Organizations end just like everything else. Departments are eliminated; teams are disbanded. People are transferred and new people replace them. These moments of ending are as important for the facilitative leader as the beginnings. While beginnings are exciting, endings are frightening. When a group stops being a particularly healthy, productive group, people go through a grieving process, and it is at this moment that the facilitative leader must be present, must share in the process. Such leaders don't short circuit the grief but are present to the grief and comfort those grieving. They are also present to those who are not leaving to help them through their grief and their guilt as survivors.

A big multinational, European data management company restructured some of its departments. One of the departments had to let go about 20 percent of its employees. Before the official announcement was made there were lots of rumors about the change. The HR manager couldn't say everything that she knew, but she did send a memo to all employees, a clear statement of what could be said. She announced that she would set aside several hours a week if people would like to discuss the situation with her. She then visited every section in the department and explained what she could. Each week she sent out memos about the current situation. When the cutbacks were announced and everyone knew who was going, she made appointments with all of them. From our perspective this HR manager was presence. She stood out in some degree because most of the other managers were to one degree or another avoiding the situation.

SENSING THE FUTURE

Perhaps it is willingness of the leader to set aside his or her own needs that enables foresight. Stilling the internal chatter allows quieter and more gentle insights to be heard. Insights into the future may also arise from being focused on the future, not in the sense of controlling it but rather being concerned about where history is going. It is more about sensing the direction of time than acting in it. Bob Dylan refers to this while reflecting on his life as a young musician in the early 1960s. He describes how you intuit that change is going to happen but it is more feeling than thought. Little clues to the change appear here and there and you may not be aware of them until the change comes and you have to go in a different direction (Dylan, 2004).

Being present to this moment and the trends of the future seems to enable foresight. Insight in this sense is not black and white. It won't tell you which stock to buy and which to sell, or whether it will rain in London tomorrow. It is instead a vague sense of the direction in which things are moving; it may elicit questions rather than certitude.

ENABLING THE IMPOSSIBLE

The facilitative leader enables the impossible rather than demanding it. They see the possible as a practical reality in the impossible.

A San Diego construction association regularly sponsors a contest in which two teams compete with each other to build a three-bedroom ranch house with garage in the fastest time. In one contest that was filmed, both teams were trying to break the world record of four hours. Nothing could be prefabricated, and the house had to meet all of the various inspections required by the city. The grounds were to be landscaped and kitchens and bathrooms in working order. Foundation had to be dug and poured, and all plastering and painting had to be completed.

The winning team completed their house in less than three hours, and the losing team in less than four hours. What seemed impossible was not so. Each team had about six hundred professionals working on site. Practice sessions had been done weeks before the competition day. Minute-by-minute project plans had been designed. Chemicals were added to cement to speed up the drying. The roofs were built a few hundred yards away from the houses with ducting and electrical wiring built in. The roofs were transported onto the house frames and wiring and ducts connected together.

When you see the film of this competition, it becomes obvious that building a house in less than four hours is possible. Viewed from the initial challenge, it sounds utterly impossible.

Some leaders put the burden of accomplishing the impossible onto those who have to carry out the work. We have all seen bosses who say, "I don't care how, I want it done now!" They do not take responsibility for what it may take to accomplish what they are asking for. Some do not even want to know.

Henry Ford is attributed with saying, "If you think you can do a thing or think you can't do a thing, you're right" (Moncur, 2005). Here the emphasis is on your own perspective; that is what makes the difference. The facilitative leader takes great care for his colleagues' attitudes, understanding that things are what we call them, be that possible and impossible, or success and failure. The facilitative leader stands at the boundary of social existence and pushes against the boundary, inventing new ways of interacting with groups and individuals. Like a scientist exploring the boundaries of physics, the facilitative leader is "discovering" how decisions are made, how teams are built, how people of different cultures and perspectives interact when working together. Actually, in today's paradigm these processes are as often invention as they are discovery.

THE FOUR LEVELS OF PRESENCE

Like the other eight disciplines, Presence has four levels of experience. They are the discontinuity, the style, the willpower and the eternal.

THE DISCONTINUITY

Discontinuity is the experience of emptiness. Jon recently attended the International Association of Facilitators (IAF) Conference in South Africa where he gave two presentations. During the conference, a post-lunch session on the first day was about laughter. The session attendees went outside and did several exercises practicing laughing. We ended each exercise with *he he, ha ha, ho*. We laughed with a partner. We laughed like a lion. We laughed in anger. We laughed as though we were floating away. It was easy to laugh. As we walked back to the seminar room, Jon experienced a deep sense of futility. After the exercises, there was a presentation about the benefits of laughter. The presenter had a body of facts and statistics showing that laughing several hundred times a day, as children often do, leads to a healthy physical, mental, and spiritual life. Jon's sense of futility increased. What he experienced was that here was laughter, a wonderful thing. It was enlivening. Most of the group seemed to get a lot out of the exercise. At the same time the presenter did not seem to believe in laughter. She seemed to be manipulating the group to a point of view. She was using statistics to justify that point of view. In the process of this experience Jon realized that the problem was not the woman doing the presentation but his interpretation of what she was doing. His understanding was not necessarily wrong. His question was, What was the most responsible way of responding to her and the group she was working with? What would the longer-term consequences of doing nothing or doing something be? The hollow feeling was nearly paralyzing.

In the movie *As Good as It Gets* (Sakai et al., 1997), Jack Nicholson plays a very neurotic writer. He is angry and hateful. He throws his gay neighbor's dog down the laundry chute out of petty irritation. He is compulsive. He goes every day to the same café, sits at the same table, and must be served the same meal by the same waitress. When someone else occupies "his" table, he becomes vicious. During the course of the film, he learns that there are other people he cares about, and he can express some of that care. At the end of the film, he is still a neurotic, nasty old man. As the title suggests, it is "as good as it gets."

In Stephen Donaldson's (1977) double fantasy trilogy about Thomas Covenant the Unbeliever, the protagonist learns that the source of evil, Lord Foul, only wins when someone succumbs to his or her despair. Lord Foul is quite accomplished at putting people in circumstances that can lead them to despair. At the end of the first trilogy, Thomas Covenant goes to confront Lord Foul in order to save the land he has come to live in. Lord Foul shows Covenant all of the destruction Covenant has done intentionally and unintentionally, often with the best of motives. There is nothing that cannot be turned to destructive purposes. While the temptation is overwhelming to despair, Thomas Covenant remembers to laugh, tentative at first, but becoming stronger and stronger. Lord Foul is not destroyed, but his power is reduced.

Discontinuity is embracing your own responsibility for the occasions of despair without succumbing to the despair. The infinite void at the center that cannot be filled is always there. The realization that you have no ultimate control of existence is always ready to come to consciousness.

This experience includes the realization that all of our actions are ultimately irrelevant. We all build monuments that crumble. The pyramids, the Aztec temples, the Twin Towers, all crumble, all turn to dust in the end.

The expression "Be yourself" is an interesting one. Either it is an incredibly naïve statement about who one "really" is, or it is a profoundly insightful rule of life.

Naïve persons, whom Kierkegaard, writing under the pseudonym Anti-Climacus (1989), called the "circumspect," know that their life will end as will all others. To avoid the implications of this realization, they don't look at who the "self" is that will die. They hide from what they really are. They have a vague feeling that something might be amiss with themselves and with others, but they close their eyes to it. They fail to see their own destructive moments, or they justify them as innocent necessity. They don't remember their own self-destructive moments, what Paul Tillich (1948) called acts of "open or hidden suicide." The circumspect also hide from those times when they do others irreparable damage through forgetfulness or neglect.

The good news for the circumspect is that they can confront the damage to themselves and others fully. Usually this is through someone offering a gentle invitation to awareness. Those of us who are circumspect need to be asked to reflect on the real situation.

Sometimes when people are confronted, they become more effective at avoiding the truth about themselves. Inviting people to awareness calls for a great deal of self-awareness and self-honesty.

Those who are aware of their "self" and are honest enough to recognize their own hand in the tragedy of the world tend to be either passively or actively defiant. The passively defiant are those who look at their own despair and say, "See, I told you so!" The actively defiant are those who try to prove existence wrong.

This journey from naïve to active defiant is one in which all of us participate. It is one of deepening understanding, an increasingly profound sense of despair accompanied by a growing capacity for effective action (Anti-Climacus, 1989). The key from the perspective of the facilitative leader is not the breadth or depth of their despair and the tragedy they perceive, but that they decide to continue in spite of these without giving in to despair. The discontinuity is the void, brutal awareness, futility and despair, lived through, day to day, without giving in.

THE STYLE

The style is the second level of Presence. At the level of style you find yourself choosing to "be" your discontinuity.

A folktale from Indonesia tells of a Javanese king conquering more and more lands. The king sent a message to a poor village in Sumatra, at the very end of the empire. The message told the elders of the village that they must give up their village and submit to the rule of the king or else they would be attacked and beheaded. The elders said to the messenger, "War is a terrible thing and should be avoided at all costs. We are weak and have no army but would propose a contest to determine if the village would be under the king's rule or not." They suggested rather than having men fight, that each side should select one of their fighting water buffalos and let the winning buffalo determine the outcome of the war.

The messenger agreed to take this proposal back to the king. Meanwhile the villagers sent word to all the villages of the kingdom, describing the terms of the contest. Sometime after the messenger had told the king of the proposed contest, the king began to hear rumors of how wise the king was to permit this contest. Although the king had not yet agreed, the rumors convinced him to allow the buffalo fight to go ahead. The messenger returned to the village and set a date.

On the day of the contest, the king and his entourage arrived at a field just outside the village. The king's buffalo was the best in the kingdom, having won many fights already. He was huge and very strong, standing proudly at the edge of the field, ready to fight. The village elders then arrived, leading a bleating buffalo calf, only a few days old, with iron horns tied onto its fluffy little head. Everyone was laughing. The king asked if this calf was really the buffalo the village had chosen to defend its fate, and the elders assured him that it was. The king called for the fight to begin. The king's buffalo looked around for its opponent. The calf, not having been allowed to nurse for more than a day, sought for milk under the big buffalo. He began butting where the udders should be. This normal preparation for nursing drove the metal horns into the belly and side of the buffalo, killing him.

The king, amazed at the resourcefulness of these insignificant, poor villagers, let them have their freedom.

There are many stories of people using what they had, however little it was, to overcome adversity. The facilitative leader likewise uses his or her weaknesses as a point of advantage.

Avis Rent-a-Car seemed to understand this some years ago when they launched their "We try harder" campaign. They were the second in the rental car market in the United States at the time, behind Hertz. They based their campaign on the common wisdom that the person or company in second place puts out additional effort while the one in first place relaxes after a time. In this sense, weakness is a potential source of strength.

THE WILLPOWER

Presence is living in and being discontinuity, style, and willpower. Willpower is a discipline within a set of disciplines.

Take top tennis players. They practice two hours twice a day, five or six days a week. They run and lift weights. They improve their service and returning serves. They increase their control in placing the ball. They get faster on the court. They learn to anticipate an opponent. They push their bodies to the point of breaking, and then they learn how to play with injuries and potential injuries. Their attitude and thinking processes become more important than their physical capacities. They make mistakes and learn to set them aside and move their game up a notch. They learn not to let a stronger or higher-ranked opponent intimidate them. As they get older and more experienced, it becomes less and less their physical ability that provides the edge to their game. New edges are found—more cunning returns for opponents, greater variety, and the capacity to surprise. Why continue with this punishing regime? Perhaps simply because they can.

In the film *The Matrix Revolutions*, mechanical monsters have invaded the humans' city and are out to destroy it. The heroine and helper of the hero is dead. The hero confronts a mechanical world that has replicated itself innumerable times. In this titanic battle, the hero is obviously defeated and yet keeps getting up to continue to fight. The mechanical replica asks, "Why do you continue?" The hero's answer is, "Because I choose to do so" (Wachowski & Wachowski, 2003).

Willpower is continuing to move on, with the knowledge that there is a good chance of failure and that even success can be easily corrupted. The facilitative leader chooses to act. She or he acts with all of the foresight and cunning available.

At the style level, you sensed the future. At this willpower level, you trust your own intuitions. By "trust your intuitions" here, we mean applying a set of self-consciously refined principles. You have refined them in the practice of sensing the oncoming future. In difficult situations thoughts come to you that are often vague and seem quite insubstantial. They may seem illogical. These frail, irrational insights are the best of your thinking emerging from your unconscious. These are the intuitions that are to be trusted.

As we grow up and become part of society, we learn what works and what doesn't within our social circle. Leadership challenges those assumptions of what works and what doesn't, adapting practice to changing times and changing needs. Leadership dialogues with society in building a revised set of images and models, which may be counterintuitive to the societies in which we grew up. So our intuitions are continually being retrained. This is a lifelong process. Presence is the restructuring, refining, and acting on new intuitions.

We have a friend who played semi-pro baseball. The position he played was shortstop. For those who don't know baseball, his major task was catching a batted ball and throwing it to a base before the batter ran there. Our friend spent days practicing catching balls that had been hit very hard. The type of pitch, the sound of the bat striking the ball, the way the hitter bats the ball, the sight of the ball as it comes off the bat are all areas in which he was refining his intuitions. In a game, the period between the bat hitting the ball and the shortstop throwing the ball to first base, according to our friend, is often a complete blank to him. He catches the ball and throws it without being altogether conscious of what he is doing.

This seeming paradox of consciously developing intuitions and then surrendering your conscious mind to the unconscious is also true of facilitative leadership. If you watch a truly great facilitative leader before a group, you are aware of dozens of tiny acts that help to move the group along. Over the years that leader has developed a complex set of gestures, facial expressions, tones of voice, ways of framing questions, verbal and nonverbal interventions. If you ask why they smiled when so-and-so said such-and-such, they are often unable to remember doing it. It was just the right thing to do at the time.

Developing and trusting intuitions is a dimension of willpower. Another aspect of willpower is being responsible for your own actions. To put it in an old-fashioned way, Presence "keeps their own conscience." Keeping your own conscience is not a stoic, "I did it my way" practice. It is making your own decisions without justifying them. We justify our decisions all the time. We use work and family. We say we felt like it, or I did it for the money or for the sake of my team. We appeal to circumstances and plans or to values and ethical systems to justify what we do.

The person of Presence knows that only their actions and choices justify. The responsibility for acting belongs personally to them. It cannot be transferred to another thing, principle or person. It is my choice. In *The Matrix Revolutions* (2003), when the hero tells the representative of the mechanical monsters that the reason he keeps on fighting is because he chooses to do so, he is keeping his own conscience. He is truly free. The discipline of willpower is maintaining that freedom in spite of the many temptations to give up. At the same time, it is offering the same possibility to others.

In Jim Collins's book, *Good to Great* (2001), he discusses Level 5 leaders. One of the characteristics of Level 5 leaders is that their companies continue to prosper after the leaders have gone. They have found and developed successors who are also Level 5 leaders to carry on their work.

Robert Greenleaf's image of the "Servant Leader" (1983) is a useful paradox. At the level of the willpower, the leader is in process of being transformed while assisting the transformation of society. While willing a new self into existence, a new society is also willed into existence. In a real sense the duality we have been describing between self and society is a false one. Society and self are bound together.

At an international conference, a session was held on servant leadership. About thirty people attended the session, seven or eight of whom came from the tax department. The leader of the session asked the participants to name some of the relationships they were involved in. People mentioned mother, father, son, daughter, employee, and boss. When someone said "Taxpayer," everyone laughed, especially those from the tax department. "Do we have a relationship with those people?" Something changed in the quality of the discussion at that point, from personal to social relationships. The group came to a clearer understanding of servant leadership, not only in its personal but also in its social context.

The Eternal

The eternal is the fourth and the most profound of the levels of Presence.

In the early 1970s, the Institute of Cultural Affairs began working on what they called "States of Being" to describe the everyday human experience of having an interior life. They called it "The Other World in the Midst of This World." They used four metaphors to describe these internal experiences: the Land of Mystery, the River of Consciousness, the Mountain of Care, and the Sea of Tranquility.

The Land of Mystery is the experience of coming to love all those moments where your thinking, doing, and being are attacked for being too parochial, too limited, too self-centered. These experiences draw out the greatness in you, and you are profoundly appreciative of the opportunity. This does not make them less painful. They are healing.

The River of Consciousness is the experience of continuing awareness that you really don't belong to the superficialities of this world. You don't belong to the interior world either. Both are necessary and of some considerable use. You are a bit like being an alien at home. Everything is familiar in a vague sort of way. After all, it is home. Yet you don't belong.

The Mountain of Care is the experience of expanding concern for the world. This care carries power to do things. You seem to be able to accomplish miracles. Everything you touch seems to be done well. This is care for the suffering of others transformed into effective actions.

The Sea of Tranquility is the experience of calm in the midst of chaos. It is a bit like the color woodcut "The Great Wave Off Kanagawa" from the series "Thirty-six Views of Mount Fuji" (1823–1829) by Katsushika Hokusai, in which a tiny boat is being rowed at the bottom of a giant wave that is about to crash over it. Something calming is present in the picture.

A friend of ours tells a story about his experience of the Sea of Tranquility. He is an architect near Chicago, and early in his career he designed and built a home for his family. It was beautiful. A wall of glass overlooked a creek running through the yard. At the time of the story, he was struggling with a number of things. The business was not going as well as he wanted it to. He and his wife were having more and more arguments. He was working later. One evening he drove home in a downpour. Already tense from the drive, he discovered that one of his boys was in trouble at school. He was simply overwhelmed. He thought of every trouble he could remember or invent. He went upstairs and starting pouring out all his problems to his wife. He went back downstairs. He looked out the glass window to see that the creek had risen and was several feet up the side of the building. At that moment, he said, total calm set in. He no longer had any problems. He had a lot to do, but he had no problems.

The internal experience is of your self being absorbed into whatever you choose to serve. Bob Dylan describes this in very simple terms writing about his encounter with other musicians during his early career:

> I . . . knew somehow . . . that if I wanted to stay playing music, that I would have to claim a larger part of myself. I would have to overlook a lot of things—a lot of things that might need attention—but that was all right. . . . I had the map, could even draw it freehand if I had to. Now I knew I'd have to throw it away. Not today, not tonight, sometime soon, though. (Dylan, 2004, p. 72)

When you are present, it is the role you have created that is present, not necessarily you. It claims a larger and larger part of your self.

At the end of *The Journey to the East* (Hesse, 1956), the hero is given three choices of penance to redeem himself for leaving the journey. He is so terrified by the first two that he refuses them. For the third task he is given a statue. As he looks at it, the statue becomes himself and HH, the leader of the community that sponsored the journey. He sees movement in the statue between himself and HH. His spirit is flowing from himself into that of HH. He realizes that his penance is to become the leader of the community, to lose himself into that venture. His self is gone, replaced by the community he desires to serve.

The hero sees that all of the destruction to himself, others, and the community are of no consequence. He sacrifices himself gladly for the journey that benefits mankind through its very existence (Hesse, 1956). While this may sound very mystical indeed, the simple fact is that we become what we serve.

Conclusion

The journey from discontinuity to style, to willpower, and finally to the eternal is one that facilitative leaders make. We all are invited to this journey in different ways and with different intensities. Frequently we refuse the invitation. A facilitative leader brings discipline into maintaining and deepening his or her capacity—whatever that may be—to be present. Being present is easy when being truthful is easy, when little power of character is needed, and when standing out is not a problem. The discipline of presence is necessary when the lie is easier than honesty, when character is demanded, and when who you are will be exposed to the world.

◆ ◆ ◆

Practices for Presence

Perhaps the practices for this discipline are in fact the practices of the other eight, and there is nothing separate at this level. Be aware every day of both the moment and the larger context. Act to serve those with you now and the coming generations. Be sensitive about the wonder present in every moment and about the larger movement of existence. Be humble and joyful. Fill your life with focus both on the immediate and on the globe.

Silencing the Mind

In the book *Presence* (Senge, Scharmer, Jaworski, & Flowers, 2004), the authors concern themselves with this discipline:

> "Isn't the key point really that study, meditation and other forms of individual cultivation over an extended period of time are essential to build the capacity to be an 'instrument of service?'," asked Betty Sue [Flowers].

> "Yes, exactly," said Peter [Senge]. "It's not just a matter of belief or wanting to be an instrument. You must develop the capacity. That's why I was saying the Buddhist notion is about the process of cultivation. There are three basic areas in which you must work. First, you must meditate of 'practice'—you must have a discipline of quieting the mind. Second, you must study—the sutras, the Koran, the Torah, the Bible or whatever helps to develop a theoretical understanding. And you must be committed to service, what the Buddhists would call 'vows.' Your cultivation grows out of all three." (pp. 231–232)

Perhaps the best practice is to spend time alone every day reflecting. Begin this reflection with twenty or thirty minutes of meditation. Slow your mind down, become at peace. Meditation is practicing "giving up." It is letting the self go so that the self does not become a block to being present. At the end of an action or a task, ask yourself, "What went well? How can what I have done be improved?" Aim at practical steps. Ask, "How has this contributed to the larger journey of humankind?" This is not intended as evaluation, but rather as a search for the truth. Pause without thought. Wait for something emerging from the heart. Let the spirit move you as it will. If your mind begins chattering away, first one direction and then another, stop and meditate for ten or fifteen minutes more. If your mind continues chattering, stop and go back to your daily work. Come back the next day. It is not time wasted if you have been present to your inner self.

We find time spent in a museum also a silencing practice. Open yourself to the art. Let each picture speak to you without arguing back or dismissing what is being said. Some pieces give their message and you can move on. Others require some time to understand, or you may need to return to them again. Return when you can and see what is being said. Leave when you have received what you can. Return again and again.

Retreats can be invaluable opportunities for quieting the mind. Many kinds of retreats are available; select one that sounds interesting and challenging to you. The key to these retreats seems to be the varied kinds of activities. One way is to spend a day or two in retreat, reflecting on your larger purpose as an individual and how that is aligned with the larger purpose of the universe. Time needs to be spent in quiet, perhaps meditation, but however it is done, your mind should quiet down, its chatter gradually decrease until long moments of stillness begin to refresh your sense of well being. Again, this is the discipline of letting go, of setting aside the ego and becoming connected to the higher self. There are retreats that focus exclusively on this quieting.

Time can be spent doing something artful, sculpting, painting, or writing poetry. If you play an instrument, take the time to play until you are content.

Writing during a retreat can also be important. It can be helpful to write down what you are experiencing. Writing short stories can also be a great exercise. They are often metaphors about your own interior state. Don't start with that in mind; start with telling a story and then look for the meaning in it.

For obvious symbolic reasons, food is important in a retreat. Some retreats are best done as fasts. If food is served, it can be simple, indicative of a life without status and adornment, a reminder of humility. The beginning and the end of a retreat might be a celebrative meal, especially in retreats that have involved fasting.

Deepening Understanding

Another useful practice is to find like-minded people who are willing to discuss important issues of the emerging future. Find ways of establishing and maintaining depth to your discussions. Finding communities is not easy, and you may need to bring them together rather than looking for one that exists already.

These communities can vary in type and focus. They can be focused on study or discussion or research or action. Whatever the focus of the discussion, growth in every member's Presence should be the result. Everyone who wants to should have a chance to lead. The whole group should agree on what is done and how it is done. The direction of the work or shared thinking can emerge through dialogue. Opinions can be valued and respected. The values and norms can be expressed openly as much as possible, open to challenge and change. The symbols that emerge can be used with care. As they evolve to the point of being mature, they can be fixed in place. Symbols that are no longer relevant can be reinvented or replaced. The boundaries of these communities can be clear enough to enable identity and process, and flexible enough to allow movement in and out.

Another practice is in-depth, intentional reading and studying. Find books or papers that are challenging—emotionally, intellectually, or spiritually. Approach your study with an open mind. An open mind does not begin with agreeing or disagreeing with what the author says; it begins by trying to understand what an author is saying, without judging it one way or another. Judgment can come later. It asks, "How can I put this in my own words?" It gives examples out of its own experience. It grasps the parts of a work, their relationship with each other and with the whole work. Once the open mind understands in depth what is being said, then it forms its own opinion. Only then does it challenge what is written by offering better insights. An open mind does not say, "You are wrong!" It gives its own perspective on what is right and true. The focus is on growing, becoming more responsible and freer, not on being right.

The whole point of study is to develop a deeper and deeper understanding of the world and of yourself. This only happens when your image changes. Sometimes this image is simply addition to what you already know, and the change is calm and not dramatic. Your behavior may not change at all. When something quite foreign to our image appears, however, a sudden revolution may occur.

While you may not look forward to this kind of dramatic change of thinking, strive to be open to it and seek it out for the sake of a deeper understanding of life.

Another practice that increases Presence is service.

Service can be a simple thing or it can be a total vocational choice. A friend of ours in Belgium heard that the local church was going to set up an elders day center and that they needed help. He spent three nights a week clearing out debris from the church basement. In a few months elders, many of whom had lived quite isolated lives, had a place to visit and have a good lunchtime meal.

Another friend left her job as a midwife in New York and moved to Afghanistan to teach and practice midwifery, knowing full well that her life was in danger.

Despite any difficulties involved, serving is an important discipline. Like all of the disciplines, it should be meeting a real need, done regularly, and connected to global concerns.

Like all of the practices described here, this is not to be taken without careful consideration. We offer practices that we have found useful ourselves and seen to be useful among close colleagues. They do not necessarily apply to others' needs and requirements. What is important is finding a set of practices that enable you to become an increasingly effective facilitative leader.

Once you begin to practice, you may find it uncomfortable. That is probably a good sign. Your life is going through a transformation, and that is not necessarily without pain. After some time you may become bored or feel as if you are not making progress. That too is good. Many of these practices lead to periods of regression. Keep at it when things are not going well. You might promise yourself one more month, and then you will decide whether you are going to continue. Do keep an open mind then during the month.

If you quit, that is also good. Go back to what you were doing before. If that is not possible, find another practice. After all, this is about developing your own discipline, not following one practice or another.

◆ ◆ ◆

Exercise for Presence

Visualization

Envision a group that you work with sitting around a table. Call to mind the challenge, issue, or problem that the group is struggling with. Think about what is the underlying cause of the issue. Envision this challenge or issue or problem as a cloud of dark grey smoke that grows and grows until it fills the whole room. The smoke is stifling, choking. It drains the energy out of the group.

Visualize that you are slowly drawing the smoke into your lungs. You keep inhaling. You hold the smoke inside yourself. You inhale more smoke and more smoke until the air is crystal clear.

Imagine the best future possible for the group. Imagine that future as a silver cloud. The cloud is inside you and you blow it into the air. Slowly you exhale, and fill the whole room with the silver cloud. The group breathes deeply of the cloud. They take that new future into themselves.

Imagine the larger community the group is part of. It could be a department or a company or town or city. Imagine the challenge, or issue, or problem that it faces. Visualize the grey smoke and silver cloud for that community.

Now imagine the country or continent that the community is part of, and repeat the process. Keep doing this until you have done the process for the whole world.

As a group discuss the experience of the clouds.

- What were some of the groups and communities you dealt with in your visualization?
- What were some of the issues?
- What were some specific things you saw during the visualization?
- What did you feel during this visualization?
- What did you think?
- What kind of thinking is this?
- When might you do this exercise in your private life?

References

Preface

Senge, P. M. (1990). *The Fifth Discipline.* New York: Doubleday.

Introduction

Block, P. (1987). *The Empowered Manager.* San Francisco: Jossey-Bass.

Clinton, B. (2004). *My Life.* London: Hutchinson.

Collins, J. (2001). *Good to Great.* London: Random House.

LaBarre, P. (2000, March). Do You Have the Will to Lead? [Electronic version]. *FastCompany, 32.*

Chapter One: Leadership: A Matter of Spirit

Abbassi, M. (n.d.). *Office of Policy & Public Services.* Retrieved April 11, 2006, from www.lacity.org/ita/itaita2c.htm.

Advanced Training Sources. (n.d.). *Joel Barker.* Retrieved April 11, 2006, from www.atsmedia.com/joel_barker_videos.asp.

Boje, D. M. (2000). *Flight of the Buffalo and Other Superleader Models.* Retrieved February 10, 2005, from http://cbae.nmsu.edu/~dboje/pages/flight_of_the_buffalo.htm.

Collins, J., & Porras, J. I. (1994). *Built to Last: Successful Habits of Visionary Companies.* New York: HarperCollins.

Denning, S. (2004). *Learn About Storytelling—How to Tell Stories: Examples and Implications.* Retrieved March 8, 2005, from www.stevedenning.com/learn.htm.

Giuliani, R. (2002). *Leadership.* London: Little, Brown.

Greenleaf, R. K. (1983). *Servant Leadership: A Journey into the Nature of Legitimate Power and Greatness.* Mahwah, NJ: Paulist Press.

Greenleaf, R. (1996). *On Becoming a Servant Leader.* San Francisco: Jossey-Bass.

Hock, D. (1999). *Birth of the Chaordic Age.* San Francisco: Berrett-Koehler.

Hodgson, D. (n.d.). *The Urbanization of the World.* Retrieved December 2, 2004, from www.faculty.fairfield.edu/faculty/hodgson/Courses/so11/population/urbanization.htm.

HSBC Group History 1865–1899. (n.d.). Retrieved November 18, 2004, from www.hsbc.com/hsbc/about_hsbc/group-history?cp=/public/groupsite/about_hsbc/en/group_history_1865_1899.html.

Hugh, B. (2004). Hans Monderman: Designing Roads for Humans. *Missouri Bicycle News,* December 9, 2004. Retrieved January 22, 2005, from www.mobikefed.org/2004/12/hans-monderman-designing-roads-for.html.

Kahan, S. (n.d.). *Accelerating Positive Change.* Retrieved March 8, 2005, from www.sethkahan.com/MeetingPlanners_SampleWorkS4L.html.

Katzenbach, J., & Smith, D. (1992). *The Wisdom of Teams.* Cambridge, MA: Harvard Business School Press.

Lyall, S. (2005, January 21). Road Design? He Calls It a Revolution. *International Herald Tribune.* Retrieved January 22, 2005, from www.iht.com/articles/2005/01/21/news/profile.html.

McGregor, J. (n.d.). Gospels of Failure. *FastCompany.* Retrieved February 22, 2005, from www.fastcompany.com/magazine/91/gospels.html.

National Commission on Terrorist Attacks upon the United States. (2004, July). *The 9-11 Commission Report: Final Report of the National Commission on Terrorist Attacks upon the United States, Official Government Edition.* Retrieved February 22, 2005, from http://www.9–11commission.gov/report/index.htm.

Owen, H. (1987). *Spirit: Transformation and Development in Organizations.* Potomac, MD: Abbott.

Owen, H. (1990). *Leadership Is . . .* Potomac, MD: Abbott.

Owen, H. (1997). *Open Space Technology.* San Francisco: Berrett-Koehler.

Rough, J. (n.d.). *Dynamic Facilitation Skills for Emergent Leadership.* Retrieved April 12, 2006, from www.tobe.net.

Scharmer, C. O. (2000). *Presencing: Learning from the Future as It Emerges.* Presented at the Conference on Knowledge and Innovation, May 25–26, 2000, Helsinki School of Economics, Finland, and with the MIT Sloan School of Management, OSG, October 20, 2000.

Smith, M. (n.d.). *Ethics.* Retrieved February 28, 2005, from faculty.winthrop.edu/smithm/MGMT%20428/ethics.ppt.

Telleen, S. L. (1996). *Intranet Organization: Strategies for Managing Change.* Retrieved February 28, 2005, from www.iorg.com/intranetorg/index.html.

Tuchman, B. W. (1984). *The March of Folly: From Troy to Vietnam.* New York: Ballantine.

Wheatley, M. (1992). *Leadership and the New Science.* San Francisco: Berrett-Koehler.

Wheatley, M., & Kellner-Rogers, M. (1996). *The Irresistible Future of Organizing.* Retrieved November 9, 2004, from http://www.margaretwheatley.com/articles/irresistiblefuture.html.

Chapter Two: Trends in Employee Participation

Infinite Innovations, Ltd. (2003). *History and Use of Brainstorming.* Retrieved May 4, 2005, from www.brainstorming.co.uk/tutorials/history ofbrainstorming.html.

Kleiner, A. (1996). *The Age of Heretics: Heroes, Outlaws, and the Forerunners of Corporate Change.* New York: Doubleday.

Lewin, K. (1951). *Field Theory in Social Science.* New York: HarperCollins.

Lyneis, J. (1980). *What Is Dynamic Complexity?* Retrieved May 4, 2005, from www.stewardshipmodeling.com/dynamic_complexity.htm.

National Center for Transit Research. (n.d.). *Conditions That Promote Creativity at Public Transit Agencies.* Retrieved May 9, 2005, from www. nctr.usf.edu/html/CreativeConditions.htm

Senge, P. M. (1990). *The Fifth Discipline.* New York: Doubleday.

A Short History of Robert's. (n.d.). Official Site of Robert's Rules of Order. Retrieved January 2, 2006, from www.robertsrules.com/history. html.

Chapter Three: The Skills of a Facilitative Leader

Argyris, C., Putnam, R., & McLain Smith, D. (1985). *Action Science.* San Francisco: Jossey-Bass.

Csikszentmihalyi, M. (1991). *Flow: The Psychology of Optimal Experience.* New York: Perennial.

Jobs, S. (2005). *"You've Got to Find What You Love," Jobs Says.* Stanford, CA: Stanford Report. Retrieved April 13, 2006, from http://news-service. stanford.edu/news/2005/june15/jobs-061505.html.

Level of Process. (2005). *IAF Methods Database.* Retrieved May 23, 2005, from www.iaf-methods.org/modules.php?op=modload&name=Sec tions&file=index&req=viewarticle&artid=135&page=1.

Morgan, G. (1986). *Images of Organization.* Thousand Oaks, CA: Sage.

Otto, R. (1958). *The Idea of the Holy* (2nd ed.). London: Oxford University Press.

Senge, P. M. et al. (1994). *The Fifth Discipline Fieldbook.* London: Nicholas Brealey.

Chapter Four: The Future of Facilitation

Brown, J. S. (2001). *Xerox: How Copiers Actually Get Repaired, Storytelling the Passport to the 21st Century.* Retrieved January 9, 2006, from www2. parc.com/ops/members/brown/storytelling/JSB8-Xerox-Eureka. html.

Cooperrider, D. L., & Whitney, D. (1999). *Appreciative Inquiry.* San Francisco: Berrett-Koehler.

Chapter Five: Detachment: Stepping Back

Chödrön, P. (2001). *The Wisdom of No Escape*. Halifax, NS, Canada: Shambhala.

Cohen, D., & Prusak, L. (2001, June 11). Making Social Capital Work. *Harvard Business School Working Knowledge for Business Leaders* [Electronic version].

Collins, J. (2001). *Good to Great*. London: Random House.

de Bono, E. (1973). *Lateral Thinking: Creativity Step by Step* (Reissue ed.). New York: Harper Paperbacks.

Hammonds, K. H. (2001, June). Grassroots Leadership: U.S. Military Academy. [Electronic version]. *FastCompany, 47,* 106.

Harris, E. J. (1997). *Detachment and Compassion in Early Buddhism*. Kandy, Sri Lanka: Buddhist Publication Society. Retrieved December 10, 2004, from www.enabling.org/ia/vipassana/Archive/H/Harris/detachmentHarris.html.

Hock, D. (1999). *Birth of the Chaordic Age*. San Francisco: Berrett-Koehler.

Jaworski, J., and Flowers, B. S. (eds.). (1996). *Synchronicity: The Inner Path of Leadership*. San Francisco: Berrett-Koehler.

Jenkins, J. C., & Jenkins, M. R. (2002). *The Personal Disciplines of a Facilitator.* Proceedings of the IAF Conference, Toronto, Canada, May 2002.

Jenkins, J., & Visser, G. (2003). *Level 5 Leadership, Imaginal Training*, at http://www.imaginal.nl/articleLevel5Leadership.htm.

Jennings, W. D. (2001). *The Ronin: A Novel Based on a Zen Myth*. Boston & Tokyo: Tuttle.

Katzenbach, J., & Smith, D. (1992). *The Wisdom of Teams*. Cambridge, MA: Harvard Business School Press.

LaBarre, P. (2000, March). Do You Have the Will to Lead? [Electronic version]. *FastCompany, 32,* 222.

Lao Tzu. (1994). *Tao te Ching: An Illustrated Journey* (ed. P. Streep; trans. J. Legge). Toronto: Little Brown.

Miller, A. (1998 [1949]). *Death of a Salesman* London: Penguin Books.

Sartre, J.-P. (1949). *No Exit and Three Other Plays*. New York: Vintage Books.

Taylor, W. C. (1999). The Leader of the Future. *FastCompany*. Retrieved February 11, 2005, from www.fastcompany.com/magazine/25/heifetz.html.

Walsh, R. (1999). *Essential Spirituality: Exercises from the World's Religions to Cultivate Kindness, Love, Joy, Peace, Vision, Wisdom and Generosity*. New York: Wiley.

Chapter Six: Engagement: Committing to the Group

Ackoff, R. (n.d.). *Mission Statements*. Retrieved January 3, 2005, from www.charleswarner.us/articles/mission.htm.

Bonhoeffer, D. (1965). *Ethics.* New York: Macmillan.

Csikszentmihalyi, M. (1991). *Flow: The Psychology of Optimal Experience.* New York: Perennial.

Greenleaf Center for Servant Leadership. (2002). *What Is Servant Leadership?* Retrieved January 4, 2005, from www.greenleaf.org/leadership/servant-leadership/What-is-Servant-Leadership.html.

Greenleaf, R. (1970). *Servant as Leader.* Retrieved January 3, 2005, from www.greenleaf.org/leadership/servant-leadership/What-is-Servant-Leadership.html.

Jenkins, J. C., & Jenkins, M. R. (2002). *The Personal Disciplines of a Facilitator.* Proceedings of the IAF Conference 2002, Toronto, Canada, May 2002.

Katzenbach, J. R. (1995). *Real Change Leaders: How You Can Create Growth and High Performance at Your Company.* London: Nicholas Brealey.

King, L. (2000). President Nelson Mandela One-on-One. *Larry King Live.* Transcript of program aired May 16, 2000, 9:00 P.M. ET on CNN. Retrieved January 11, 2005, from http://transcripts.cnn.com/TRANSCRIPTS/0005/16/lkl.00.html.

Owen, H. (1990). *Leadership Is . . .* Potomac, MD: Abbott.

Russell, B. (1979). *Second Wind: The Memoirs of an Opinionated Man.* New York: Random House.

Sun Tzu. (1963). *The Art of War* (trans. S. B. Griffith). Oxford: Oxford University Press.

Chapter Seven: Focus: Willing One Thing

Bingham, H., King, G., & Peters, J. (producers), & Mann, M. (director). (2001). *Ali* (motion picture). Culver City, CA: Columbia Pictures.

Bonhoeffer, D. (1954). *Life Together.* New York: HarperCollins.

Caffey, F. (producer), & Schaffner, F. J. (director). (1970). *Patton* (motion picture). Century City, CA: 20th Century Fox.

Collins, J. (2001). *Good to Great.* London: Random House.

Collins, J., & Porras, J. I. (1994). *Built to Last: Successful Habits of Visionary Companies.* New York: HarperCollins.

Covey, S. R. (2004). *The 8th Habit: From Effectiveness to Greatness.* New York: Simon & Schuster.

Csikszentmihalyi, M. (1991). *Flow: The Psychology of Optimal Experience.* New York: Perennial.

Herbert, F. (1965, 1970, 1976, 1981, 1984, and 1985). *Dune, Dune Messiah, Children of Dune, God Emperor of Dune, Heretics of Dune,* and *Chapterhouse Dune.* New York: Putnam's Sons.

Kierkegaard, S. (1969). *Purity of Heart: Is to Will One Thing* (trans. D. V. Steere). Scarborough, ONT: HarperCollins Canada.

Koudsi, S. (2003). Kimberly Jordan, New Belgium Brewing Co, *Fortune Small Business*, Retrieved May 2, 2005, from www.fortune.com/fortune/smallbusiness/articles/0,15114,456077,00.html.

Lao Tzu. (n.d.). Retrieved August 5, 2005, from http://www.brainyquote.com/quotes/authors/1/LaoTzu.html.

Lawrence, D. H. (1972). *Poems* (Selected and introduced by Keith Sagar). London: Penguin.

Musashi, M. (1974). *A Book of 5 Rings: The Classic Guide to Strategy* (trans. V. Harris). Woodstock, NY: The Overlook Press.

Senge, P. M. (1990). *The Fifth Discipline*. New York: Doubleday.

Soper, J. H. (August 26, 1999). *Facilitator Disciplines*. Retrieved March 28, 2006, from the State University of New York at Albany Group Facilitator's ListServ archives Web site: http://listserv.albany.edu:8080/archives/grp-facl.html.

Wesley, J. (1951). *The Journal of John Wesley*. Chicago: Mood Press. Retrieved March 22, 2006, from www.ccel.org/ccel/wesley/journal.pdf.

Williamson, M. (1996). *A Return to Love: Reflections on the Principles of a Course in Miracles*. New York: Harper Perennial.

Chapter Eight: Interior Council: Choosing Advisors Wisely

Acosta, E. (n.d.). *The Wolf I Feed or the One I Feed Story*. Retrieved September 23, 2004, from www.story-lovers.com/listswolfifeedstory.html.

Arbinger Institute. (2002). *Leadership and Self-Deception: Getting Out of the Box*. San Francisco: Berrett-Koehler.

Boulding, K. E. (1961). *The Image*. Ann Arbor: Ann Arbor Paperbacks, University of Michigan Press.

Clapton, E., & Jennings, W. (n.d.). Tears in Heaven. Retrieved August 15, 2005, from www.ercl-clapton.co.uk/ecla/lyrics/Tears-in-heaven.html.

Everything You Wanted to Know About Courage . . . But Were Afraid to Ask. (2004). *FastCompany*. Retrieved February 3, 2005, from www.fastcompany.com/magazine/86/courage.html.

Jenkins, J. C., & Jenkins, M. R. (2002). *The Personal Disciplines of a Facilitator*. Proceedings of the IAF Conference 2002, Toronto, Canada, May 2002.

Kazantzakis, N. (1960). *The Saviors of God: Spiritual Exercises* (trans. K. Friar). New York: Simon & Schuster.

McCartney, P. (2001). *Blackbird Singing: Poems and Lyrics 1965–1999*. London: Faber & Faber.

Peck, M. S. (1983). *People of the Lie: The Hope for Healing Human Evil*. New York: Simon & Schuster.

Senge, P. M., Scharmer, C. O., Jaworski, J., & Flowers, B. S. (2004). *Presence: Human Purpose and the Field of the Future*. Cambridge, MA: Society for Organizational Learning.

Senge, P. M. et al. (1994). *The Fifth Discipline Fieldbook*. London: Nicholas Brealey.

Wademan, D. (2005, January). The Best Advice I Ever Got. *Harvard Business Review*, 35–44. Retrieved March 31, 2006, from http://harvard-businessonline.hbsp.harvard.edu/hbrsa/en/hbrsaLogin.jhtml;jsessi onid=4TBX43LACNRGEAKRG5BR5VQBKE12MISW;$urlparam$k NRXE2ULYRiR52NiwJYH5SF?ID=R0501C&path=arc&pubDate=Jan-uary2005&_requestid=6761.

Chapter Nine: Intentionality: Aligning the Will to Succeed

Briskin, A., Erickson, S., Lederman, J., Ott, J., Potter, D., & Strutt, C. (2001). *Centered on the Edge: Mapping a Field of Collective Intelligence and Spiritual Wisdom*. COTE. Kalamazoo, MI: Felzer Institute.

Ruete, N. (1999). *Facilitator vs Moderator*. Retrieved May 18, 2006, from http://listserv.albany.edu:8080/cgi-bin/wa?A2=ind9909&L=GRP-FACL&P=R475&I=-3&X=420DE27A9AFF6278F3&Y=jon%40imagi nal.nl.

Scharmer, C. O. (1999). *The Heart Is the Key to All of This*, Conversation with Joseph Jaworski, Generon and SoL, Cambridge, MA, October 29, 1999. Retrieved March 31, 2006, from www.dialogonleadership. org/Jaworski-1999.pdf.

Spurgeon, B. (2005, August 17). The Arduous Work of the Eternal Optimist. *International Herald Tribune* (Paris). Retrieved March 31, 2006, from www.iht.com/articles/2005/08/16/news/wilson.php.

Walsh, R. (1999). *Essential Spirituality: Exercises from the World's Religions to Cultivate Kindness, Love, Joy, Peace, Vision, Wisdom and Generosity*. New York: Wiley.

Chapter Ten: Sense of Wonder:
Maintaining the Capacity to Be Surprised

Boulding, K. E. (1961). *The Image*. Ann Arbor: Ann Arbor Paperbacks, University of Michigan Press.

Campbell, J. (1949). *The Hero with a Thousand Faces*. New York: Bollington Foundation.

Jenkins, J. C., & Jenkins, M. R. (2002). *The Personal Disciplines of a Facilitator*. Proceedings of the IAF Conference 2002, Toronto, Canada, May 2002.

Kennedy, J. F.(1956). *Profiles in Courage*. New York: HarperCollins.

Kuhn, T. S. (1970). *The Structure of Scientific Revolutions*. Chicago: University of Chicago Press.

Lawrence, D. H. (1972). *Poems* (selected and introduced by Keith Sagar). London: Penguin.

Otto, R. (1958). *The Idea of the Holy* (2nd ed.). London: Oxford University Press.

Owen, H. (1990). *Leadership Is . . .* Potomac, MD: Abbott Publishing.

Peck, M. S. (1983). *People of the Lie: The Hope for Healing Human Evil.* New York: Simon & Schuster.

Sartre, J.-P. (1969). *Nausea* (trans. L. Alexander). New York: New Directions.

Senge, P., Scharmer, C.O., Jaworski, J., & Flowers, B. S. (2004). *Presence: Human Purpose and the Field of the Future.* Cambridge, MA: Society for Organizational Learning.

Chapter Eleven: Awareness: Knowing What Is Really Going On

Bergdall, T. D. (2005). Facilitating Participatory Evaluations. In S. Schuman (ed.), *The IAF Group Facilitation Handbook* (Chap. 27). San Francisco: Jossey-Bass.

Boulding, K. E. (1961). *The Image.* Ann Arbor: Ann Arbor Paperbacks, University of Michigan Press.

Brown, J. S. (2001). *Xerox: How Copiers Actually Get Repaired, Storytelling the Passport to the 21st Century.* Retrieved January 9, 2006, from www2.parc.com/ops/members/brown/storytelling/JSB8-Xerox-Eureka.html.

Campbell, B. (n.d.). *The Naturalist Intelligence in Multiple Intelligences.* Retrieved April 2, 2006, from www.newhorizons.org/strategies/mi/campbell.htm.

de Bono, E. (1985). *Six Thinking Hats.* Toronto: Little, Brown.

Denning, S. (2002). *The Narrative Angle: The Seven Most Valuable Forms of Organizational Storytelling: A Managers Handbook on Narrative.* Retrieved January 20, 2005, from http://www.line56.com/images/articles/attachments/km0302.denning_ch1.pdf#search='Storytelling%20values%20transmit'.

Gardner, H. (n.d.). Intelligences in Seven Steps. In D. Dickinson (ed.), *Creating the Future: Perspectives on Educational Change.* Retrieved April 2, 2006, from www.newhorizons.org/future/Creating_the_Future/crfut_gardner.html.

Jenkins, L. (2005, January 8–9). His Eyes Wide Shut, Brees Saves Career. *International Herald Tribune,* p. 20.

Jennings, W. D. (2001). *The Ronin: A Novel Based on a Zen Myth.* Boston and Tokyo: Tuttle.

Korten, A. (2003). *Core Value Storytelling.* Transcript of the April 12, 2003, Session at the Smithsonian Associates. Retrieved January 20, 2005, from www.creatingthe21stcentury.org/Values.html#CoreValueStories.

Mathews, J. W. (1996). Transparent Knowing. *Golden Pathways* (CD-ROM). Chicago: Institute of Cultural Affairs.

McLellan, H. (2002). *Introduction to Corporate Storytelling.* Retrieved January 23, 2005, from http://tech-head.com/cstory1.htm.

Murdoch, A. (2004, May). Make Your Company a Real Success Story. *Glasgow Herald.* Retrieved January 17, 2005, from www.stevedenning. com/SIN-154-Glasgow-Herald-on-storytelling.html.

Ortega y Gasset, J. (1962). *Man and Crisis* (trans. M. Adams). New York: Norton.

Pink, D. H. (2003). How to Make Your Own Luck. *FastCompany.* Retrieved on January 26, 2005, from www.fastcompany.com/magazine/72/ realitycheck.html.

Ransdell, E. (2000). The Nike Story? Just Tell It! *FastCompany.* Retrieved January 20, 2005, from www.fastcompany.com/magazine/31/nike. html.

RedWorld.biz. (2004). *People: How to Be Lucky.* Retrieved January 26, 2005, from www.redworld.biz/redbusiness/issue/vol3/issue03/people.

Taylor, W. C. (1999). The Leader of the Future. *FastCompany.* Retrieved February 11, 2005, from www.fastcompany.com/magazine/25/ heifetz.html.

Webber, A. M. (2000). New Math for a New Economy. *FastCompany.* Retrieved January 12, 2005, from www.fastcompany.com/magazine/ 31/lev.html.

Wheatley, M. (1992). *Leadership and the New Science.* San Francisco: Berrett-Koehler.

Whitmore, J. (1996). *Coaching for Performance* (2nd ed.). London: Nicholas Brealey Publishing.

Wiseman, R. (n.d.) *People: How to Be Lucky.* Retrieved January 26, 2005, from www.redworld.biz/redbusiness/issue/vol3/issue03/people.

Chapter Twelve: Action: Effective Doing

Gladwell, M. (2002). *The Tipping Point: How Little Things Can Make a Big Difference.* London: Time Warner.

Herrigel, E. (1989). *Zen in the Art of Archery* (trans. R.F.C. Hull). New York: Vintage.

Hock, D. (1999). *Birth of the Chaordic Age.* San Francisco: Berrett-Koehler.

Katzenbach, J., & Smith, D. (1992). *The Wisdom of Teams.* Cambridge, MA: Harvard Business School Press.

Locke, M. (2003). *The Weapons of a Japanese Warrior.* Retrieved March 14, 2005, from www.detarver.com/The Weapons of a Japanese Warrior. htm.

Maijka, C. (n.d.). *What Is Tai Chi?* Halifax, NS, Canada: Empty Mirrors Press. Retrieved August 13, 2005, from www.chebucto.ns.ca/Philos ophy/Taichi/what.html.

Mandela, N. R. (1994). *Statement of the President of the African National Congress Nelson Rolihlahla Mandela at His Inauguration as President of the Democratic Republic of South Africa Union Buildings, Pretoria, May 10, 1994.* Retrieved April 6, 2006, from www.anc.org.za/ancdocs/speeches/inaugpta.html.

Musashi, M. (1974). *A Book of 5 Rings: The Classic Guide to Strategy* (trans. V. Harris). Woodstock, NY: The Overlook Press.

Ortega y Gasset, J. (1962). *Man and Crisis* (trans. M. Adams). New York: Norton.

Theroux, P. (2003). *Dark Star Safari: Overland from Cairo to Cape Town.* Boston: Houghton Mifflin.

Chapter Thirteen: Presence:
Inspiring and Evoking Spirit in Others

Anti-Climacus. (1989). *The Sickness Unto Death: A Christian Psychological Exposition for Edification and Awakening* (ed. S. Kierkegaard). New York: Penguin Classics.

Collins, J. (2001). *Good to Great.* London: Random House.

Donaldson, S. (1977). *The Power That Preserves.* New York: Holt, Rinehart & Winston.

Dylan, B. (2004). *Chronicles: Volume One.* New York: Simon & Schuster.

Greenleaf, R. K. (1983). *Servant Leadership: A Journey into the Nature of Legitimate Power and Greatness.* Mahwah, NJ: Paulist Press.

Hesse, H. (1956/1970). *The Journey to the East* (trans. H. Rosner). New York: Noonday.

Moncur, M. (2005). *The Quotation Page,* Retrieved March 28, 2006, from www.quotationspage.com/quote/2330.html.

Sakai, R., Mark, L., & Ziskin, L. (producers), & Brooks, J. L. (director). (1997). *As Good as It Gets* (motion picture). Culver City, CA: Sony Pictures.

Senge, P. M., Scharmer, C. O., Jaworski, J., & Flowers, B. S. (2004). *Presence: Human Purpose and the Field of the Future.* Cambridge, MA: Society for Organizational Learning.

Tillich, P. (1948). *The Shaking of the Foundations.* New York: Scribner.

Wachowski, A., & Wachowski, L. (directors). (2003). *The Matrix Revolutions* (motion picture). Burbank, CA: Warner Bros.

INDEX

A

Abbassi, M., 23
Absurdity, as level of focus, 141–143
Academic specialization, 219
Accelerated learning facilitation, 70
Acceptance, 108–109
Accessibility, expectations of, 133
Accountability, fear of, 177–178
Accounting, 222
Ackoff, R., 111–112
Acosta, E., 149–150
Acrobat pilot, focus of, 131–132
Action: awareness and, 215–216, 242–243; caring as, 114–115, 181–182; courage for, 199–200; difficulties of, 245; discipline of, 242–261; exercise for, 260–261; intentionality and, 171, 174, 181–182, 185–187, 246–247, 256–257; issues of, for facilitative leaders, 245–253; levels of, 253–259; overview of, 8, 9, 242–244; planning and, 244, 245, 246–248; practices for, 259–260; responsibility for engagement and, 120–121; thinking and, 242, 244
Actors, Method *versus* character, 175
Adaptability, organizational, 49–50
Addictions, 100
Address, as level of interior council, 160–161
Adoration, in sense of wonder, 207–209
ADSL, 107
Advanced Training Sources, 31
Adversarial stance, 21–22
Affirmation, 142
Agassi, A., 15
Airline industry leaders, 221
Ali, M., 140
America Online, 84
American Revolution, 45

Anger, in grieving process, 42
Annual Story practice, 143–144
Anti-Climacus (Kierkegaard), 271, 272
Antibiotics, 48–49
Anxiety, self-limitation and, 2
Apple, 64
Applications, 59
Appreciative Inquiry, 70, 232
Arbinger Institute, 151
Argyris, C., 61
Armstrong, N., 6
Art, 70–72, 280
As Good as It Gets, 270
Ashby, W. T., 19
Assimilation, 104, 119
Attachment: to command-and-control mode, 84, 86–88; indulging in, as practice, 99–100. *See also* Detachment
Attentionality, 223–225
Attractiveness, of vision, 33
Auntie Mame, 130
Austrian Army, 106
Authenticity, authority *versus,* 26
Authority, in old paradigm, 26, 221–222
Automobile designers, 47–48
Autonomy, detachment and, 5–6
Avis Rent-a-Car, 273
Avoidance: action *versus,* 244, 253; of reality of death, 41–42, 271; of reality of emptiness, 271–272; of responsibility, 276–277; of truth, 28–29
Awareness: action and, 215–216, 242–243; attributes of, 216–220; difficulties of, 218–220; discipline of, 215–241; exercise for, 240–241; issues of, for facilitative leaders, 220–233; levels of, 233–237; overview of, 8–9, 215–216; practices for, 238–240; of transitoriness, 80–81

Awe, 64, 194, 196, 198, 201, 236–237. *See also* Wonder (sense of)

B

Backlash, against new thinking, 31
Bacteria, hyper-virulent, 48–49
Balance: in engagement, 107–109; in focus, 127–129, 134
Barker, J., 31
Baseball, 275
Bay of Pigs, 199
Beatles, 168
Beer Game, 177–178
Behavior change, focus and, 130–131
Behavior Modeling exercise, 125–126
Belasco & Stayer, 19, 24
Belgrade, 206–207
Bergdall, T. D., 228
Best companies lists, 26
Big Hairy Audacious Goals, 32
Bigness, of vision, 32–33
Bingham, H., 140
Blaming others: freedom with responsibility *versus*, 122–123; pervasiveness of, in organizations, 177–178; self-justification and, 153; walking away from failure *versus*, 82
Block, P., 2
Body language, cultural differences in, 73
Boje, D. M., 19
Bombay, 125
Bonhoeffer, D., 121, 131
Book of 5 Rings, A (Musashi), 141–142
Boulding, K. E., 153, 196, 216–217
Boundaries: collapse of, 173; freedom and, 171–172; pushing one's, 255–257
Bowerman, B., 230
Brainstorming, 53, 91
Breadth, in problem diagnosis, 225
Brees, D., 235
Briskin, A., 184–185, 187
British Airways, 221
British men, study of stress in, 132
Brown, J., 184
Brown, J. S., 71, 231–232
Brussels, 23, 39–40
Buddhism, 17; fasting in, 99; on mastery, 243; meditation and practices of, 279; non-activity in, 244; non-attachment concept in, 81; on self-

awareness, 234; teachings of, application of, 95–96, 97; true way in, 258
Built to Last (Collins and Porras), 130
Burden, as level of intentionality, 182–183
Burke, J., 229
Business of Paradigms (Barker), 31

C

Caffey, F., 129–130
Calabrese, J., 51–52
Callanen, T., 187
Calmness, 277
Campbell, J., 208
Care and caring: as action, 114–115; awareness and, 219–220; betrayal of instinct for, 151–154; as emotion, 114; engagement and, 109–110, 114–115; intentionality and, 181–182, 190–191; interior experience of, 277; of managers for employees, 190–191; sacrifice and, 94–95
Carlzon, J., 221
Catholic fasting, 99
Cause-and-effect complexity, 48–49
Celebrations, 36
Celtics games, 109–110
Centering Prayer, 98–99
Central Europe, 73, 206–207
Central New York Regional Transportation Authority (Centro), 51–52
Centralization, 18–19, 40
Challenge: creativity and, 51–52, 110; interior council and, 159–160; love and, 108–109; spirit and, 65
Challenger disaster, 196
Chance, 235, 236
Chang Yü, 116
Change: contextual, 22–25, 35; disruptive, 35; engagement and, 106–107, 117; indicators of, 250; intuiting, 268; levels of, 106; in modern organizations, 47–52; paradigmatic, 16–27, 31; seeing the need for, 51; setbacks and, 180–181; stability and, 106–109
Change leaders, 115
Change processes, action discipline and, 247–253

Change programs, 225
Charisma, 263–264, 266. *See also* Presence
Chavez, C., 184–185
Children: detachment learned by, 79–80; rights of, 47
Chödrön, P., 95–96, 97
Choice: awareness and, 215–216; fear of commitment and, 103; freedom and, 122–123; intentionality and, 171–172; risk taking and, 115; in sense of wonder, 194, 207–209
Christian community life, 131
Christianity: fasting in, 99; vigil in, 145
Circumspect persons, 271–272
Civil rights movement, 9, 46
Clapton, E., 163
Clarifying questions, 58–59
Clinton, B., 6
Clock building, 31–32
Co-creation, 207–209, 263
Coaching, 82–83, 225
Coaching for Performance (Whitmore), 225
Cohen, D., 88
Collapse of Boundaries, 173
Collective illusions, 196
Collegiality, in sense of wonder, 205–206
Collins, J., 4, 31–32, 82, 130, 141, 276
Columbia shuttle disaster, 29
Command-and-control model: adversarial relationships and, 21; attachment to, 84, 86–88; charisma based on, 263–264; paradigm of, 18–19, 32
Commitment: action and, 242; communities of, 41; employee, 53–54; engagement and, 5, 102–126; failure of, 102–103, 117–118; fear of, 102–103, 136; group decision making and, 87–88; intentionality and, 188; multiple, 118–119; sustained, of facilitative leader, 110–114. *See also* Engagement
Communication: complexity and, 49; demands of, on time, 133, 176; and expectations of accessibility, 133; failure of, 29–30; and focus on group, 134–135; online, 67–70; responsiveness and, 50; stories for, 36–37; through art, 70–72
Communications technology. *See* Technology

Communities: of commitment, 41; Deepening Understanding practice with, 281; organizations as, 41; of practice, 41, 230; of reflection, 41; stories about, 230–231
Community development work: awareness in, 220; detachment in, 90; evolutionary vision in, 34; growing spirit in, 37–38; providence in, 257; spirit of intentionality in, 187–188
Competence, 243–244
Complexity: dynamic, 48–49; facilitative leadership in situations of, 73–75; organizational, 47–49; oversimplification of, 251–252; of relationships, 236–237; of rhythms, 23–24; storytelling and, 37
Conflict management, in meetings, 63–64
Conflicting demands, 132–133, 175–176, 189–190
Connection: experience of, 208; through stories, 231
Consequences: avoidance of, 176–177; unintended, 253
Contemplation practice, 210–213
Content: detachment to, 85, 92–93; management of, 58–59
Context, awareness of larger, 220
Contract *versus* covenant, 117–118
Control: box of, 198–199; fear of losing, 84, 86, 103; of nature, 198–199; over thinking, 137–138
Cooperrider, D. L., 70
Core-value stories, 229–230
Countryside Agency, 228
Courage: self-mastery and, 2–3; sense of wonder and, 199–200, 208–209
Covenant of engagement, 117–119
Covey, S. R., 135
Creativity: challenge and, 51–52, 110; employee participation and, 50–52; environment of trust and, 88–89; intentionality and, 173–174; sense of wonder and, 201; unifying models and, 219
Credit sharing, 65, 82, 141
Criticism, 277
Csikszentmihalyi, M., 35, 64, 65, 110, 129
Cullman, J., 82
Cultural asymmetry, 28

Cultural diversity: group norms and, 63, 73; new reality of, 23–24, 72–73
Culture, organizational: of success, 29, 42; transmitting, through stories, 229–230
Curiosity, 221
Customer service, 49–50
CVs, 233
Czech Republic, 73

D

Dark moments, 96–97
Dark side, 138, 234, 263–264
Dating industry, 24–25
David, 263
de Bono, E., 90, 218
Death and dying: avoidance of, 41–42, 271; emptiness and, 271; fear of engagement and, 103; sense of wonder and, 200–201; sensitivity to reality of, 93–94
Death of a Salesman (Miller), 86
Decentralization, 40
Decision making: advantages of group, 86–88; avoidance of consequences in, 177; employee participation in, 44, 45–54; facilitating resolution and, 57–65; facilitator's detachment in, 86–93; implementation commitment and, 87–88; multiple perspectives in, 86–87
Deepening Understanding practice, 281–282
Definitions, 58
Dehumanizing, 155–157
DeKoven, B., 83
Dell Computers, 50
Demagoguery, 263–264
Denial, in grieving process, 42
Denning, S., 36, 228–229
Despair, 270–272
Destructiveness, 138, 243, 271; interior council and, 150, 151–154; self-deception and, 151–154
Detachment: action and, 243; dimensions of, 81–84; discipline of, 79–101; everyday experience of, 79–80; exercise for, 100–101; focus as balance between engagement and, 127–129, 134; to goods, 81–82; issues of, for facilitative leaders, 84–93; learning, in childhood,

79–80; levels of, 93–98; overview of, 4–5, 80–81; practices for, 98–100; to relationships, 82–83; to self, 83–84; to work, 82
Details: in complex situations, 73–74; interaction skills and, 57–58
Developmental paths, overview of, 3–9
Dharma, 95–96. *See also* Buddhism
Diagnosis, facilitating, 56–57
Dialogue, as level of interior council, 161–162
DiGiorgio Corporation, 184–185
Digitization, 35
Direction, possibilities of, 185–187
Disciplines: of action, 242–261; of awareness, 215–241; of detachment, 79–101; of engagement, 102–126; of focus, 127–146; freedom and, 172; of intentionality, 170–193; of interior council, 147–169; levels of intensity of, 93; life-related, 3, 8–9; matrix of, 4; others-related, 3, 4–5; overview of, 3–9; of presence, 262–283; self-related, 3, 6–7; of wonder, 194–214. *See also* Action; Awareness; Detachment; Engagement; Focus; Intentionality; Interior council; Presence; Wonder
Discontinuity, in presence, 270–272
Disruptive change, 35
Distraction, 74, 175–176, 213
Do-ability, of vision, 33
Donaldson, S., 270–271
Downsizing, 43, 253, 267–268
Drilling projects, 135–136, 172
Dualistic paradigm, 16–17
Dune, 130
Dutch telephone company, 107
Dylan, B., 268, 278
Dynamic complexity, 48–49
Dynamic Facilitation, 21

E

E-mail, 133
Eastern Europe, 204
Ecstasy, as level of action, 258–259
Ecumenical Institute, 34, 216
"80–20 rule" of information accuracy, 30
Einstein, A., 16, 130
Eisley, L., 142
Elder phase, 103, 104–105

Election, as level of action, 257
Electronic purse company, 119–120
Emotions, in groups, 62–64
Empathy, 181–182. *See also* Care and caring
Employee participation: historical precedents to, 45–47; organizational complexity and, 47–49; organizational creativity and, 50–52; organizational movements toward, 52–54; organizational responsiveness and, 49–50; trends in, 44, 45–54
Employee satisfaction, 26, 50–51
Employee termination, dehumanizing approach to, 155–157
Emptiness, experience of discontinuity and, 270–272
Encounter, in sense of wonder, 203–204
Endings, 41–43, 267–268
Energy, aligning, 179
Engagement: difficulties with, 102–103; dimensions of, 105–110; discipline of, 102–126; everyday experience of, 103; exercise for, 125–126; focus as balance between detachment and, 127–129, 134; issues of, for facilitative leaders, 110–116; levels of, 116–123; overview of, 5, 102; phases of group, 103–105; practices for, 123–125. *See also* Commitment
Entrapment, in sense of wonder, 204–205
Environment: facilitating the, 55–56; online, 67–70; setup of, 39
Essential Spirituality (Walsh), 99–100
Established Adult phase, 103, 104
Eternal, the, 276–278
Ethics: lapses in, 27–28; multiple roles and, 118
Evil, 151
Evolutionary vision, 33–34
Execution, 246–247
Executive Champion's Workshop, 163
Exercises: for action, 260–261; for awareness, 240–241; for detachment, 100–101; for engagement, 125–126; for focus, 145–146; for intentionality, 191–193; for interior council, 168–169; overview of,

10–11, 98; for presence, 282–283; for sense of wonder, 213–214
Expenditure, as level of intentionality, 187–188
Explicit knowledge, 37
Exposure, 172
Extended family, 25, 133

F

Facilitative leaders and leadership: action issues of, 245–253; awareness issues of, 220–233; defined, 1; detachment issues for, 84–93; engagement issues for, 110–116; external, 91; focus issues for, 134–137; intentionality issues of, 178–182; interior council issues of, 154–158; internal, 91–92; need for self-mastery in, 1–3; for new ideas, 54; for new paradigm, 31–32; presence issues of, 266–269; sense of wonder issues for, 200–202; skills for, 55–66; trends in, 67–75. *See also* Leadership
Facts, 221–222
Failure: of commitment, 102–103, 117–118; courage to acknowledge and correct, 199–200; detachment from, 82, 84, 89–90; enabling learning from, 89–90; fear of death and, 103; intentionality and, 174; range of responses to, 264–265; taking responsibility for, 65, 82, 141; of traditional leadership, 27–30; willpower and, 274
Family events, 254
Fascination, 195
FastCompany, 2, 83, 160, 222
Fasting, 99, 280
Fear: of accountability, 177–178; of commitment, 102–103, 136; of death, 103; of freedom, 121–122; of greatness, 141, 151, 265–266; of losing control, 84, 86, 98; self-limitation and, 2; sense of wonder and, 195; of standing out, 265
Feedback, personal, 239–240
Fifth Discipline, The (Senge), 127, 140
Fifth Discipline Fieldbook, The (Senge), 61, 166
Filtering, 30, 197–198
Financial reports, 224, 225
Fish, 137

Flexibility, 57
Flood control, 198–199
Flow, 35, 64, 65, 129, 187
Flowers, B. S., 163, 197, 279
Floyd, M., 235
Focus: difficulties of, 132–134; dimensions of, 129–132; discipline of, 127–146; exercise for, 145–146; issues of, for facilitative leaders, 134–137; levels of, 137–143; overview of, 5, 127–129; practices for, 143–145; on present moment, 129–130; on present situation, 130–131, 136; on whole being, 131–132
Focused Free Writing, 238
Food, 280
Football, sensory awareness in, 235
Ford, H., 269
Foresight, 268
Forestry and wildlife management, 199
Fortune 500 list, 26
Free writing, 238
Freedom: in detachment, 97–98; in engagement, 121–123; intentionality and, 171–172; obedience and, 121; responsibility and, 121–123; types of, 172; willpower and, 275–276
French Revolution, 45
Freud, S., 2
Frustrate an Addiction practice, 100
Functions, different perspectives of, 224
Fund-raising, 257
Future: awareness and, 220; bringing, to the present, 129–130, 195; emerging, 34–35, 220; gap between past and, 258–259; and honesty about present situation, 127–128, 136; honoring greatness and, 140–141; intentionality and, 195; presence and, 263; sense of wonder in, 195, 203; sensing the, 268; storytelling of, 37

G
Gardner, H., 217–218
Giuliani, R., 44
Gladwell, M., 255–256
Globalization, 22–25, 35, 72–73
Good to Great (Collins), 4, 82, 141, 276

Graphic facilitation, 70, 71–72
Gratitude: intentionality and, 180–181; sense of wonder and, 208
"Great Wave Office Kanagawa," 277
Greatness: absurdity and, 141–142; fear of, 141, 151, 265–266; interior council and, 151, 162–163; as level of focus, 140–141
Greenleaf, R. K., 31, 32, 114–115, 276
Grieving, 41–43, 267–268
Ground rules: for groups, 62–63, 73; for online meetings, 69
Group Context practice, 213
Group methods, 52–53
Group norms, 62–63, 73
Groups: emotional expression in, 62–64; getting to know, 60–61; managing individuals in, 60–65; managing information in, 58–59; managing process in, 59–60; phases of engagement in, 103–105; practices for sense of wonder in, 210–213; profiling yourself in, 191–193; spirit in, 64–65; stuck thinking in, 108; transferring power to, 86–88
Groupthink, 196
Guns of Will Sonnett, 170
Gymnastics, 235

H
Hairdresser, 186–187
Hammonds, K. H., 84
Harris, E. J., 81
Harvard Business Review, 148
Harvard University, Kennedy School of Business, 85
Heifetz, R., 85
Herbert, F., 130
Hero with a Thousand Faces, The (Campbell), 208
Heroes and heroines, 150, 154, 278
Herrigel, E., 243
Hesitancy, 242
Hesse, H., 278
Hewlett-Packard, 228
Hierarchy, 30, 40
High-performance teams: dreams versus reality of, 131, 136; interdependence in, 26
History: being part of, 142; dynamic versus static, 17

Hock, D., 20, 32, 43, 93, 242
Hodgson, D., 23
Hokusai, K., 277
Hole, The, 203
Honesty, difficulties of, 127–128, 264–265. *See also* Truth
House styles, 36
Householder phase, 103
HSBC Group, 21
Hugh, B., 20
Humility: honoring greatness and, 141, 142; intentionality and, 174, 179; sense of wonder and, 208–209; technology and, 68

I

IBM, 104, 228; Worldjam event of, 67
Icons, 36
Idea of the Holy, The (Otto), 64, 195
Ideas, detachment to one's, 83, 89. *See also* New ideas
Identity: detachment and, 84; intentionality and, 174–175, 178–179; self-story for, 233
"If only's," 42
Ikebana, 260
Illusions, 151–154, 159–160, 196
Image, messages about, 216–217
Imaginal Training, 239
Imagination, in grieving process, 42
Impact: of action, 248–250; as level of interior council, 159–160
Impatience, 251–253
Implementation, serial *versus* parallel, 247–248
Impossible, enabling the, 268–269
India, 94–95, 103, 125, 139–140, 182–183
Individualism: detachment and, 84; fear of commitment and, 102–103
Individualization, 35
Indulge an Attachment practice, 99–100
Industrial Revolution, 46
Inferences, 61–62
Infinite Innovations, 53
Information: acquiring, 223–225; awareness and, 221–233; filtering, 30; handling, 2225–233; managing, 221–223; in meetings, 58–59; multiple perspectives and, 86–87; over-load, 222–223; processing, 61–62; structuring, 225–227. *See also* Knowledge management; Storytelling
Innovation, employee participation and, 50–52
Institute of Cultural Affairs (ICA), 34, 70, 103, 172, 174, 239, 258, 276–277
Intangibles, 29–30
Intelligences, types of, 217–218
Intentionality: action and, 171, 174, 181–182, 185–187, 246–247, 256–257; difficulties of, 175–178; dimensions of, 171–175; discipline of, 170–193; exercise for, 191–193; issues of, for facilitative leaders, 178–182; levels of, 182–188; overview of, 6, 7, 170–171; practices for, 189–191; sense of wonder and, 194–195
Interaction skills: at meeting level, 58–65; at organizational level, 57–58
Interior council: choosing internal advisors in, 154–155; difficulties with, 150–155; dimensions of, 148–150; discipline of, 147–169; exercise for, 168–169; issues of, for facilitative leaders, 154–158; levels of, 158–163; listening to the right voices in, 155–158; overview of, 6–7, 147–148; practices for, 164–168; self-deception and, 151–154; sense of wonder and, 194–195
Interior experiences, 276–277
Internal disciplines. *See* Disciplines
Internal state, importance of, 27
International Association of Facilitators (IAF), 3, 270; Methods Database of, 59
Internet: new economy and, 35; online meetings and, 67–70
Interrelatedness, 17, 24
Intervention: in groups, 59–60; as level of intentionality, 185–187
Intuition: acting in the now with, 129; awareness and, 223–224, 236; interior council and, 154; presence and, 268, 274–275; trusting, 274–275
Irish fable, 208–209
"Irresponsible genius," 121
Italy, development planning in, 108

J

Jackson, P., 15
Japanese arts, 260
Japanese car manufacturers, 50, 197
Japanese folklore, on three selves,
    174–175
Japanese management, 89
Japanese sword art, 141–142, 223,
    249–250, 260
Javanese King folktale, 272–273
Jaworski, J., 94, 163, 173, 197, 279
Jenkins, J. C., 23–24, 80, 82, 90, 91,
    94–95, 104, 108, 111, 114, 119–120,
    132, 154, 158, 160–161, 177, 179,
    182–183, 187–188, 195, 200, 202–
    204, 205–207, 210, 219–220, 270
Jenkins, L., 235
Jenkins, M. R., 23–24, 80, 90, 91, 111,
    114, 132, 135–136, 138, 154, 158,
    161–162, 182, 187–188, 195, 200,
    205, 210
Jennings, W. D., 82, 163, 223
Job selection, 24
Jobs, S., 64
Johnson & Johnson, 229
Jordan, K., 136–137
Journal Writing practice, 238–239
Journey to the East, The (Hesse), 278
Judgment, suspending, 5, 84–85,
    90–92
Justification, of destructive behavior,
    151–154, 155–156

K

Kahan, S., 36
Kant, I., 121
Katagini, D., 97
Katzenbach, J. R., 21, 26, 85, 115, 245
Kazantzakis, N., 157
Kelleher, H., 221
Kennedy, J. F., 33, 65, 199
Kierkegaard, S., 133–134, 271, 272
Kimsey, J., 84
King, L., 122–123
King, M. L., Jr., 9, 65, 130
King-vassal relationship, 32
Kleiner, A., 53
Knight, P., 230
Knowing, ways of, 217–218
Knowledge management: complexity
    and, 49; storytelling in, 37, 71, 228,
    230, 231–232

Knowledge workers, 53–54
Koestenbaum, P., 2, 83
Korten, A., 229
Koudsi, S., 137
Kuhn, T. S., 196

L

LaBarre, P., 2, 83
Labeling, of experience, 198–199
Labor movement, 46
Ladder of Inference, 61–62
Lakers, 110
Land of Mystery, 276–277
Language diversity, 23, 24
Lao Tsu, 84, 141
Larger purpose, engagement and,
    111–114, 116–117
Laughing, 270
Lavoisier, A., 17
Lawrence, D. H., 139, 200–201
Lazarus, S., 148–149
Leadership: backlash against new para-
    digm and, 31; global changes and,
    22–25; Level 5, 141, 276; new chal-
    lenges of, 16–27; in new world,
    31–32; paradigm shifts in, 16–22,
    31; spirit and, 15–16, 32–43; tradi-
    tional, failures of, 27–30; traditional
    versus new, 16–27. *See also* Facilita-
    tive leaders
Leadership Is . . . (Owen), 32, 108–109
Lebesch, J., 136–137
Left-Hand Column/Right-Hand Col-
    umn, 166–168
Lego Serious Play, 232
Lepers, 182–184
Letter writing, to interior council, 164
Lev, B., 222
Level 5 leaders, 141, 276
Levels of Contribution practice,
    123–124
Lewin, K., 52–53
Liberation, 107
Life, disciplines of, 3, 8–9. *See also*
    Action; Awareness; Presence
Life, living fully, 139–140
Life purpose, uncertainty about,
    133–134
Life Timeline Chart, 145–146
Limits, pushing one's, 255–257
Linsky, M., 85
List Writing, 239

Listening, 221
Locke, M., 249
Logos, 36
Lonely Hearts Club Montage exercise, 168–169
Long-term effects: of action, 249–250; dynamic complexity and, 48–49
Long-term problems, 225
Los Angeles, City of, 23
Los Angeles Lakers, 15
Love, 108–109
Love making, 128–129
Loyalty, 32, 105
Lucidity, 172
Luck, 235–236
Luther, M., 154
Lyall, S., 20
Lyneis, J., 48

M

Machine paradigm, 17–18, 40, 46, 56–57, 109
Magical places, 163
Mahmad, India, 94–95
Maijka, C., 259
Mandela, N. R., 6, 122–123, 258–259
Marathon training, 120
March of Folly, The (Tuchman), 28
Marriage partner selection, 24–25
Marshall, C., 221
Martial Arts practice, 259–260
Marx, K., 46, 154
Mathews, J. W., 93–94, 216
Matrix Revolutions, The, 274, 275–276
McCartney, P., 158
McDonald's, 24, 56–57
McEnroe, J., 267
McGregor, J., 29
McLellan, H., 228
Meaning: engagement and, 111–113, 116–117; group spirit and, 65; interior council and, 162–163
Measurement, 222, 250
Meditation: for detachment, 98–99; for presence, 279–280
Meeting the Rock exercise, 240–241
Meetings: content management in, 58–59; creating trust in, 56, 62–63; diagnosis for, 57; dominant participants in, 252; facilitating resolution in, 58–65; online, 67–70; people management in, 60–65; process management in, 59–60; spirit in, 64–65
Memories: in grieving process, 42; in interior council, 148–149; of what is given up, 96–97
Mendel, G., 17
Mental toughness, 189
Messages, awareness and, 216–217
Met Office, 228
Metaphors, organizational, 56–57
Method actors, 175
Methods and models, 59
Metropolises, 23
Michelangelo, 263
Middlebury College, 187
Miller, A., 86
Mind Mapping, 238
Mindful Music exercise, 213–214
Mission, as level of action, 253–254
Mission statements, 111–112
MIT, 35
Modeling, 89, 116; exercise regarding, 125–126
Models: building, 227; characteristics of, 226; for structuring information, 225–227; unifying, 219
Moncur, M., 269
Moon, putting a man on, 33, 65
Moon rock, 6
Moral influence, 116
Morgan, G., 56–57
Motivation: action and, 246–247; caring for spirit and, 109–110; sense of wonder and, 201
Mountain of Care, 276–277
Mumbai, India, 182–183
Murdoch, A., 228
Murray, W. N., 242
Musashi, M., 141–142, 258
Museums, silence practice in, 280
Music, 70–71, 72, 213–214, 278
Muslims, 99
Mystery, intentionality and, 173
Myth, 35–36, 70. *See also* Storytelling and stories

N

NASA, 28–29, 31
NATO, 207
Nausea (Sartre), 194
Networked structures, 35, 40–41
Neutrality, 91–92, 93

New Belgium, 136–137
"New Heaven and New Earth" (Lawrence), 200–201
New ideas: employee participation for, 50–52, 53–54; environment of trust for, 88–89; facilitative leadership for, 54; sense of wonder and, 201; storytelling for, 37; suspending judgment on, 91
"New Individual and New Society," 205–206
New York City, subway crime prevention in, 255–256
Nicholson, J., 270
Nike, 36, 228, 230, 267
9/11 Commission Report, 28
9/11 terrorist attacks, 28, 31, 44
Nixon, R., 94
No Exit (Sartre), 96
Novartis, 159

O

Obedience, 121
Obligations, avoidance of, 176–177
Observation, impact of, 21–22
Odyssey, The, 175
Ogilvy, D., 148–149
Ogilvy & Mather Worldwide, 148–149
Olympic athletes, 255
Online meetings and learning, 67–70
Open Space stage of grieving, 42
Open Space Technology, 21, 32, 247
Openness: for deep understanding, 281; to sense of wonder, 195, 199, 236–237
Opportunities: losing, through distraction, 176; risk management for, 190; sensitivity to, 235–236
Organizations: archetypes of, 40–41; beginnings of, 266–267; changes facing, 47–52; as communities, 41; as containers of spirit, 40–41; creating trust in, 55–56, 88–89, 202; creativity and innovation in, 50–52; diagnosis of, 56–57; endings and grieving in, 41–43, 267–268; interaction skill in, 57–58; larger purpose of, 112–114; as machines, 17–18, 40, 46, 56–57; metaphors for, 56–57; movements toward participation in, 52–54; phases of

engagement in, 103–105; responsiveness and adaptability of, 49–50; as self-organizing systems, 19–21; sensing the health of, 235; stability in, 105–109; stories in, 36–37, 228–233, 266–267. See also Structure
Ortega y Gasset, J., 215–216, 242–243
Osborn, A., 53
Others, disciplines regarding, 3, 4–5. See also Detachment; Engagement; Focus
Ott, J., 187
Otto, R., 64, 195, 196
Oversimplification, 251–252
Overwhelm, 132–133
Owen, H., 21, 22, 32, 41–42, 108–109, 198

P

Paper manufacturer sales reps, 49–50
Paradigm and paradigm change: backlash against new, 31; facilitative leadership for new, 31–32; information management and, 221–223; old versus new, 16–27, 109, 221–223
Paralysis, 177, 183, 244
Parochialism, 23
Passion, as level of intentionality, 183–184
Past: awareness and, 220; bringing, to present moment, 129–130, 195; gap between future and, 258–259; group connection through, 65; interior council and, 194–195; sense of wonder in, 195, 203; stability and, 106
Patterns: constructive versus destructive use of, 177; discernment of, 90–91
Patton, 129–130
Peck, M. S., 151, 196
People management, in meetings, 60–65
People of the Lie (Peck), 151, 196
People sketches, 239
Perception: attentionality and, 223–224; filtering, 197–198; of impact of action, 248–250
Personal Feedback practice, 239–240
Personal mastery. See Self-mastery
Personal Values exercise, 100–101

Perspectives, multiple, 86–87, 218, 224
Peru, 37–38, 79, 81–82, 230–231, 251
Philip Morris, 82
Photocopy machine repair stories, 71, 231–232
Pink, D. H., 236
Planck, M., 16
Planning: action and, 244, 245, 246–248; detachment in, 83; dynamic complexity and, 48–49; revision in, 246; storytelling for, 37. *See also* Strategic planning
Poland, 203–204
Porras, J. I., 130
Positive attitude, 151, 236
Possibility, sensitivity to, 235–236
Power: in detachment, 97–98; fear of losing, 84, 86
Practical Care practice, 190–191
Practices: for action, 259–260; for awareness, 238–240; for detachment, 98–100; for engagement, 123–125; for focus, 143–145; for intentionality, 189–191; for interior council, 164–168; overview of, 10–11, 98; for presence, 279–282; for sense of wonder, 210–213
Precognition, 35, 195, 196, 237
Prefontaine, S., 230
Preparation, for focus on group, 135
Preparing the Space practice, 124–125
Presence: collective side of, 266; dark side of, 263–264; difficulties in, 264–266; discipline of, 262–283; exercise for, 282–283; issues of, for facilitative leaders, 266–269; levels of, 269–278; overview of, 8, 9, 262–263; practices for, 279–282
Presence (Senge et al.), 279
Present moment: awareness of, 220; focus on, 129–130; as gap, 258–259; sense of wonder in, 195, 200, 204
Presley, E., 36
Prisons and prison camps, 4, 6, 122–123
Privatization, 217
Problem solving: addressing root causes in, 206; avoidance in, 244; diagnosis in, 225; jumping to solutions in, 252; sense of wonder in, 201; storytelling for, 231–232

Process: focus on, *versus* content, 85, 92–93; management of, 59–60
Product development and improvement, 50
Profiles in Courage (Kennedy), 199
Profiling Yourself in the Group exercise, 191–193
Progress tracking, 74
Promise, as level of focus, 139–140
Prompts, 239
Providence, in commitment to action, 242, 257
Prusak, L., 88
Purity of heart, 133–134
Putnam, R., 61

Q

Quarterly financial reports, 225, 251

R

Ransdell, E., 230
Real Change Leaders (Katzenbach), 115
Reality tests, 196
RedWorld.Biz, 235–236
Reflection: interior council and, 150–151; presence and, 279–280; written dialogue and, 70
Relationships: adversarial *versus* cooperative, 21–22; commitment difficulties in, 102–103; detachment to, 82–83; sense of wonder and, 202, 205–206; social trends in, 22–25, 35
Renunciation, 95–97
Reorganization efforts, 107
Resistance, 217
Resolution, facilitating, 57–65
Responsibility taking: avoidance of, 176–177; awareness and, 219–220; detachment and, 83–84; in engagement, 120–123; for failures, 65, 82, 141; fear of, 177–178; freedom and, 121–123; intentionality and, 176–177; for life purpose, 134; presence and, 275–276
Responsiveness, organizational, 49–50
Retirement crisis, 86
Retreats, 280
Return to Love, A (Williamson), 140
Reverence, 208–209
Revolutionary vision, 34–35

Rhythms: complexity of, 23–24; structuring, to sustain spirit, 39–40
Rich man, parable of, 96
Risk and risk taking: detachment and, 84; engagement and, 115; focus and, 135–136; freedom and, 172; identifying personal, practice of, 189; for sharing new ideas, 52
Risk Management practice, 190
Risk Planning exercise, 260–261
Rituals: organizational, 36; for practicing engagement, 123–125
River of Consciousness, 276–277
Robert, H. M., 53
Robert's Rules of Order, 53
Role models, 150
Roles: different perspectives and, 224; engagement and, 103–104, 117, 118–119; identity and, 174–175, 178–179; intentionality and, 174–175, 178–179; separating self from, 84, 85–86
Ronin, The (Jennings), 82
Ross, R., 61
Rotterdam, 202–203
Rough, J., 21
Royal Mail, 228
Ruete, N., 179
Russell, B., 109–110

S

Sacrifice, in detachment, 94–95
Sakai, R., 270
Sartre, J.-P., 96, 194
SAS, 221
Scale, attentionality and, 224–225
Scenarios, 232
Schaffner, F. J., 129–130
Scharmer, C. O., 35, 40–41, 163, 173, 197, 263–264, 279
Schooling systems, 219
Scientific paradigm, 17, 25–26
Scientific revolutions, 196
Scottish Himalayan Expedition, The (Murray), 242
Scram jet, 22–23
Sea of Tranquility, 276–277
Second Wind (Russell), 109–110
Seduction: of demands on time, 176; inner voices of, 150
Self: awareness of, 234, 271–272; creating, with intentionality, 174–175;

detachment to, 83–84; emptiness and, 270–272; highest, 263; sensitivity toward, 234; separating, from role, 84, 85–86; society and, 276. *See also* Identity; Whole being
Self, disciplines of, 3, 6–7. *See also* Intentionality; Interior council; Wonder
Self-actualization, 171
Self-care, 43–44
Self-censorship, 30
Self-confidence, 115; humility and, 208–209
Self-deception, 151–154
Self-limitation, 2, 172
Self-mastery: honesty and, 127–128; journey of, 75; need for, 1–3, 43–44; for online meetings, 68; spiritualization and, 35
Self-organizing systems, 19–21
Self-stories: to create identity, 233; to develop focus, 143–144; interior council and, 151–154, 164–166
Self-talk, 6–7, 147–148, 236. *See also* Interior council
Senge, P. M., 35, 48, 61, 127, 140, 143, 154, 163, 166, 197, 279
Sensitivity: to awe, 236–237; freedom and, 172; levels of awareness and, 234–237; to possibility, 235–236; to reality of detachment, 93–94; toward self, 234; to the world, 234–235
Sensual perception, 197–199, 223, 234–235
Serbia, 206–207
Servant as Leader (Greenleaf), 114–115, 276
Servant leadership, 31, 32, 114–115, 158, 276
Service industries, 29–30
Service practice, 279, 281
Setbacks: intentionality and, 180–181, 189; as motivation, 65. *See also* Failure
Sgt. Pepper's Lonely Hearts Club Band, 168
Shell, 67, 247
Shock, in grieving process, 42
Short History of Robert's, 53
Short-term effects: of action, 248–249; dynamic complexity and, 48–49

Short-term focus, ethical lapses and, 27
Silence, 220, 279–280
Silencing the Mind practice, 279–280
Silo behavior, complexity and, 47–48
Sitting Bull, 154
Situation, current: attentionality to, 223–225, 234–235; focus on, 130–131, 136; gratitude for, 180–181; honesty about, 127–128, 136
Six Thinking Hats, 218
Skills, facilitation: for diagnosis, 56–57; in environment, 55–56; for resolution, 57–65
Skype, 67
Slavery, abolition of, 46
Smith, D., 21, 26, 85, 245
Smith, D. M., 61
Smith, M., 27–28
Social capital, erosion of, 88–89
Social Processes model, 226–227
Social responsibility, 136–137
Social science research, 52–53
Socialism, 46
Songwriting workshops, 70–71
South Africa, 258–259
Southern Peru Copper, 81–82
Southwest Airlines, 221
Space: awareness of, 220, 234–235; magical, 163; practice for engagement in, 124–125; workplace, 39
Specialists, 26; complexity and, 47–48, 74
Spirit: caring for, in engagement, 109–110; comforting, at the end, 41–43; conditions for, 65; evoking, in engagement, 109–110; evoking, with presence, 9, 266–268; evoking, with vision, 32–35; facilitating, in a meeting, 64–65; growing, by collective storytelling, 35–38; leadership and, 15–16, 32–43; organizations as containers of, 40–41; revitalizing, 267; sustaining, with structure, 38–41
Spirit or Consciousness Conversation, 210–213
Spiritualization, 35
Spontaneity, 244
Spurgeon, B., 174
Stability: balancing change with, 107–109; engagement and, 105–109
Standards, responsibility for, 116
Standing out, fear of, 265

Stanislavski, C., 175
Star Wars, 170
States of Being, 276–277
Staying Alive (Heifetz and Linsky), 85
Stockdale, J., 4
"Stockdale Paradox," 4
Storytelling and stories: awareness and, 228–233; communication through art and, 70–72; to develop focus, 143–144; functions of, for leaders, 229; in grieving process, 42; growing spirit through, 35–38, 266–269; of interior council, 148–150, 164–166; for knowledge sharing, 37, 71, 228, 230, 231–232; in organizations, 36–37, 228–233; for problem solving, 231–232; self-, 143–144, 151–154, 164–166, 233; for sustaining commitment, 112–113; for transmitting values, 229–230; types of organizational, 228–229; of "us," 119
Strategic planning: identifying root causes in, 206; importance of process in, 92; practical proposals and strategic directions in, 186; storytelling in, 232. *See also* Planning
Stream-of-consciousness writing, 238
Stress: as condition for spirit, 65; focus and, 132–133
Structure, sustaining spirit with, 38–41
Structure of Scientific Revolutions, The (Kuhn), 196
Study, 279, 281
Style, as level of presence, 272–273
Submission, in engagement, 119–120
Success: culture of, 29, 42; intentionality and, 170–171, 188; presence and, 268–269s
Summary documents, 74
Summary writing, 166
Sun Tzu, 115, 116
Supplier relationships, 50
Support networks: luck and, 236; stress and lack of, 133; traditional *versus* new, 25, 133
Suzuki, D. T., 243
Symbols and symbolism: acts as, 250–251; in practices for engagement, 123–125
Synchronicity (Jaworski), 173

T

Tacit knowledge, 37
Tagore, R., 182
Tai Chi, 259–260
Tan, A., 175
Task break-down, 47–48
Taylor, W. C., 85, 221
Tea ceremony, 124, 260
Teams: complexity and, 49; development of, 245; executive and board, 85; new paradigm of, 21; storytelling of, to develop focus, 144. *See also* High-performance teams
"Tears in Heaven" (Clapton), 163
Technical limit, 172
Technique, transcending, 242
Technology: control and, 198; and demands on time, 176; and expectations of accessibility, 133; impact of, on social relationships, 22; for online meetings, 67–70
Teleconference, 69
Telleen, S. L., 18
Tennis players, 273–274
Thinking, control over, 137–138
Thomas Covenant the Unbeliever, 270–271
Threaded discussion, 69–70
Tillich, P., 271
Time: action and, 245, 248–250, 251–253; awareness and, 225, 237; in complex situations, 73–74; creating trust and, 55–56; demands on, 175–176, 189–190; focus in, 129–130; frenetic, 23–24; structuring, to sustain spirit, 39–40
Time frame, organizational, 225, 245, 251–252
Time management, 132, 189–190
Tipping Point, The (Gladwell), 255–256
Tito, 207
Traffic management, 20
Transitoriness, 80–81, 93–94
Transparency: in decision making, 44; in leadership, 141; presence and, 265
Transportation changes, 22–23
Trend analysis, 226
Trust and trust building: consequences of lack of, 88–89; creating an environment for, 55–56, 88–89; detach-

ment and, 84; emotions and, 62–63; sense of wonder and, 202
Truth: authority and discernment of, 221–222; avoidance of, 28–29, 271–272. *See also* Honesty
Trying *versus* doing, 170
Tuchman, B. W., 28
Tuning out, 68–69
Tupe, B., 95
"Two Wolves," 149–150
Tylenol recall, 229

U

Ukrainian folk song, 255
Uncertainty, about self, 133–134, 217
Unconscious: aligning conscious with, 131–132, 135, 173–174, 182; awareness and, 223–224; competence and, 243; interior council and, 158; intuition and, 275
Unifying models, 219
Unintended consequences, 253
Union, as level of interior council, 162–163
United Farm Workers, 184–185
U.S. Air Force, 22–23
U.S. military, commitment in, 102
U.S. Navy, 39
Urbanization, 22, 23
Useem, M., 160

V

Values: commitment to standards and, 116; Eastern *versus* Western, 73; exercise in personal, 100–101; information interpretation and, 30; for professional facilitators, 3; traditional *versus* new, 25–27; transmitting, through stories, 229–230
Vasella, D., 159
Venezuela, community development planning in, 90
Venture, as level of action, 254–257
Videoconference, 69
Vietnam War, 28, 102, 160
Vigil practice, 144–145
Visa, 20
Vision: evoking spirit with, 32–35; evolutionary, 33–34; holding, with focus, 136–137; and honesty about current situation, 127–128, 136;

honoring greatness and, 140–141; as level of focus, 137–139; qualities of, 32–33; revolutionary, 34–35; stage of grieving, 42
Visser, G., 82
Visualization exercise, 282–283
Vocation, 133–134
Voting rights, 46

W

Wachowski, A., 274
Wachowski, L., 274
Wademan, D., 148–149, 159
Walking in Bombay practice, 125
Walkway construction, 198
Walsh, R., 98, 99–100, 182
War, art of, 116
Warrior phase, 103
Water, contemplative conversation about, 210–213
Watergate, 94
Watson, A., 236
"We Are Transmitters" (Lawrence), 139
Weakness: acknowledging one's, 179; using, to advantage, 272–273
Weariness, 200
Webber, A. M., 222
Wesley, J., 130
Wheatley, M., 17–18, 222
Whitmore, J., 225
Whole being: action with, 244; focus on, 131–132
Will: focus and, 127–146; intentionality and, 170–193; interior council and, 147; presence and, 273–276. *See also* Intentionality
Williams, S., 15
Williams, V., 66
Williamson, M., 140

Willpower, as level of presence, 273–276
Wilson, C., 174
Wisdom of No Escape, The (Chödrön), 95–96, 97
Wisdom of Teams, The (Katzenbach and Smith), 21
Wiseman, R., 235–236
Women's right to vote, 46
Wonder (sense of): difficulties of maintaining, 197–200; discipline of, 194–214; exercise for, 213–214; issues of, for facilitative leaders, 200–202; levels of, 202–209; as nexus between interior council and intentionality, 194–195; overview of, 6, 7, 194–196; practices for, 210–213
Wood, D., 112–113, 116
Work/life balance, 253–254
World Bank, 228
World Café, 184
World Trade Center, 44
Worldview, disruptions to, 196
Worst-case scenarios, 28–29
Writing, 164, 238–239, 280
Written dialogue, 69–70
Wrong, courage to be, 199

X

Xerox Park, 71

Y

Yoda the Jedi, 170
Young Adult phase, 103, 104
Youth, phase of, 103–104

Z

Zen, 234, 243, 244
Zen in the Art of Archery (Herrigel), 243
Zone, the, 187